Long Time No See

Long Time No See

A memoir of fathers, daughters and games of chance

Hannah Lowe

periscope
www.periscopebooks.co.uk

Long Time No See
A memoir of fathers, daughters and games of chance

First published in Great Britain in 2015 by

Periscope
An imprint of Garnet Publishing Limited
8 Southern Court, South Street
Reading RG1 4QS

www.periscopebooks.co.uk
www.facebook.com/periscopebooks
www.twitter.com/periscopebooks
www.instagram.com/periscope_books
www.pinterest.com/periscope

Copyright © Hannah Lowe, 2015

ISBN 9781859643969

A CIP catalogue record for this book is available from the British Library.

This book has been typeset using Periscope UK, a font created specially for this imprint.

Typeset by Samantha Barden
Jacket design by James Nunn: www.jamesnunn.co.uk

Printed and bound in Lebanon by International Press: interpress@int-press.com

To my mother and Lorna, for their unfailing memories
and in memory of my dad, Ralph Lowe

AUTHOR'S NOTE

*T*his book is a reconstruction – part fiction, part truth. The early chapters set in Jamaica are loosely based on a notebook my father kept, discovered after his death, in which he wrote about his childhood.

And either I'm a nobody, or I'm a nation

– Derek Walcott, *The Schooner* Flight

CONTENTS

1

1935

*T*he boy was ten when he discovered his mother had sold him, but by then he hadn't seen her in a year. He and his father were together all day serving in the shop, and at night, they ate together at the table in the shop's back room. The room was small and served as kitchen, bedroom and stockroom. In the corner stood a wood fire and hotplate where they cooked; a sink. The walls were lined with ramshackle floor-to-ceiling shelves packed with the shop's goods – rolls of cloth, pots and pans, plimsolls, bags of dried beans, tins of oil. On the floor, hemp sacks of rice and grain were piled wherever there was space, and at the long wall, placed a few feet apart, were two low cots on which the boy and his father lay at night listening to each other's breathing. They were constant companions, knew the other's habits as well as they knew their own, but the boy never spoke to his father unprompted, and the man only ever spoke to the boy when issuing a command related to the shop which was their livelihood. The boy hated his father, and the father's hatred in return sang itself in the cracking of his leather belt on the boy's small limbs, named itself in the dark bruises and red welts on his skin.

Hannah Lowe

It was a one-storey wooden building, the only Chiney shop in Yallahs. This was backwater Jamaica, the green land wrapped in mist before the sun came up to heat it, one main track running inland from the coast, joining all the villages. The shop stood at the junction. The boy and his father rose in darkness to the silent work of lighting oil lamps and heating water, and from a mile away the silhouettes of villagers were visible walking the road in the purple light of early morning. They made their purchases of johnny cakes or salt-fish fritters wrapped in brown paper, simple food for the day's work in the fields. Most customers had credit and it was the boy's job to note their transactions in the shop's large, yellowed ledger.

This was the third shop they had owned. Two before in other towns, Mocho and Hearts Ease, had gone up in flames, as though tragedy followed them; that's what some said. But other rumours went around the Yallahs market – that James Lowe burned down his own shops for insurance money, owed so much in gambling debts he had to torch his shop, his home. And the boy knew this was the truth, remembered sitting by his father in the truck crossing the Yallahs River, the shop building still smoking, a hulk of wood and ash behind them, the smell of petrol on his father filling the small cabin, so acrid that the boy had to look away and cover his nose.

Now they were miles away. His mother had lived close to the last shop and had sometimes passed by, bringing the boy a treat – a notebook or piece of sugar cane – nothing the shop didn't sell, but he loved her gifts, craved them and the way her eyes searched his face for pleasure at them. Her name was Hermione and she was just a girl really, a light-skinned girl in a pale dress. He was forgetting her face but still recalled the smell of her, of frangipani and oranges. He knew that he had lived with her once, a long time ago, as a baby. She had sung to him. He thought he remembered this, searched hard through his mind for those memories, but they were like bright, tangible dreams you woke from but could never recall, both real and unreal. He missed his mother, was scared of losing her from his mind. After his father's worst beatings he had run to her, to the small shack by the river. She cleaned the cuts made by the leather, rubbed arnica on his bruises, and, standing shaking in the doorway, he had begged to stay with her, but no matter how he pleaded – *Please ma, please ma* – she always, always sent him back.

There was no one to run to now. The boy's days filled themselves with the routine of the shop and school, when he went. It was a three-mile walk to the classroom with its galvanised roof and Teacher Lewis or Miss Harvey sat at the table on a raised platform at the front. There might be forty children crammed at the small square desks and on the window ledge; some sat on the floor by Mrs Harvey's feet – boys with small hand mirrors who tried to look up her skirt. She was a fat woman in bright, billowing clothes, conducting the children through hot afternoons, chanting times tables, spelling simple chalk words on the board which they would scrape onto their slates.

School was too easy for the boy, whose quick mind had been honed in the shop, who could add and multiply big numbers in his head, and could already read the newspaper cover to cover. His father couldn't read English and sometimes when the shop was quiet, ordered the boy to read the news to him aloud. The boy almost liked doing this, could not understand how, even hating his father, he wanted to impress him with reading, wanted him to be proud.

He went to school less and less often these days, his father demanding he run the shop when he went to Kingston to buy and trade stock. Most times his father was gone for a day, returning with a laden truck. But other times he might be gone for two days and nights, returning with bloodshot eyes, looking thinner and meaner in his creased clothes. The boy knew then that his father had been to Chinatown, to the illegal gambling dens that lined Barry Street, and lost himself in all-day-and-night *mahjong* games. The smell of rum would be thick on his breath and no matter how hard the boy tried to keep away from him, a beating always came in the days that followed the Chinatown trips, where money had been lost. The tiredness and hangovers made his father more brutal and he beat the boy with more ferocity, as though he were beating the man who'd taken his cash.

The shop was a hub in the village, busy all day and open long after the sun went down. At dusk, the boy and his father would light the oil beacons, and from miles away the glow could be seen, luring the village men to come and sit at the small tables, to drink beer or rum and play dominoes. An awning overhung the veranda, keeping them dry if a storm broke, and James Lowe knew this social time was good for business, would stand in the doorway making light conversation, asking after wives, children, sometimes ordering the boy to bring a plate of fritters to share. The mood was light, no sign of the tension that snagged between the blacks and Chinese, the resentment at Chinese wealth, the stories from the other side of the island of Chiney shops looted and burned. James Lowe liked to keep things sweet, and meanwhile fixed the scales he weighed their goods on, bedded rocks of salt in fish to give it weight, mixed new flour with old.

The boy liked these nights and the company of the men. The less time spent alone with his father the better. He liked their talk, listening from his spot in the shadow at the side of the porch as he played dice against himself. Sometimes Rufus or Luther, his friends from school, would come and they would play against each other. Rufus was the same as him – had a mother who didn't want him, a father who beat him. They bet pennies on the roll, and the boy loved the clicking of the ivory cubes in his fist, loved the chance of the dice. But in truth, the boy loved to play alone the best, testing the laws of probability against the truth of the dice.

When his father was away and the boy was left in charge it was his job to clear the veranda when the men left, to lock the wooden shutters, bolt the door and grille. His father's absence brought a kind of peace, a quiet time the boy did not feel scared in, safe in the company of the lime-green geckos that clung to the shop's whitewashed walls and the cicadas clicking in the grass.

It had rained on the night he couldn't find the dice, and he spent the evening fetching drinks for the men or sitting to the side listening to their banter, sometimes thinking of his mother. When the men had gone, the boy moved through the shop with a lamp, casting tall shadows on the shelves, holding it up to light the cabinets behind the counter where they kept the dice and dominoes sets, the packs of playing cards. He thought to help himself to another pair, but the shelf was empty and so he carried the lamp across to where they slept, setting it down on the table between the low beds. The boy wanted another pair of dice badly, and thought he might find some among his father's things, an old pair from a *mahjong* set, perhaps. There was a wooden chest on his father's side that had many thin drawers, each with a brace for a written label, but there was no paper in them, no indication of what the drawers held.

The boy wondered what he might find in the drawers he had never opened, never even thought to open. He pulled the top one out and reached in. There were letters from China that looked the same as those he sometimes saw his father reading intently while sat at the kitchen table. They were written in calligraphy, delicate black marks the boy traced below his fingers. He could feel the texture of the ink but it gave no clue to what was written there. He tucked the letters back in place and opened the next drawer, which held his father's passport and official-looking papers, stamped. Here was his father's Chinese name – Lowe Shu-On. Lowe Shu, Lowe Shu. He'd heard other Chinese men call his father by this name. And here was a date of birth. The boy quickly did the maths. His father was thirty-one. He had not known his age before. No birthdays were celebrated in the room behind the shop.

There was a tattered photograph of a young Chinese woman, staring impassively at the camera. She was thin-faced, delicate looking. The boy thought the photo looked older than other photographs he had seen. Who it was it? A sister? His father's mother? In another drawer was a cufflink box that held two gold cufflinks with black onyx stones. The boy had never seen his father in anything but a vest and so the cufflinks surprised him – everything in these drawers surprised him – and suddenly he was pulling open every drawer and examining its contents – holding papers up to the lamp light, as though the answer to the riddle of his father might be found here if he looked closely enough, as though the reasons his father could barely look at him, never in the eye, might be found here in this drawer or that drawer, the reasons for the beatings, the slaps and punches, the reason the father did not love the boy. The rain began outside again, hammering on the tin roof of the room. And it was there, in the fifth drawer down, that the boy caught sight of his own name on a slip of paper. It was a handwritten receipt like the ones they gave for large purchases in the shop, but here, where the goods were usually described, was his father's writing and own name spelt out in block capitals, and the words altogether read *For the Care and Upkeep of Ralph Lowe, a sum of £25 received*. And there below it was his mother's name, signed and printed in her shaky hand.

2

FLOWERS SHAPED AS DICE

I can't give you anything but love, baby

My father died on a Tuesday in March. Three days later, we sat on the hard seats of the cold crematorium at Manor Park, the light filtered by the high stained-glass windows. The pews were full. My father had been as zealous in his atheism as any religious fundamentalist and so the ceremony was led by a Humanist official – a tall, bony man with a neat moustache who gave a careful eulogy about my father's life, notable for what it left out as much as included.

The service was punctuated by the old jazz music my father had loved – Ella Fitzgerald and Billie Holiday. My brother read *Invictus*, one of his favourite poems. My mother stood at the end, smiling brightly, thanking everyone for coming. The ceremony was over. We sat in silence as the conveyor belt slowly moved the coffin through the hatch towards the furnace. It didn't seem feasible to me that my father's body was in that box, just as it seemed impossible his ashes were in the plastic urn delivered home by the undertaker a few days later, and all this just as inconceivable as the fact that he was dead.

We trailed outside into the rainy afternoon where already other mourners were arriving for the next service. There was space on the flagstone terrace for flowers to be placed. We hovered beside the display for my father, noticeably different from other arrangements nearby. There were a number of garlands shaped as dice, bright red with white spots on each side, and as a centrepiece, an enormous white and red playing card made of roses and carnations – the ace of hearts.

A way off stood a circle of middle-aged men in suits and overcoats or leather jackets, one or two in trilby hats. All of them were smoking. There were black faces and white faces, some I recognised, others I'd never seen, and yet, in a way, I knew them all. Over the years I had come to distinguish their voices on the phone when they rang to speak with my father, always asking for Chick or Chan or Chin. I knew their names too: Sylvester, Mac, Felix, Ray the Pilot, John the Carpenter. They were the gamblers who had known my father for decades, with whom he had spent long nights at card and dice tables in clubs and casinos all over London. They were here to pay their respects.

The wake was held at my parents' home in Ilford, an unremarkable semi-detached house, identical to others on the street opposite the park with its small front garden and pebble-dashed walls. The doorbell rang as the mourners arrived, more and more, too many for the cramped back room and kitchen. The front living room was off limits since we hadn't had the heart to move the single bed my father had died in, placed there when he could no longer climb the stairs. It hadn't seemed right to open that room up yet. My family had no religious beliefs, but I, at least, felt that room was still charged with sadness and the strange energy of illness and death.

There are photographs from that afternoon, evidence of the strange mix of people at the wake. My mother's elderly relatives stare into the camera from their upright chairs against the wall, looking twee and confused. Our old next-door neighbours, Irish Bridget and her husband Dick, raise their glasses to the camera. In other photographs my own motley crew of friends stands together, young and casual, getting stuck into the wine and beer. I was moved by how many of them had come – friends from university, friends from college, even friends of Sid, my newish boyfriend. It was strange to see them in their best clothes, in a different setting from the nightclubs and house parties where we danced into the early hours.

Visible in a corner behind them were the gangster-suave men from the crematorium, all younger than my father. *They looked up to him*, my mother said. *Like apprentices, I suppose you'd say.* In that crowd was Charlie White, a man I'd known as long as I could remember. He was a plumber, a hard-looking man, squat and muscular, his face webbed with red from his early years of hard drinking. He'd been wild as a young man – *a real delinquent*, my mother said. Some unspeakably violent act had put him in borstal for a time, but that rage had mellowed. He was often stoned, and never without his tin of Rizlas and tobacco. When I'd turned thirteen, he'd shocked me by rolling a joint and holding it out to me to light. He'd done the same with my brother four years earlier, as though it were a coming-of-age ceremony. I had taken up his offer, inhaling the heavy black hash he crumbled, exhaling a thick tongue of smoke and trying not to cough.

Charlie was a regular at our house, often found sitting in an armchair in the front room, or opposite my father at the table, the two of them drinking tea and discussing the state of the world. He'd bring a crossword with him and they would work through the clues together, Charlie filling in the boxes neatly with his biro.

There's a photo of him with Angie, his wife, a kind, gossipy woman who'd been a hairdresser when he met her, still glamorous in her fifties. Charlie was twenty years younger than my father, but six months later he too was dead, collapsed at work from an aneurysm. He left a surprising amount of money to Angie. *Now where did that come from?* my mother said, and we all wondered. I thought well of Charlie for leaving her enough, unlike my father, whose belongings fitted into three cardboard boxes. He didn't even have a bank account, let alone a will.

Charlie was devastated by my father's death. He was the only one of my father's friends to visit every day in the last week of his life when Dad lay unconscious in the front room. Charlie sat in silence at his bedside, in the room where they had passed hours together, a mug of tea in his hand, talking gently. 'Chick's still listening,' he said. 'I know the fella.'

There's a photograph of my mother, her hand on the shoulder of Wes, another of my father's friends. She is smiling broadly, but looks dishevelled, her hair awry, the half-there, half-absent look I had come to know well since her stroke two years before. It had changed her in strange and subtle ways – no serious paralysis, no loss of speech, but a softening inside, a new gentleness, confusion, tears that came easily and often. She'd become extremely sentimental about animals. Their injuries, illnesses and rescues from cruelty, as aired on various TV shows, would leave her bereft, speechlessly weeping in the blue flicker of the screen. Yet in the days leading up to my father's death, and on the day of the funeral, she didn't cry, or if she did, no one saw. She was proud and always concerned with keeping up appearances. This didn't change with the stroke.

Wes was someone whose name I remembered, but didn't recognise at the funeral. Years ago, when I was eleven or twelve, and for reasons I can't recall, my father had taken me to the card club owned by Wes in Canning Town. It was winter and grey snow was thawing on the side street where we parked up by the club's dark green door. The blinds inside were half closed and held the daylight from the large hall that smelt of cigarettes, perfume and stale sweat. It looked more like a community hall than a casino – worn-looking men and a few women sat in plastic chairs at chipboard tables, cards fanned in their hands. A television hung in the corner of the room showing horse racing with the sound turned down. People nodded to my father as he led me past the tables to the back of the club where a hatch revealed a strip-lit kitchen and a bored-looking black woman leaning on her elbows on the counter. He bought me a can of Coke and disappeared through a side door to attend to whatever bit of business he had come for. Wes popped his head out to wave at me, saying my name as though we knew each other.

Wes was Jamaican, very light skinned, almost yellow, in his late sixties when my father died, dressed in a good black suit, white shirt, his thin Clark Gable moustache slicked down. Outside the crematorium he had introduced himself and offered me a lift back to the house, and I'd accepted, intrigued, I suppose, by these men who knew my father, wanting to know more.

It was only a few miles in Wes's little red sports car. A Christmas tree air freshener swung from the rear-view mirror. He drove with one hand on the steering wheel and with the other kept reaching for a paper bag of sweets on the dashboard, holding them out to me and saying 'You like sweeties?' again and again, before dissolving into high-pitched laughter. I sucked an aniseed twist. 'How pretty you get,' he said, looking over, one eyebrow raised, then laughing again as I willed the drive to be over, to be out of the car. 'Your daddy never say how pretty you get.'

Later, at the house, he brought me glass after glass of Baileys, as though he could seduce me with sweetness. I prayed for him to leave. *That old lech*, my mother said when I asked about him later. Wes was on his fourth marriage, the most recent to a girl he'd brought over from Jamaica. She was twenty, two years younger than me. Imagine my surprise when I answered the phone a week later to hear Wes's womanly laughter. He'd known my father for thirty years but was phoning to ask if I wanted to meet him 'to have a nice time'.

Another picture: my brother's friends – men in their late twenties, Essex boys grown. The twins, Jonny and Scott Morris, Mickey Walker and handsome Colin with his short dreadlocks – all of them in suits. I had loved these boys since they first came knocking for my brother, teenagers in their baggy jeans and Adidas trainers. I'd run to the front door, fascinated by the look and smell of them, by the rituals that went on behind my brother's bedroom door where they drank lager and listened to old soul music and hip hop, their easy laughter sounding through the walls.

The strangest photo is of my father's four children standing together – my half-sister Gloria, a small middle-aged black woman, born in America to my father's first wife. Next to her is Tom, with wavy black hair and glasses, nearly fifty, my half-brother from my father's second wife, and behind them, Sam and me, full brother and sister, both of us taller than the other two and entirely white in appearance. You wouldn't believe our father was a black man or that the four faces smiling sombrely for the camera are biologically related. It was the first time we had been in the same room together.

◆

The rain continued. The water clung in wobbling beads to the patio doors. Inside, the gathering had a surreal, cheerful atmosphere. My Jamaican friend Claudette had come early to cook a feast of my father's favourite food – what he'd asked for in his final days. Speaking through the fog of pain and morphine, he called for stewed chicken, plantain, rice and peas. Now we stood balancing our paper plates, gnawing chicken bones. The hum of conversation grew louder, cigarette smoke clouding the hot room. Billie Holiday sang in the background.

One last photo: me and Mac, one of my father's oldest friends, but a man I hardly knew. His arm is slipped through mine. He wears a jacket with a leather collar, a gold chain, expensive clothes. His face is tanned below the neat crew-cut. A week later, he posted three plane tickets to the house, a set of keys and directions to his villa in a tiny village in Spain. He had money. He wanted to buy us a week in the sun, time to recover. *Chick would have wanted it*, he wrote. *It's the least I can do.*

I am smiling in all these photos, like my mother, caring always about impressions. I remember trying to put everyone at ease, highly conscious of the dynamics of that group, the intermingling. What would my well-to-do sister, who'd flown all the way from her comfortable life in America, whose relationship with my father was disjointed and strained, make of the shady characters he had fraternised with? And my friends – I couldn't bear their sympathetic looks, the awkwardness. So I drank, I laughed, I chatted for hours, repeating the same hackneyed phrases: 'He'd have loved to see everyone here' and 'This is the way he'd have wanted it.'

But was it? My father died in shock and pain. He wasn't ready to die, he hadn't decided the time was right. Cancer decided that.

Escaping from the room for fresh air, I stood in the hall to look at the photographs I'd pinned to a cork board the night before: my father as a young man and an old man. He was fifty-two when I was born, and my memory did not register this handsome fellow, light-skinned, black-Caribbean-looking, his Chinese blood apparent, perhaps, in the high cheekbones and broad forehead. In the older photographs, he was lean and sharply dressed.

An old man in a black overcoat and hat caught my arm. 'You're Chick's daughter,' he said in an East End accent so strong he sounded like a parody of himself, like something from an old film. His face was gnarled and barky. 'I know who you are, darling, but do you know who I am?' I didn't, and I can't remember now the name he told me. 'I knew your dad for years,' he said, 'You know what your daddy did?'

Did I know? I thought I did. He laughed.

'He played poker, darling. Dice. And oh, he was the best in London, what he could do with his hands. You should be proud. He was the best. And I'm not kidding you.' He was suddenly serious. 'The best, I'm telling you.' He was holding my arm more tightly as I looked back into his wet blue eyes.

Outside, I stood alone on the front door step. I was exhausted. The cold March air was a relief from the heat of the house. Across the road, the high trees in the park were in silhouette against a purple sky. My father was dead. Chick was dead. I knew so little about him. *The best in London?* Sometime in the afternoon the undertaker must have brought the flowers from the crematorium back to the house. They were laid on the grass at the side of the path, lit by the street lamp's glow and shimmering from the rain. Red dice and the ace of hearts.

3

A TOUCH OF THE TAR BRUSH

There are no stars tonight
But those of memory

> – Hart Crane, *My Grandmother's*
> *Love Letters*

My earliest memories are of Nan – a rocking chair, a crochet blanket on her lap, a teaspoon of sweet tea from her mug. Nan came from Kennington – *the slums,* my mother said, but Nan had married up and out. My eccentric middle-class grandfather brought her from south London to his home in Ilford, the sprawling suburban town that joins east London to Essex, sometimes called the gateway to Essex. Ilford was always a place where the rich and poor rubbed shoulders – the north side of Gants Hill had big white houses set back from tree-lined streets, and the east side – Goodmayes and Seven Kings – was poorer, but not quite run down: road after road of identikit homes with pebble-dashed walls and small front yards. My grandfather lived in-between at Newbury Park, in a two-up-two-down he bought in 1910. Ilford has changed enormously since then. It still has those enclaves of affluence but it's a shabbier place. It was shabby when I was growing up. I remember the shopping parade of pound shops and shops boarded up; the scrappy, vandalised parks; the rough pubs where boys hankered for fights on a Friday night.

My dad was lovely, my mother said. *Not like my mum.* My grandfather, Walter Hart, died long before I was born, so I never met the man who made himself the black sheep of his well-to-do family – spurning a job in their stockbroking firm, denouncing God, refusing to fight in the First World War – who got divorced and married Nan, his cleaner, and, apparently, spent long hours teaching himself Sanskrit in order to decipher ancient Hindu scriptures. *He must have loved her I suppose*, said my mother, *though God knows why.*

Nan was the only grandparent I knew and everything about her spoke of another time. Her rooms downstairs were musty and old – the kitchen worktops of yellow, cracked Formica, the fragile china mugs and tiny antique silver teaspoons, the bobbly cardigans and drab blue housecoat she wore every day. There were dusty hairnets on her mantelpiece, dusty ashtrays full of her crumpled butts. Even her pale hair seemed to have a coat of dust. She is only half there in my memory, as though she were already slipping away. The images I have of her possess a certain quality, like the faded lustre of cinefilm. I see her in the flower garden in her polyester bathing suit, her scraggy legs of knotted veins, or her shaking hands spooning jam into pastry cases, or pushing an old-fashioned pram along the road, a floral headscarf tied under her chin. It might be me in the pram, as though I see us from the outside now. Of all the memories, the most striking and clear to me is the morning I pushed open her bedroom door to find her and two of her sisters, Edith and Lily, sleeping top-to-toe on the brass bed's white eiderdown. Old ladies in pale nightgowns with loose, long hair, snuggled into each other like small girls.

I remember the cups of sweets Nan gave to Sam and me – the strange ritual each morning when we went downstairs to her like Hansel and Gretel, lured by sweetness and sugar, knowing she'd have filled a cup for both of us with broken chocolate and honeycomb, bonbons wrapped in greaseproof paper, barley sugars, cubes of fudge. We loved it, of course, but my mother hated Nan giving us sweets and begged her not to when she'd just got us into the routine of cleaning our teeth.

The day I turned eighteen, she tried to rule my life, she said, *decide my friends, my boyfriends, who I married, how I brought you children up*. My mother originally met my father through his cousin Joe, whom she had dated some years before, when my grandfather was still alive. Joe was a saxophonist and my mother loved jazz. Every weekend, she'd tell Nan she was staying with a friend and catch the bus up to the East End club he played in. Joe was Jamaican – tall, handsome, always broke, often drunk, and devoted to music more than any woman, and there were many overlapping women. He was thirty-two, my mother eighteen.

'Joe? Who's Joe?' Nan said. 'A darkie? No! Not on your nelly, lady!' She was appalled when she found out and wouldn't look or speak to Joe the one time he came to the house. She cried into her mixing bowl. She couldn't sleep. My grandfather begged my mother to lie to Nan, to say they'd broken up – he thought the fret might kill her. But Nan needn't have worried. Eighteen months of lending Joe money, enduring his drunken rages, not knowing where he was, was enough for my mother. She gave him the elbow in a letter she handed him solemnly at Ladbroke Grove Tube station.

By then, she'd already met my father at the house he had shared with Elsie, his second wife, when Joe took her there one Sunday for tea. Joe loved to gamble and thought his cousin was the bee's knees. Six years later my parents bumped into each other at a hardware shop in Seven Kings. My mother was back from teaching college, dispatched by Nan to buy iron wool. My father had just split with Elsie and was living up the road in a rented room. He was out buying saucepans and asked my mother's advice. *And that was that*, she said. They rented a flat together three months later, much to Nan's disdain.

By anyone's standards, my parents were an unusual couple. She was a young, white teacher – he was twenty-three years older, an immigrant gambler. Only later did I wonder what drew them together. On my father's part, my mother was young, attractive and educated. He had a great respect for education. He loved that she was a teacher. She was also English. My father's upbringing in colonial Jamaica had left him conflicted – on the one hand he was committed to anti-imperial politics, on the other, he revered England and all things English. Socially, my mother might well have represented a 'step up' to him. Or maybe this didn't come into it at all. On a simpler level, my father was in his mid-forties, living alone, two marriages behind him, two children. He might just have been glad that anyone would have him.

As for my mother, she'd already been out with Joe, who spent half the time ignoring her, half the time sponging off her. My father compared well. Like Joe, he was handsome and well dressed. Unlike Joe, he was charming and thoughtful, had money and liked to spend it, although it took my mother a while to realise where he got it. He was well-read and articulate. He had a sense of humour. He liked to cook. He came from another place, a million miles from Ilford. He was a way out from her mother. Or so she thought.

One Boxing Day they drove out into Essex, to Theydon Bois, where my mother's elderly aunts lived in a little bungalow. They managed to feign politeness towards the only black man they'd ever had in their house, serving tea and cake and trying not to be caught staring at him. Driving home along the country roads, my parents got to talking about my father's past, and somehow he found himself telling her the story of his life – his sad childhood, running away, leaving Jamaica. They pulled up on a lovers' lane somewhere – a freezing night, snow melting on the banks. They put the heater on and sat smoking and talking past midnight. That's when she fell for him, she said – when he told her his story.

If going out with a black man caused her trouble beyond Nan, my mother never said so. She was broad-minded and expected other people to be the same. While Nan was bigoted and full of class anxiety, my grandfather was a progressive free-thinker, irreverent of convention and fascinated by other places in the world. My mother inherited his liberalism. Years later, I asked her what she saw in Joe and my father. *I just found them fascinating*, she said. *Compared to local blokes. All the things they'd seen and done.* Just as my father might have had an investment in my mother's Englishness, she was pleased to be married to a foreigner.

They lived for a year and a half in a flat on Empress Avenue in Ilford, a place my mother always mentioned with a wistful look in her eye. Then my grandfather died, and Nan, scared of being lonely, made my mother a proposition. She had some money, my parents had none – she would put down a deposit for a house they could share. Despite my mother's reservations, together they bought a house in

Ashgrove Road in Goodmayes, a semi that backed onto the
railway tracks. My childhood home. Nan lived downstairs
and we lived above. *I must have been mad*, my mother said.

When Nan found out my mother was expecting Sam
she told her, 'What a mess you're in. You'll have to keep
on working. I'll look after the baby.' *Over my dead body*,
my mother told my father, but she couldn't stop Nan from
interfering. My mother used to put Sam in the pram and
park him on the lawn so she could see him from the upstairs
window. She had a theory babies should be in the garden,
rain, shine, or snow. But every time Sam so much as blinked
or whimpered, Nan came running out the door, whisked him
up and took him in. *She wouldn't give him back*, my mother
said. *We used to have a tug of war.*

The wedding came later. A photograph outside the registry
office shows my mother plump and smiling. I worked the
dates out – she was four months pregnant with me already.
'I suppose we should get married,' my father said the night
she did the pregnancy test. *Always a one for romance*, my
mother said. *I said, I suppose we better.* Nan didn't like my
father any better than Joe, and she didn't want my mother
marrying him, even though they had one child together
and were expecting another. In Nan's mind, the immigrants
were taking over, and her only daughter planned to marry
one and parade their miscegenation right above her head.

Every plan they had, Nan was against. They saved up for an
extension to give her a bigger kitchen. Weeks talking about
it, all the plans made. Nan would stay with us because she
couldn't breathe with all the dirt and dust. But the day before
the work was meant to start Nan declared that all she needed
was a cooker and a sink, and when the workmen arrived
– Charlie White and two Jamaican chaps – she refused to

come upstairs. 'Didn't know the blacks were coming in,' she said. 'I can't be leaving all my things for them to get their grimy paws on.' *I could have killed her there and then*, my mother said. When she told my father, he went down and grabbed the sledge hammer, flung it through the window of her kitchen, shouting, 'Now you have to come up, don't you, don't you?' Nan went running out the house without her coat, and into next door, telling the neighbours about the terrible son-in-law she had, the black man who'd just assaulted her. She stayed there all day. But in the evening she was upstairs at the dinner table. Nan never missed her dinner, and knew my mother had a bit of liver in. *She always loved a bit of liver and bacon, your Nan*, my mother said.

My mother was relieved when Nan died, but I remember loving Nan – her spindly hands, her smoky breath, her long face with its deep grooves. The evening she fell ill I was curled on her lap like a cat. She was fidgety, wheezy, out of breath. She had emphysema. They took her away in an ambulance in the middle of the night. In the morning there were no sweets, no knees in the rocking chair to rest against, no more teaspoons of sweet tea.

Nan died just after I began school. Cotton Lane Primary. Days of tapping the xylophone and cake-baking – soft pink and yellow sponges I took home wrapped in foil. Gymnastics, painting, Christmas mobiles made from wire coat hangers and tinsel, angels cut from silver cardboard. I can't remember learning to read or write or do sums, only the classroom's corner library of bright picture books, the sugar-paper walls, the neat click of the abacus on the teacher's desk.

The children in my class are locked in time, back in that classroom with their paintbrushes and potato printers, sat in their little chairs, or lined up at the wall ready to be led to the school hall or playground. I don't know any of them now or where they are, what happened to them. My best friend was Mina, a Pakistani girl who wore pink plastic clips in her hair and had tiny, furry wrists. She was so light. I used to swing her on the field, round and round, her head thrown back laughing. There were lots of Pakistani children, children from India and Bangladesh, Sikh boys with topknots, girls who wore saris beneath their winter parkas. I was fascinated by the children who spoke different languages, walking home with their mothers or fathers, chatting in Gujarati or Urdu. Nirpal Singh gave me Punjabi lessons as we sat on the bench in the playground watching the others kick a tennis ball around. He taught me how to count from one to ten and every swear word he could think of. There were black children too, whose parents came from Africa or the Caribbean, like my father: Marvin Pearl, who told me he loved me in the stock cupboard, who saved me his biscuit at milk-time and tried to hold my hand.

My mother had a new job teaching at my school and that was the reason I was there. I had swapped schools, making it easier for her to bring me with her in the morning. We walked the mile from our house. Sam had stayed at the school where she had taught before, because he'd been there for years and could walk there by himself. We didn't get on, or rather he didn't get on with me. Like lots of little sisters, I worshipped my brother and wanted to endear myself to him. Despite, or perhaps because of this, he found me intensely annoying, an annoyance which most often expressed itself as a Chinese burn to my wrist or a quick jab in the ribs. His temper was changeable, from a relaxed coolness to sudden black anger. I put him on a pedestal but I was scared of him. I was glad he wasn't at my new school.

My mother's income provided stability, but even if it hadn't, she would have wanted to work. She loved teaching, she loved the children at Cotton Lane and all the challenges that went with teaching children who couldn't speak English well, or refugee children who were often traumatised.

She ran a gardening club for the worst behaved in the school – local children, more often than not – *my little delinquents*, she called them. I'd watch from my classroom as she led them across the asphalt to the school's small garden, where they would plant raspberries and runner beans and fight over whose shoots were whose or where the boundaries of each child's patch lay. There were biters and spitters and scratchers in her wayward cohort. She spent much of the time keeping the peace.

Her work was consuming. The hours were long, and most mornings she left my father a note with a list of instructions for when he woke: *Defrost chicken. Pick up dry-cleaning. Book dentist.* It suited her to have him at home taking care of the domestic tasks, and he didn't seem to mind. Just as my mum was a liberal thinker, my dad was open-minded about gender roles. He always cooked dinner. He tidied up and hung the washing out. He liked to experiment with making puddings and cakes – his 'colonial fusions', he called them. Traditional English puddings with a Jamaican twist – coconut sponge, ginger roly poly.

At the end of the school day, my father usually picked me up because my mother had to stay for meetings or to plan lessons. I'd come through the gates to find him waiting, occasionally on foot but usually parked up with the radio on, a cigarette in the hand on the steering wheel. 'Hello, Han!' he always chimed as I appeared at the school gate or by the side of his car with my satchel and lunch box. 'Hello, Han!', as though he hadn't seen me in years and what a surprise it was for us to bump into each other. All my life he greeted me this way, whether I'd been upstairs in my bedroom for an hour or, years later, flying back from a year living in California to find him, unexpectedly, waiting for me at the airport arrival gates. He was in his seventies by then, and dying, stood looking out for me in his old mustard cardigan, his hair gone wild and cartoonish. We never hugged or touched. 'Hello, Han!' he said, reaching out his thin arms to help me with my suitcase.

♥

'Is that your dad?' Solomon Kallakuri asked me one morning as we hung our coats on the pegs in the cloakroom. We were six. Solomon was my new friend since we'd been paired on a school trip to the farm, ordered to walk round hand in hand. He wasn't white but he wasn't black either, or Pakistani, and I still don't know where his tanned skin came from, or his surname. He had a cheeky face with big, thick eyebrows that joined in the middle. 'Yes,' I said, but I didn't say anything more, knowing only that I couldn't lie, though I'd have liked to. We went into the classroom. Later, washing our paintbrushes at the sink, Solomon had more to say:

'Your dad looks really old,' he said. 'How old is he?'

My dad was really old, I knew that. 'I think he's sixty.'

His eyebrow went up. 'That's *well* old! That's older than my grandad.'

This wasn't the first time I'd had this conversation. 'My mum's not that old,' I offered, as though it might compensate for the outrage of my dad's years.

'And he's black.' He turned off the tap. 'It's weird that he's your dad.' He was dabbing his brushes on the rainbow-blurred kitchen roll at the side of the sink.

'Mum, am I half-caste?' She was washing up, lost in thought. 'Mum!' I spoke louder. I had just returned from a sleepover at Anna Faulkner's house, where her dad had expressed surprise after he'd seen my father dropping me off. 'I didn't know you were a half-caste,' he said thoughtfully. 'You look English, doesn't she, Pam?' Pam was Anna's mother, a nervous woman with fluttery hands who looked even more flustered at her husband's remarks. I said nothing, carefully carving the steamed kidneys we were having for dinner. They were disgusting but I forced them down out of politeness. Anna's dad also whispered I was 'very pretty' the moment Anna and her mother left the room to fix the pudding. I'd found this more disquieting and decided not to mention it. 'Am I half-caste, Mum? Yes or no?'

'No, love. That's not a nice term. You're not half anything.'

'But am I half Jamaican?'

'Well, your dad is from Jamaica. But his dad was Chinese, and his mum was black, which makes you part white, part Chinese and part Jamaican.' Right. My mother had it sorted. Jamaican was synonymous with black, then, I assumed, and since my father was from Jamaica, and looked like a black man, that part made sense. But the Chinese aspect always threw me a little, since my father didn't look like other Chinese people I knew, like Eileen Ng in my class at school with her shiny flat hair. And my father never mentioned anything about China or his Chinese father. As far as I knew, he couldn't speak Chinese. China showed itself in the ornate chopsticks we kept alongside the knives and forks in the cutlery drawer and the small bowls painted with red and gold dragons he sometimes ate Chinese food from. And he liked to drink jasmine tea from little porcelain cups. I did too. Steaming cups of aromatic tea. The twig-like leaves sunk to the bottom and looked like tiny bird's nests.

But Jamaica, Jamaica. I knew the sound of the word long before I had any clear idea where Jamaica was, who lived there, or why my father had come all the way from that island in the sun to Ilford, Essex. Jamaica showed itself in the sing-song lilt he would sometimes put on to make us laugh. He was rarely jovial, but occasionally after dinner he might lean his head back and break into an old calypso song about a woman selling herbs and weeds at the village market:

> She had the man piaba, woman piaba,
> Tantan, Fallback and Lemon Grass,
> Minnie Root, Gully Root, Grannie Back Bone,
> Bitter Tally, Lime Leaf and Toro, Coolie
> Bitters, Caralia Bush,
> Flat o' the Earth and Iron Weed, Sweet
> Broom, Fowl Tongue, Wild Daisy,
> Sweet Sage ...

I loved the names of these weeds, imagining what they looked like and what magic they held, but my father loved the final line the most, as though he sang the whole song through just to reach a climax we never found as funny as he did:

*The only one she didn't have ... was the
wicked ganja weed!*

He would hold his stomach and fall around laughing.

Jamaica also revealed itself on the telephone – long
conversations in the hall where he would suddenly switch
to a thick Jamaican accent. I stood listening through a crack
at the dining-room door. Was he talking to someone actually
in Jamaica, I wondered, picturing a payphone below a palm
tree on a beach, turquoise sea in the background, and the
man who had decided to phone his long-lost friend Ralph
standing there shouting into the receiver, 'Man, long time no
see!' Now I realise it was often his cousin Dolores in Canada.
Other times it was London-based West Indians, as he called
them (and himself), discussing some business of home or
family but more likely a card game, or a dice table someone
needed making, or a croupier wanted for an all-night game.

Jamaica named itself most regularly at dinner time. My
father loved to cook and he loved to boast about his cooking.
'I can cook anything,' he said. 'I don't need a recipe! Trust
me, I know what I'm doing!' He did most of the cooking in
the week, an arrangement that fitted my parents' disparate
lifestyles – my mother at work all day while he went out
gambling after dinner, returning around dawn to sleep
through to lunchtime. Before she came home from work
he'd already be at the stove, lifting the lid of a pan of rice and
peas, stirring chicken, chopping ginger, crushing star anise.
He concocted soups and stews of yam and dumpling, back
bacon flavoured with pig-snout and pig-tail, or fried johnny
cakes of flour and salt to dip in stewed tomato – *poor man's
food*, he called these – the fare of the field workers from his
childhood.

His cooking had legendary status among my mother's friends, other teachers who came often for dinner. They were solid left-wing women like her who wore floaty clothes and ethnic earrings, who cooed over my father's culinary inventiveness, his knack of making everything taste good. It was at these times I could see my mother was proud to be married to a Jamaican man. He'd cook lavish dishes – mainly Caribbean food but sometimes Chinese food too – nothing like Chinese takeaway, but salty won ton soup or steamed egg that had the consistency of slime but tasted delicious. Sometimes he returned from the butcher with a whole pork belly, rubbing salt and five-spice into the skin, stringing it across the oven to roast all afternoon. My mother was less pleased with this – the sizzling pork filling the kitchen with smoke, spitting fat onto the oven that *someone, i.e. me, will have to scrub off*, she said.

She also objected to the sweet sausages of pork and chilli he made every summer and hung in clusters on our washing line to dry and preserve. Nan was dead by this time but if she hadn't been, she might have dropped down from a heart attack to see those sausages hanging in the garden. They were a deep, dark red, gristly looking with twisted ends and oily skins, swinging in the English breeze. In Jamaica, the hot sun would have dried them out nicely, but here they hung limply for a week between the bed-sheets and tea-towels and might easily be ruined by a sudden downpour. I can still see him pulling the back door open, crying, 'Oh no, oh no!' and running down the path through the rain to pull the clothes pegs from the strings and shelter his precious sausages in his shirt. My mother's objection was never specified, but I suspect she found them a troubling symbol of my father's exoticism in Ilford and his efforts to save them an embarrassing spectacle in front of the neighbours.

The cooking arrangements in our house were unlike those of my friends, whose fathers didn't cook and whose mothers, for the most part, served up bland dinners of fish fingers and peas, pizza, chicken nuggets, everything with chips and everything English, except chilli con carne or spaghetti bolognese. We ate English food as well. My mother liked us to eat traditional Sunday lunch together, and on Sunday evenings, when my father was always out playing cards, a tea of egg sandwiches, buttered scones and fruitcake, accompanied by endless cups of strong teapot tea. I hated this ritual. It went hand in hand with the awful dullness of Sundays and the night-before-school feeling. Sam and I would disagree, arguments that often ended in violence, then an hour of tears before *The Antiques Roadshow* and *Last of the Summer Wine*, and maybe before that *Songs of Praise*, because my mother liked the singing. All of this had the effect of making Sundays more English than other days, but it was an Englishness I had little experience of – countryside and church halls and cake sales and *boredom* – an Englishness I didn't want to know about, not from the television, and definitely not in real life.

My mother was also enthusiastic about frozen food. This was the 1980s and a trip to Sainsbury's Freezer Centre delivered different delights each week. 'Try these,' she said, marvelling at the crunchiness of Findus crispy pancakes or Birds Eye potato waffles, or the convenience of Brussels sprouts and chopped carrots you didn't have to peel. When my father was older, and in fact, when he could no longer eat very much – the doctors took half his stomach, trying to remove all the cancer cells – his enthusiasm for food unsurprisingly diminished, and he resorted to the freezer when he had to cook dinner, serving up anaemic sausages and pale oven chips. By then he was uninterested in the whole ritual of dinner time and if we ate at the table, he would excuse himself halfway through, his plate still full, and sit a way off, thumbing the paper or watching television as though eating was no longer something that he could be wholly concerned with – his stomach had betrayed him.

I think my father must have learned to cook because he had to. He left Jamaica in 1947, sailing to Liverpool on the HMS *Ormonde*, one of the immigrant boats before the *Empire Windrush*. Over a hundred young men were on board, hoping for better opportunities in England. My father had lived with his friend Lionel in a damp cellar with one bed they had to share. I see the two of them in the drab light of their digs, frost on the windows, cooking on a single hotplate – simple, inexpensive food. And I remember the one-man meals my father would cook for himself when he was home alone – a tin of sardines steamed over a pan of rice, potato hash cakes, callaloo mashed with nutmeg. He never spoke about this period of his life and much of what I know is gleaned from my mother – how he came to London, found a job as a shunter at King's Cross, joining and decoupling the heavy steel train carriages. She told me how he hated that work – a whole winter when he bandaged his hands and wore two pairs of gloves to protect his fingers, but how they still cracked and bled from pulling the freezing metal.

There are no letters from this time and few photographs, apart from his old passport and two pictures of his mother, Hermione Harriott. I loved looking at the images of my other grandmother, long dead, the Nan I would never meet. In one, she stares face-on into the camera. She is very light-skinned but her features are African – a broad nose, high cheekbones, wide lips. Her hair is pinned in a chignon and she wears a white lace dress, her best perhaps, as though the taking of the portrait was an important occasion. Her young face has a kind, dignified look. The resemblance between her and my father is strong. The other photograph is from a wedding. Hermione is dressed in an organza frock on the left side of the bride, her niece, but her face is fixed in an angry frown, whereas the other guests are smiling. My father told me that his mother disapproved of the groom, because her niece, in her view, was marrying down. In the strict shade hierarchy of Jamaica, the paler you were the better – the higher in class, the more socially superior – and the groom in the photo, compared to his bride, is much darker.

But surely these intricacies of shade and colour are unpredictable? I used to look for myself in the image of Hermione, but there is little likeness. I am white, fair-haired, green-eyed. No one would ever think I was mixed race. I wonder if my father cared that my brother and I looked so white, if he wanted us to look more like him, more easily recognisable as his children. That question – 'Is that your dad?' – was a common one throughout my childhood. It came from children at school who, not bound by the laws of polite social interaction, looked at me with that old black man and wondered aloud what their parents would think, but not dare say.

◆

Charlie White was never reticent in his opinions. A scholar of the 'university of life', he had a range of hare-brained theories about the world and universe. His views on racial mixing were extraordinary, and more so that he would share them with my family and me. 'Look, it's like this,' he said one day while my father was making us tea. 'You like dogs. You buy a dog. Let's say you buy an Alsatian. Great big dog, big ears, slobbering tongue – you know the deal. Let's say your neighbour's got a Chihuahua – a little poncy dog, cross-eyed. Now they're both dogs, right? But they're different breeds. They're different *species*. You're not gonna mate them. There's no way you're gonna mate them. Cos what would you get?'

'A medium dog?' I asked. 'But a weird-looking one.'

'Precisely!' He looked pleased, as though I had proved his point. '*Weird* is the key word. It wouldn't be right, would it? I'm not a racist, but it's the same thing with humans. We're from different parts of the world, we're from different *civilisations*. Some of us need to be out in the sun so we've got black skin. Others live where it's cold, like this poncing country, so we're white.' He prodded himself. 'Then you've got your Indians, your Pakistanis, all different, job done. But we're not meant to mate, no way. I've read a book about it. I've *thought* about it. It's not about race, it's the same with dogs – we're just different breeds, it's obvious.'

'But what about normal mongrels, who don't look weird?' I asked, unable to follow his logic. I was thinking about our dog Chloe, whom Charlie loved.

'Well, they're not right either,' he said. Chloe was sat at his feet. He bent forward to tickle her. 'Chloe's a sweet dog and all, but she's not a pedigree, is she? She's not the best that she could be.' Chloe jumped into his lap and licked his face.

'She likes you though,' I said.

'That's as may be.' He leant back in his chair, straining his neck to see if my father was in earshot, stroking the dog. 'Now your dad, he's all right. You know he's my best mate. I've known him half my life. But bloody hell, we've had some rows about this one. We're never gonna agree on this one.' He was speaking conspiratorially, as though I could surely see the reason of his argument, even if my father couldn't. 'I told him, "Chick, it's like two different dogs – no reason not to get on, but just don't mate them." But he sits there in his bloody armchair, lights his cigarette and looks straight back at me – like I'm a fool, like *I'm* a bleeding idiot!'

♠

My father liked to remind me that I was, in Charlie's words, a mongrel. 'You've got a touch of the tar brush,' he would say. 'Don't forget now.' He'd be laughing, knowing well enough how loaded that phrase was – its origins in the bigoted slang of those obsessed by racial purity. He found it funnier because of that. His humour was often irreverent and sometimes careless – a sort of schoolboy insolence. He took the joke one step further once or twice, finding a ruler in the bureau drawer to measure the width of my nose. I was seven, completely unaware of the implications of this, long before I knew about scientific racism that used this type of anatomical investigation to prove its awful theories. I laughed along as he measured my nose from side to side, then let me measure his. It was strange to be so physically close to him, to be touching his face. But his nose was 6.5cm across at the widest part, a figure I was impressed with.

'Your nose is *massive*, Dad!' I worried that mine might grow to match the size of his.

♥

Up close to my father was too close to his moles. There were literally hundreds of them, covering his face and neck, down his arms, across his back. The ones on his back were large, the size of five-pence pieces. Others were smaller and resembled sultanas, raised from the skin and gathered in clusters with waxy surfaces. In some places, there were more moles than actual skin. Once he went to the doctor's about a mole that had become irritated and had an operation to remove it. Apparently the hospital dermatologist had been fascinated by the volume of moles covering my father's body and had wanted to conduct tests on them. But my father didn't want to be experimented on. He seemed unfazed by the moles, which he called his *black spots*, even though there were more and more every year.

But those black spots horrified me and he knew this. I had a few dark moles on the side of my face he used to point at or try to touch. 'Oh dear, Han,' he said, 'looks like you'll be covered soon, like me!' I ran to the mirror in the hall to check the size of the moles and search for the appearance of more.

It was a rare skin condition – *Seborrhoeic keratosis* – although I don't think he was actually ever properly diagnosed. Sufferers develop multiple benign moles from the age of forty onwards. *They weren't so bad when I met him*, my mother said. But by the time he was sixty, his black spots covered the surface of his skin and one day, driving with them, I announced my decision to stop kissing him. 'I don't want to catch black spots,' I said, pulling a face.

'They're not catching,' my mother turned round from the front seat. 'They're just moles. We've all got moles.' My father said nothing, his hands on the steering wheel.

'Well, I'm not kissing him anymore, just in case.' Although I didn't mean it, I really didn't kiss him again, not once, not a kiss, not a hug, for fifteen years, until he was lying unconscious in our living room, the night before he died.

♣

The Ashgrove Road house was a place of mysteries. I both knew and didn't know it. It was so familiar, my house, my home, but *something* made me a snoop there. I was in everything. No drawer unopened, no cupboard I hadn't rooted through. For a while I was a thief and liar too.

One morning I rose early and found a packet of meringues in the kitchen cupboard. Six perfect white meringue nests. I crunched through them, one after another, washed them down with orange squash. There were crumbs on the carpet in front of the television where my cartoons played. I was happy. It was good to be awake at 6 a.m., alone with myself and sated with sugar as Wile E. Coyote pranced across the screen.

But hours later, at lunchtime, my mother went to look for those meringues. It was Sunday and we had a guest at the table – not just anyone, but Dolores, all the way from Canada. She was my father's cousin, but much younger. They had known each other in Jamaica, but had lost touch for years. Then out of the blue, she was on the phone and coming to visit in her red blouse with a jewelled brooch pinned to it. She had long fingers with red painted nails and wore gold rings. The lunch was special. The good white-and-brown china was on the table, and – how could I know? – raspberries from our garden and a pot of whipped cream were waiting in the fridge to be spooned onto those meringues.

To lie well you have to shift reality to match your truth. For a second before you tell a lie, you must believe that what you are about to say is unequivocally the truth and hold your nerve about it. Stick with the lie and not betray it. So when my mother came back into the room, I already knew I hadn't eaten the meringues. When she asked, the denials came easily. Even when I saw she really knew – because, after all, what other explanation was there? – the only thing that mattered was to hold the lie, to keep denying, and so I lied and lied. 'I swear, Mum, I didn't eat them.' She sat down at the table and watched me. 'I didn't, I didn't.' It was all planned – the raspberries, meringues, whipped cream, and I had ruined it all, ruined the lunch, the visit. 'I promise, Mum, I didn't eat them. I didn't eat them.'

We sat around the table and watched the lie, like a ball I rolled towards my mother. Every time I rolled it, she rolled it back, harder each time. So then I rolled it to my father, who was keeping the conversation going with Dolores as though they couldn't hear the lie rolling on the wood, and without even looking, he raised his hand and stopped the ball and rolled it back. Sam sat smiling at the other end of the table. Slowly he shook his head. By then, of course, I was crying, and there was only one place for me to go, and I was grateful when my mother sent me away to my bedroom. Yet I still felt *I* was the victim of a terrible miscarriage of justice, even as I lay sobbing into my sheets, the tears were not of guilt, but of indignation – sorrow, not remorse.

Was it minutes or hours after that Dolores held me and told me everything was all right? She smelt of a sweet perfume. We were on the bed and she was leaving. I was crying still because she couldn't give me what I wanted – her belief in the lie. Instead I took what was offered – forgiveness. It made me heavy in her red silk arms, still sobbing: 'I didn't, I didn't.'

♦

My mother's younger brother, Uncle Terry, lived a mile away from us with Auntie Lyn and my three cousins, Susanna and Maria – 'the girls' – both older than me, and little Alfie, a year younger. Lyn had been my mother's close friend at teaching college, which is how she'd met Terry. I was sometimes scared of my uncle, of his big dark beard and loud voice. My aunt was gentle and pragmatic. I liked her and I pretty much worshipped Susanna and Maria, just for being older than me and for being my cousins. *In each other's pockets*, my mother said about the five of us together before my brother outgrew us, leaving the girls with me trailing after them, and Alfie trailing after me through long summers in the bright garden and the park with its hideaways and secrets, the endless games of leapfrog and hide-and-seek, dressing up in Nan's old dresses and old hats with peacock feathers, our small feet in her old-lady shoes, and the sleepless sleepovers and camping holidays, Christmas Day not starting until they arrived at our house, or us at theirs.

In 1982, I was desperate to join the girls at Margie Sparrow's Dance School in the church hall at Chadwell Heath and my mother finally agreed. On Wednesday evenings after school would-be ballerinas aged five to fifteen would train under the tutelage of Margie herself. Some looked as though they were born to dance, while others had been pushed into the class by their mothers. They looked dazed and lonely, loitering at the back of the hall to fidget with their leotards and pink tights, until we were called to our places to warm up. Then we rested our hands on wooden chairs as Margie, frail and ancient in a yellow gauze dress, her dyed black hair in a tangled beehive – swept down the rows, turning our knees out with her wooden cane, her rheumatic eyes locking with ours as though she could see the bad inside of us.

Susanna was ten by then. She was studious and bookish and didn't like dancing at all, but Maria was a natural dancer, full of self-confidence. Even Alfie had a go at ballet, wanting to be wherever we were. He was the only boy in a class of fifty girls, his thin body clad in black tights and a wrap-around cardigan. The older girls laughed at him when we lined up to run and leap, one by one, across the hall's polished floor, even though Alf could jump higher than all of us, and looked so lithe and elegant moving through the air. '*Saut de chat*, girls!' cried Margie Sparrow. 'Your arms are wings! Reach for the stars!' Alfie looked like he was flying. I thought he was brave for joining in, and said so, but he stopped coming at the same time as Susanna, then Maria moved to the advanced class on Saturday mornings, leaving me to fend for myself.

At seven, I was as tall as the ten-year-olds and it soon became clear to me that long limbs were not an advantage in ballet, in the way that they were in netball or running. I wasn't going to excel at dancing. Joy and Suki Lovell were in the same set as me – small, blonde, angelic sisters, who stood at the front and executed every plié and jeté perfectly. I persevered through the twice-yearly exams – always Commended, never Highly Commended, never a Distinction

– and through the annual shows at Ilford Town Hall, which required our parents to pay out for garish pink or lilac tutus and obliged our mothers to spend hours stuffing us into our costumes in the dressing rooms, slicking us in blue eyeshadow and red lipstick, before the curtain rose and we spun and polka-danced across the stage.

My father never came to these events but he dropped me off and picked me up from every lesson. We spent more time together in his car than anywhere. He patiently ferried me to choir and piano lessons, to and from school, to birthday parties and back again. After ballet, I would come out to find him standing among the Essex mothers in their leopard-skin leggings and stiletto boots and gold jewellery. Once, after a particularly gruelling class in which I had failed to master a series of chassés, my feet seemingly too large for one to 'lightly chase' the other, an exasperated Margie Sparrow had ordered me to stand aside to let the other girls pass. 'Fairy steps, girls!' she cried, 'Don't wake the fairies up!' Her look told me I was more elephant than fairy. I don't think I've ever felt as horribly body conscious as I did at that moment. Afterwards my father was in the foyer, standing to the side looking dishevelled in his old suede jacket and jeans, grey hair uncombed, jingling his car keys. 'Hello, Han!' he called out to me. Why couldn't I just be normal, I thought, the same size as other girls, with a normal father, who looked like other fathers?

I saw Suzette Bryce, a portly girl who struggled with dancing even more than I did, look at him, and then look quizzically at me. As we went to the pegs to retrieve our coats and shoe bags, I turned to her and whispered, 'My mum's at work so she sends a cab driver for me,' and she whispered back, 'Oh right, I wondered.'

Penny Hodge, another little dancer, was nearby, listening. 'I always wondered too,' she said, leaning in. She looked in my father's direction. 'Is it always the same man?'

We were conspiratorial. I nodded. 'They always send the same one.'

'Well,' said Suzette. 'I could ask my mum to give you a lift if you like.' We all looked at my father again, who suddenly looked exactly like a cab driver.

'Oh no, it's OK,' I said quickly. 'I don't really mind.'

'See you next week, then?' Penny asked, picking up her bag.

'Oh, I suppose,' said Suzette. She looked miserable at the thought.

'Yep, next week! See you!' I replied brightly, pulling on my coat. I turned away to my father, who reached out for my shoe bag, completely unaware of my betrayal.

4
1938

*T*he boy and his father were living in a small village near to Yallahs. They worked in Mr Ho Choy's grocery. The old shop was gone. The boy did not know why there had been a change of fortune but his friend Rufus told him his father had pledged the shop in a *mahjong* game and, unable to pay the debt, had been forced to hand it over. Once again they had tied their mattresses to the truck, packed their clothes and whatever goods were left, and gone off into the night, along the yellow dust lanes, past moonlit banana fields and coffee groves, the storm debris of branches cracking under their wheels.

Mr Ho Choy was an old man who limped behind the counter. He had white whiskers and a bald head. He was kind to the villagers, who all had credit with him, and his business had grown from a simple grocery to a sprawling store that sold hardware and timber, with a rum shop attached and a kitchen selling snacks. He lived with his wife in a large white house half a mile away and allowed the boy and his father to sleep in the shop's back room, among the sacks and crates.

A makeshift curtain split the room in two and on the other side, Linda Bloomfield, the shop's servant, slept with her two small children. She was young and very black but reminded the boy of his mother with her wide doe-eyes and the coils of plaits she wore wrapped above her ears. Her children whimpered and cried and the boy lay awake listening to Linda's cooing. The soft lull of her songs floated out of the window into the blue night, reminding the boy of his mother's singing. Sometimes the boy awoke to hear another noise – not children, but something animal behind the curtain, a low grunting, rhythmic and breathless, and a woman's soft cries. The boy sat up and looked over at his father's empty cot, the bare sheets crumpled in the moonlight.

He was thirteen now. He didn't go to school but worked all day in the shop, often left alone with Mr Ho Choy when his father was sent to Kingston for goods. He was grateful, always, to be out of his way. His father still beat him, his violence sudden and chaotic.

One night he had been reading the newspaper to his father in the back room of the shop. The news told of workers demanding more wages and rioting at the sugar factory in Westmoreland. People had been killed. Caught up in the injustice, the boy blurted out a curse: 'Damn the factory owners! The workers have a right to stand up for themselves.' Before he could continue reading, the blow struck his ear. His father's left fist first, then his right, again and again as the boy stumbled round the lamp-lit room, trying to duck the punches, until finally he lay on the floor, curled against the bare feet kicking his back.

Sometimes the boy would wake in the morning, the first light sloping up the wall, to find his father sitting on his own cot, bent forward and staring at him, a brooding look on his face. Before the boy could speak, his father's hands would be on him, pulling him up and pushing him towards the door, the two of them in a strange, silent dance, out across the yard and towards the trees. There was no one else awake to see the man dragging the boy, naked but for his shorts, fallen to his knees and clawing at the dirt. There would be rope, the boy's body tied to the trunk, and then his father's punches, quick in succession, sharp jabs to his back and sides, the boy's cheek scraping on the bark, his body waking up to pain, the snap of his father's belt before the buckle whipped against his thighs. Sometimes his father neglected to tie him, but he still leant there, nailed to the tree by the force of his father's fists.

Afterwards the boy watched his father's back heaving as he walked away, out of breath. He would bend to wash his hands in the bucket on the veranda, as though the boy had dirtied him somehow, as though he needed to be rinsed off. He never looked back. The boy would pick himself up from the ground, slowly unfurling. He never cried. He would go inside and dress slowly and carefully in the back room, examining the bruises already showing on his torso, dark blooms on his skin, dabbing the bright cuts with a cloth. Then the day would begin, as though he had just risen.

♠

One day he was alone minding the shop, leaning on the counter, his mind busily running over the accounts, only vaguely aware of a small child skipping back and forth in the yard outside the door. Customers came and went and each time they left the boy would look up to see the child, a boy of five or six, playing hopscotch, throwing a stone into the dust, the sound of his counting just audible. The boy looked down again. Then suddenly the child was before him, bare-chested, his nose just touching the counter, his grubby fingers gripping the wood. 'What you doing?' the child asked, looking at the ledger, the pen in the boy's hand, then immediately, 'My mummy says we brothers.'

'Hmm?' The boy looked up, pretending not to hear. 'Take your hands off the counter.'

'I'm your brother,' the child said proudly. 'I'm Kenneth.' His smile showed his pink gums and the threat of a nervous laugh rippled in his thin chest. The boy took him in – the pretty face below his scalp shaved and scarred by a careless razor. They had the same slant eyes, the same cheekbones, the same nose. He could see that what the child said was true. But quietly he said, 'No,' looking him in the eyes, 'is not true,' and then a whisper: 'Your mummy is lying because she don't know who your daddy is, I promise you.'

Something flickered in the child's smile and the boy pulled himself up a little taller behind the counter until he loomed above the child blinking up at him.

'Yes, we brothers!' he insisted.

'Get out my shop,' the boy said, pronouncing each word carefully. 'You're no brother of mine.'

'Yes, my mummy said!' The child looked hurt. 'We brothers. Same daddy, the Chinaman.'

The boy pointed at the doorway, spoke louder. 'Out! Get out of here!' The child turned to the door, then slowly back to the boy and said simply, 'Because we look the same, you can't see?' and he walked fast out the door and began to run, across the yard and through the gate. He was barefoot. The boy watched him disappear along the road.

He had seen his own face so clearly in the smaller boy's he couldn't bear it, and didn't know what it was he couldn't bear, the sight of his own self, or of his father. And how many children did his father have with girls from Mocho, Hearts Ease or Yallahs? Linda Bloomfield's belly was growing and he knew what was in there. How many others, a mile away or thirty miles away? Did he pass them on the road, these children who were not owned like he was, who had loving mothers to care for them and time and leisure to throw stones into the dust, hopping back and forth in the midday sun?

Mr Ho Choy was kind. He helped out the poorest in the village, didn't chase credit if he knew a family couldn't pay it, give small loans of cash he knew he wouldn't see again. He had worked hard, had enough for himself and could afford to be kind. He was kind to the boy too, as though he could sense the sorrow in him, could see below his clothes the scars and marks put on him by his father. When the shop was quiet, and the boy's father gone to trade, he showed him card tricks – the boy following the queen in Three Card Marney, pointing at the card he knew must be the one because his eyes told him so, even as he knew Mr Ho Choy had somehow swapped it. 'You sure, you sure?' the old man laughed in his croaky voice, turning the cards over, fooling the boy again.

Mr Ho Choy was old but his hands were nimble. They were small, strangely pale and reminded the boy of the fragile shells the tide washed up in Yallahs Bay. Mr Ho Choy showed the boy how to hold his fingers still and pressed together, curving his palm just so, to hold a card out of sight, then how to flick his wrist so quickly a swap could not be seen. The boy practised this manoeuvre for hours at the counter, until he too could do the three-card trick.

Some nights he sat outside the shop with the village men, their rum and beers and dominoes set out on the table. He would take out his cards and the men would gather round, one by one trying their luck against the boy, tossing him a penny to deal the three cards face down side-by-side. Then slowly at first, the boy would slide the cards around, swapping them into each other's places, but always turning them over to show their faces. He knew the banter needed for the trick, the constant talk the confidence man should spin a punter. 'So *there* she is,' he'd say, turning the queen, 'and there she is again.' His audience hummed and ahhed along, bent towards the table, the punter's eyes fixed on the boy's hands moving the cards faster and faster until finally they came to rest. 'Now which one is it?' the boy would ask, looking up, and the fellow would point to a card with conviction, his eyes wide, and say 'That one! It *has* to be that one,' and 'I haven't looked away – I *know* it's the queen!'

'You sure, you sure?' the boy would ask, before turning the card to show a three of hearts or two of diamonds. 'No way! No way!' the man cried, outraged but half laughing, and the other men slapped their thighs and shook their heads. All evening, they would play the boy, drunker and drunker, but more determined to outwit him. And sometimes he let them win, enough times to keep them playing, their pennies knocking against each other in his pocket.

5

IF YOU CAN'T WIN IT STRAIGHT, WIN IT CROOKED

It matters not how strait the gate
How charged with punishments the scroll
I am the master of my fate:
I am the captain of my soul

– William Ernest Henley, *Invictus*

My grandfather Walter had played the piano, my mother played the piano and then I began to play the piano. My father drove me to weekly lessons at Miss Phelps's house on Breamwood Road, with its dark rooms of brocade furniture, the windows blocked by ornate nets and velvet curtains, the lingering smell of polish. Miss Phelps was in her eighties with thin white hair pulled into a bun and half-moon spectacles she peered over to observe my hands misbehaving on the keys of her piano.

'Stop, stop!' she would cry in her croaking voice, yanking my wrists up with a pencil, 'Lift them, lift!' Sometimes she would shut the piano lid altogether, sighing, and would bring me an orange from her fruit bowl. '*Feel* the orange,' she ordered and I had to sit in her upright chair and roll the fruit between my palms, to mould my hands into the proper shape to play – fingers spread like claws, high wrists.

Miss Phelps had a brain tumour. I didn't find this out until my mother announced that we needed to find a new piano teacher because Miss Phelps was in hospital and not expected to come home. I didn't have the chance to see her before she died, to thank her for her teaching and her patience. By then, I was quite good at the piano, having left behind *Teaching Little Fingers How to Play* for *Step by Step to the Classics*.

My father used to see Miss Phelps every time he came to pick me up from lessons. They would pass the time of day while I stood between them, squirming, wanting to be gone. He was upset when he found out how ill she was, worried that she didn't have any family to visit her. She'd never married and didn't have children. He bought flowers and drove to the hospital to sit at her bedside, returning the next day and all that week until the last time, when the staff told him Miss Phelps had died in the night. He came home looking sadder than I'd ever seen him.

After Miss Phelps I went to Maisie, who was barely eighteen, a punk who wore long black skirts and slashed T-shirts, painted her nails blue and had three rings in her nose. She was a virtuoso, her long fingers dancing on the piano keys in her mum's back room where she gave lessons. I wanted to play like her. At nine years old, I wanted to *be* her. She hennaed her hair and smelt of cigarettes. I practised more and more.

After Nan had died, my mother inherited the rest of the house and we took over the rooms downstairs. The brass bed was removed and Nan's bedroom became our front room and home to the piano. It was a space rarely used except by me – a quieter, stiller room somehow, with pale green walls bathed in light from the tall bay windows. I was only allowed to play the piano in the afternoons and evenings – morning practice was banned because it disturbed my father in the room above, sleeping off a night of poker. When I could practise, I'd play for hours at a time, until my arms and shoulders ached. I found it peaceful and was rarely interrupted, unless by my father. 'Play me a song, Han?' His head popped through the front-room door. For him, the piano was a serious pastime with the genteel associations his upbringing in colonial Jamaica encouraged him to admire. Sometimes I just refused, but other times I'd shut the lid heavily and leave the room, stalking past him. Worse was when he had a friend round and wanted to show me off. I couldn't bear it and I never would. Often I'd hear him shuffling outside when I practised and would fling the door open to find him standing listening.

'Honestly, Dad! Go away, will you!' I'd say, and like a chastised child he'd turn and slope off down the hall.

I resented the pride he showed in me. It made me angry in a way I didn't understand then and still don't entirely. Looking back, I see how he claimed his children's successes as his own, as though we existed as reflections on him, despite his hands-off parenting. He would boast to anyone about my half-brother Tom's first-class degree in Maths from Durham, or my half-sister Gloria's glamorous work in Atlanta. 'Yes, my daughter is Head of Cultural Affairs,' he'd say. 'She's clever, like me,' and 'Brains are in the family.' Most children want to make their parents proud, but I sensed a desperation in his pride, his need to prop himself up through me. Because what did he have? No qualifications, no job, no access to the institutions he so admired. No bank account, no mortgage, no pension. Nothing of any import. Nothing that carried any currency or status. Even aged nine, I knew I had the opportunity for those things and that my life would take a very different path from his. I looked down on him because of it. And of all the things he coveted, the one he wanted most was my respect.

♣

Your father didn't know how to be a father, my mother once said. *He had no role model.* I remembered the silky scars on my father's legs, pale and raised, made by the belt of his father, my grandfather. They haunted me – I was horrified that marks made so long ago could endure.

I wondered what a good father might be. A breadwinner? When my father slapped cash onto the dinner table, he was claiming that status, but we all knew our household needed our mother's income too, that his winnings were erratic and unreliable. Was a father supposed to make the rules, perhaps, to be the disciplinarian of a family? I'd heard that threat – *Wait until I tell your father* – from the television and from the mothers of my friends, as though the father was the chief justice of punishment, the last recourse when you were *really* bad. But my mother was our judge and jury, and my father was soft as butter – he never told me off, never raised a hand to me.

Half the time he wasn't there – out in the evening, asleep half the day. My mother tried to compensate, to be both mother *and* father to us – but perhaps this undermined him even more, although it seemed to suit him to let her. 'Ask your mother,' he'd say whenever I would ask to bake a cake, or walk to the shop, or watch TV. 'Ask your mother. Ask your mother.' Until I didn't ask him any more.

Many of my friends' fathers had *enthusiasms* – football, sailing, DIY, stamp collecting – some activity they might share with their children. But what were my father's hobbies? Going to the bookies? Nothing we shared, although he'd sometimes do a card trick for me, and we spent a lot of time in the car together, driving from A to B, or the occasional trip to the park, where I would push the roundabout, working up a speed before jumping on, while he stood a way off under a tree, smoking a roll-up.

In the car, he'd boast: 'I know the streets of London like the back of my hand.' A cliché, but one he often used, and of course he did – his gambling took him everywhere, all over London, at times all over England, and later even overseas. He spent hours driving, the talk-show chatter from the radio keeping him company. One night, somewhere near Bow, he said, 'Come on, Han, let's see if you can get me lost.' He was smiling. 'I bet you any money you can't.' I saw his need to impress me in that smile – 'Look what I can do,' it said, and although I didn't want to, I played along, giving him instructions, 'Turn right here, Dad,' and, 'Turn left, then left again.' I see us from the outside now, crossing the river onto a dual carriageway, past a dilapidated art-deco factory, a huge estate of high-rise blocks with their balconies crammed with crates and bicycles and laundry on the washing lines. Past traffic lights and down a noisy street where men crowded at the pavement cafés, past neon signs in kebab shop windows, below a railway bridge. And finally, sure that he must be lost, that I had led him miles from our starting point, we stopped and he reversed and turned to drive us back a different way, laughing the whole time and saying, 'I know my way, I know my way, you see?' I wished I didn't feel as though I'd made a child happy.

The card tricks were an uncommon occurrence, but one I liked. 'Cut open the deck anywhere, Han,' he'd say, and I would, carefully lifting a section of the deck and turning it over, handing it to him. 'So that's the four of clubs, you want that one?' I nodded, stood in front of him, my eyes fixed to the card. 'You sure now, yes? You sure?' I nodded again. 'Right then, now blow!' He held the deck open where I'd made the cut. I blew. He would make the smallest movement with his hand, almost imperceptible, and suddenly the four of clubs had disappeared, replaced by eight of spades. 'How? How, Dad?' I always asked, or my cousins begged if he'd performed the trick for them. We'd pull his trousers. 'Show us, show us!' But he just offered the trick again, or sat back and crossed his legs, laughed and tapped his nose. 'That's for me to know, and you to find out,' he said, but of course we never did.

I used to watch as he sat on the sofa with a pack of cards. He could shuffle them in twenty different ways, arching and flexing the deck between his thumb and middle finger, so they looked as pliable as rubber, then split them, stack them, flip them. I can still hear the pitter-patter of a riffle shuffle, when he split a pack in two, cascading the cards into an interwoven pile. It looked so easy, but it wasn't. The cards would fly away from me when I tried to copy him, scattering on the floor.

I liked the names of the games he played too. Some were common – blackjack, poker, rummy – but others sounded foreign and sophisticated – baccarat, kalooki, chemin de fer. I loved the feel of cards, playing patience for hours or building card towers, balancing the cards in pyramids, one on top of the other. I imbued the royal cards with personalities. The jack was suave but impetuous, the worst of these the jack of diamonds. The queen was stoic and unflinching. The king was wise but passive, and of course, ruled by the queen.

One of the clearest memories I have is watching my father asleep upstairs – it was always daytime, the curtains holding back the light. I was intrigued by his slumbers. Why else would I have so often held my breath and quietly opened the door to stand observing the rise and fall of his chest below the covers? I knew the smell of him asleep – a pungent scent, completely physical, but not unpleasant.

Over the years he must have adapted to those strange hours, driving in the city in the early light from games in Ladbroke Grove or Kentish Town or Pimlico, through the West End then out along the littered East End streets, the shuttered shops and garages of Romford Road, below the flyover where Ilford's one-way system starts. Then turning through the tidy maze of residential streets that brought him home, often around dawn. Sometimes if a game had gone on, we'd all be up and having breakfast when his car pulled into the drive, Sam and I on stools at the kitchen counter, my mother buttering toast for us. He'd appear fleetingly in his suede jacket, car keys in hand, the smell of cigarettes on his breath. While the kettle boiled he'd dig into his pockets for a roll of money, counting out the notes and handing them to my mother, who would slip them into her handbag. Then he'd make himself a cup of tea and vanish off to bed. He was a ghost-father – gone all night or in the house but asleep – a present absence, hovering at the edges of our lives.

◆

I woke one morning and, through my bedroom window, saw my father standing in the garden with three other Caribbean

men. On the grass were a pile of timber and several long rolls
of bright green fabric. It was a warm day and they were in
their vests, heads bent together, talking. Every now and then
one of them would gesticulate, as though drawing a diagram
in the air. My mother carried a tray of mugs out to them,
and they smoked and sipped their tea, eyeing the wood on
the ground.

'What's he doing?' I asked my mother when I came down.
She was in the kitchen, sifting flour into a mixing bowl.
'Making tables,' she replied.

'What sort of tables?'

'Snooker or dice,' she said. 'Not sure. Why don't you
ask him?'

John from St Lucia was on the patio, sawing wood,
singing under his breath. He had a strange, hollow face
with big eyes, but I thought he was kind-looking. I knew he
was completely bald under his trilby hat as he sometimes
took it off and let me rub his shiny head. My father called
him John the Carpenter, a biblical-sounding name befitting
John's religious convictions, his penchant for quoting the
Bible. I'd known him all my life. He lived round the corner
and had six children. Last time I'd seen him, he'd pulled out
a crumpled photograph of 'his people', as he called them.
The eldest girl was twenty-one and the youngest two were
baby twins, a boy and girl. 'Look how sweet they are,' he
said, pointing to the picture. 'Children are a heritage from
the Lord. Sweet God, I'm blessed.' The children were all dark
like John, posed in their Sunday best around a Christmas
tree. *He had more than six kids*, my mother said. *He'd probably
lost track. Too busy in the bookmakers.*

'Good morning to you,' John said when he saw me. He
dipped his hat. There was a sheen of sweat on his face. My

father and the others were kneeling on the lawn, nailing beams of wood together.

'What are they for, Dad?' I asked, enticed by the green felt, the same shade as the grass, an overload of colour in the bright garden. 'Dice,' he said. 'The club want two new tables, so we making them.' He introduced me to the other men – 'This me daughter.' He had adopted his Jamaican accent. The men, Frank and Sylvester, looked up from their hammers to greet me.

They were out there all day, and all the next, making those tables, enormous when finished, with the green felt tacked tightly on their tops. And they were beautiful. John spent hours sanding and waxing the legs and frames until the curved wood gleamed, and as the sun went down, the four of them stood around the table, my father shaking dice and rolling them out across the baize. I stood at the side. John put his arm around me.

'Watch this, Han,' my father said, 'two sixes.' And he threw the ruby-coloured dice so they bounced against the table's rim, rolling back to land with twelve dots facing up.

'You' daddy always get the numbers,' John said. 'You see? Boy, he's skilful. Every good gift and every perfect gift is from above.'

'Your call, Han,' my father said, looking up at me.

'A two and a four?' I said, and he took the dice and shook them, rolling a two and four on the green table top. I called the numbers again, then Sylvester called, then Frank, and my father rolled the call every time, the dice spinning off the high wood rim. Then they all threw the dice – Sylvester, Frank and John – but none of them could do what my father could.

'Darlin', have a go!' Sylvester said, dropping the dice into my hand. He wore a gold ring on his little finger. 'Blow some luck into your fist.' I blew into my balled hand and rolled the dice, then scooped them up, and rolled them again. It was a hot evening in the garden, the sky a soft shade of pink. I felt small and safe with those tall men on either side of me.

'Yes, yes, we training you,' Frank said, and put his hand on my head. They were laughing. I knew I'd been included in a ritual I wasn't meant to be a part of, and I liked it.

Afterwards, they carried the tables upended down the alleyway at the side of our house and put them into the truck pulled on the drive. It was nearly dark. I was feeding the fish in the pond, letting them kiss my fingers, when John came through the alley gate, his hat in his hand, showing his shiny head.

'You like the dice,' he said. 'You see your daddy play?' His smile showed his gold teeth. 'Not bad, not bad.' I didn't know what to say. We stood side by side, watching the fish.

'I see you liking it,' he said. 'Your daddy is a good man.' He sat down on the grass and crossed his legs. 'Let me tell you a story.' He paused to make sure he had my attention. I took my hand from the pond reluctantly, not sure I wanted to hear it.

'I came from Castries, thirty years ago,' he began. 'You know where Castries is?'

'St Lucia?' I asked.

'That's right, clever girl.' He winked. 'My mother told me, "John, go on now. Be always good. Whatever you do, work heartily, as for the Lord and not for men." She said, "You have a gift for wood and England will be rosy."' He pointed to himself. 'I was seventeen. Oh, it was a scary place, the ship, the sea. I couldn't sleep, played cards the whole long journey; what I lost the first night, took me sixty days to win again.' He sighed dramatically, his head bowed. 'I came to Paddington. So lonely. I met your daddy dealing on the Edgware Road. All the fellows in the upstairs room, below a yellow bulb, and no one going home.' He raised a finger. 'A gambler is never lonely – is another man who always wants his money.' I realised I was listening to John's confession, and he was in no hurry to let me go, lost in his own reveries.

'Every gambler has his curse,' he said authoritatively. 'For me it's horses. The devil prowls around, seeking someone to devour. Then a letter in my post box said my mummy is dying, am I coming home?' He looked up, tears in his eyes. 'It was thirty years since I came from Castries.'

Suddenly I felt sorry for John. 'What happened?' I asked.

He sighed. 'I took my money to the bookies and I lost it all. In bets there is a fool and a thief.' He shook his head. 'It was your daddy give me work and lend me what him can. Iron sharpens iron, and one man sharpens another.' He smiled, showing his gold teeth. 'I made it home. Her hand in mine, I help her on from this life to the next. Amen. Amen.' He stood abruptly, put his hat on and tipped it. 'Be good. Listen to your father who gave you life. God loves you. And love your daddy, don't forget.' He was whistling as he walked away.

Clearly my father had magical powers when it came to dice, and could manipulate playing cards in all kinds of ways, but beyond knowing this, his night-time activities were a mystery to me. There was a cupboard in our hall, below the stairs, where the hammer and screwdrivers were kept, along with tins of varnish, buckets, rollers, a paint-splashed stepladder. A bare bulb lit the space, which always seemed mysterious, as though its dark corner might slope off to a secret room. The shelves held an assortment of cake and biscuit tins of different shapes and sizes. Inside these were my father's dice – not the small white dice of a Monopoly board, but large red and green dice, transparent, the shades of rubies and emeralds with big white spots. Other tins held packs of cards, always Kem, the American brand, plastic backed with swirling red or navy blue patterns. Alongside them were marker pens and pots of ink, pins and needles, Stanley knives and razor blades, and right at the back of a shelf was a very small guillotine. I didn't know it then, but these were the tools of my father's trade.

It was my mother who filled me in, years later, repeating my father's motto – *If you can't win it straight, win it crooked*, meaning that he cheated when he needed to, in a variety of ways. These included counting cards, marking them, or slipping them in and out of play. She didn't know about this when they first met, but later she saw him practising and he would leave things out around the house – the pens and the blades for shaving cards, a dentist's drill for loading dice. Back then he was playing all the time, out all afternoon at dice games in Whitechapel or Bow. He'd come home for dinner and to change his shirt, blow her a kiss and be gone. He might come back at twelve if things were slow, or he mightn't come home until the following day. *We needed the money*, she said, *so I didn't complain*. He was winning big all the time – three hundred pounds here, four hundred pounds there – a fortune in 1968 for one night's work. My mother was simultaneously fascinated and repelled by the way my father earned his living; in her mind, there was a distinction between his methods – counting cards and using sleight of hand were expert skills, but marking cards was dishonest.

Regardless, all of them required hours of practice. *Your dad had a photographic memory*, she said. 'He might have been born with it, but he honed it well.' Here, my own recollections corroborate her words. I used to watch him dealing out cards to memorise them, mouthing the numbers and suits to himself. He'd be at it for hours. *He could recall the order of an entire deck, so he always knew which cards were in the pile and which were still in play. He used to deal the other players what they needed, but he always had the better hand.* One time he came home raging mad, complaining to my mother that a man he'd dealt a jack of spades to hadn't played it. *Like he'd done your father wrong*, my mother said, *and not the other way around!*

He also had incredible sleight of hand, and was able to slip cards in and out of play. *I think he learned all that in Jamaica*, she said. *Some Chinese fellow used to show him tricks. He was brilliant at it. But he marked cards too. I wasn't sure about that. It wasn't moral.* Indeed, the whole world of gambling, according to my mother, was immoral and dangerous. A few people – 'confidants', my father called them – knew what he could do, and would pay him to prepare a deck or load a pair of dice. *It was a nice earner*, she said, *but I worried that they'd tell on him.* Nothing good would come of getting caught.

I always thought my father had false front teeth because he was old, but in fact some fellow who thought my father had cheated him had knocked them out. Another time, in Ladbroke Grove, another chap accused him of palming a card. Things got nasty and my father had to leave. It hadn't ended there. There were lots of phone calls and worry – who knew what and who'd seen whom – but one way or another my father finally charmed his way out of it.

He was older than many in the gambling fraternity and he was renowned among them, for his dexterous dealing and his winning streak, no doubt. He was considered a kind-hearted gentleman in that tough, edgy world, but surely his cronies can't have known the truth of what he did? My mother didn't think so. *If you can't win it straight, win it crooked.* They can't have known my father lived by that motto.

My father was a complicated man, full of contradictions and morally ambiguous – on the one hand, seemingly happy to cheat his fellow gamblers out of their money; on the other, happy to lend or give money when he had it, to just about anyone who asked. From either side, it was as though he didn't value money in the way that other people did. Some days he had it, some days it was gone.

Years of gambling must have taught him to read situations well. Yet there were other times when his skills of intuition failed him completely. He'd once been arrested for, in his words, 'doing a friend a favour'. This friend was Ginger Brian, a local criminal everybody thought was mad. He had a shock of red hair and small, rabbity teeth, and was missing a finger and a thumb, apparently lost to a dog. Brian organised illegal dog fights and rumour had it he beat his dogs with chains to toughen them up.

My father knew Brian from the bookies, but they weren't close. It was a mystery as to why he phoned the house one day and asked my father for a lift to town because his car had broken down. Anyone else might have smelt a rat, but my father told him yes, no problem, and arranged to pick him up in Forest Gate. But in the car, Brian pulled out a gun and started waving it around, telling my father that he planned to kill a nightclub owner in Piccadilly who allegedly owed

Brian money. The details are a little fuzzy here. For some reason, perhaps because he was scared, my father drove Brian to the club, but as soon as they got there, before they'd even stepped out, the police surrounded the car – and not just any police, but *armed* police, and my father and Ginger Brian were arrested. They kept my father in a cell overnight, and all the next day *and* the following night.

My mother was frantic with worry and phoned every number in my father's phone book. He finally called her from the police station, asking could she come and get him and could she ask her brother Terry if he could put some money up for his bail? He'd been charged with intent to commit affray and possession of a firearm. *The silly git*, my mother said. *I should have left him there.*

In the end, the case was thrown out. It turned out that Ginger Brian and the club owner had been waving guns at each other for weeks, but no one was quite sure of the reason, including them. Nevertheless, my father had to spend two nights in jail for doing Ginger Brian a favour, or, as my mother said, *for being bloody thick.*

You might expect a gambling man to be reckless or profligate, unconcerned with the affairs of the wider world, but in fact my father felt his responsibility as a citizen and was surprisingly political – a committed socialist, in fact, since, as a young man in Jamaica, he'd been involved in the country's struggle for independence. In England he'd joined the Communist Party and sold the *Daily Worker* outside the Tube. Then, when Harold Wilson became prime minister in 1964 – the year my parents got together – they both joined the local Labour Party, went to all the meetings, posted leaflets at election time. My mother used to staff the polling station on election day, keeping a list of who'd been in, while my father drove his car around our neighbourhood, knocking on people's doors. He would bring old ladies to the polling station to cast their vote, or teenagers who hadn't known they were old enough.

Aged six or seven, I remember trailing with him up and down our neighbours' garden paths, a stack of bright red Labour leaflets in our hands. I didn't understand elections or politics. I used to watch the police attacking the miners on the television and Margaret Thatcher speaking in her bright blue suits, her bouffant hair always looking thin and wan. I didn't understand the things she said, knowing only that I didn't like her. When I misbehaved, my father used to hunch his shoulders, pull a face and say, 'You better watch your step, or I'll send in Mrs Thatcher.' From this, I gauged her villainy. In my childish world, it was enough to know Labour liked the colour red and were the good guys, while the Conservatives were blue and bad.

♣

The incident with Ginger Brian was not my father's only run-in with the law. Apparently he had been caught at an illegal poker game sometime in the sixties, just before getting together with my mother. Betting shops were already legal but card gambling was still prohibited, and police raids on gambling parlours were common. My father been arrested at a card table – red-handed, as it were – playing cards in hand, a pile of cash in front of him.

In court, he chose to represent himself, taking the stand in his smart suit to give an impassioned speech against the current gambling laws. His argument had two threads – the first was that the criminalisation of gambling was a moral censor initiated by the church, who associated gambling with the sin of selfishness and could not tolerate participants' faith in chance over God; and secondly, related to the first, the laws were a paternalistic form of social control, penalising and patronising the working classes whose agency and self-determination they denied. The transcript of the speech was printed in the evening newspaper and my father preserved the cutting, proudly glueing it onto the first page of an empty scrapbook, perhaps hoping to fill the rest of the pages with further reports of his campaign. Like many of my father's ideas, it came to nothing in the end. The judge in the case listened with amusement as my father extolled his views, then imposed a hefty fine.

There were other minor misdemeanours. Small-time criminality went hand-in-hand with gambling, and my father often brought home 'swag' from the clubs – leather coats and shoes, plates and silver cutlery, expensive towels. He brought home a microwave and a Moulinex food mixer my mother loved. Everything knocked-off, of course. She turned forty in 1984 and the day before her birthday he dragged a bin-liner of dresses in from the car – 'No tat,' he said. 'Upmarket frocks.' She hung them in her wardrobe: glitzy dresses with pleats and shoulder pads, not her style at all, and she never put them on, except for the bright red dress she wore the night of her birthday party. It was red satin with a black sash across the middle, like something worn by a character from *Dynasty* or *Dallas*, my favourite TV shows at the time.

My memories of the party are slightly hazy, mainly because I was blind drunk. My mother's friends arrived at Ashgrove Road in droves – mostly teachers she had known from the different schools she'd worked at over the years and neighbours from our street. Sam and I and the three cousins were banished upstairs with Joseph, my father's niece's son, all the way from Peckham. At fifteen, he was the oldest. He wore his Afro in a flat-top and when he laughed, his eyes creased up and made him beautiful. The girls and I swooned.

We sent Alf down to steal the alcohol, bottle after bottle, then, clueless what to do with it, we mixed it in the way we'd seen our parents do, on the ironing board we set up as a bar in the big spare room. We had no mixers, so gin was mixed with lager and rum with Babycham, concoctions we then downed with great bravado, grimacing, until our heads fizzed and we couldn't stop laughing. *Hits Five* was playing on the tape recorder, the volume turned right up. We drew the curtains and put the lamps on for a nightclub feel.

'Let's limbo!' Maria shouted, holding up the broom, and the six of us straddled, bumped and shook below it, lower and lower, until I bent so far I thought I'd snap in two, as though the alcohol had made me bendier. Then Susanna had a nosebleed and had to lie on her bed with her head hung back while Alf pinched her nose. It didn't work. I was sent downstairs for ice to stem the flow of blood.

From the top of the stairs I saw a small man with highlighted hair standing by the front door. He was naked except for a leopard-skin loincloth. In his shaking arms he held my mother, who must have weighed three stone more than him. The red dress was hitched above her knees to show her shiny thighs, a black lace garter sunk into the flesh. She was flushed in his arms, her head thrown back, laughing. Everyone, including Tarzan, was singing 'Happy Birthday' at the tops of their voices.

'Everyone! Tarzan's downstairs!' I ran upstairs and shouted, but the limbo dance had resumed with Joseph nearly on his knees to slide below the broom while the others cheered him on. By the time I went back to look, Tarzan had disappeared, as though I'd dreamt him. My father was standing in the hall with Charlie Walker, both smoking and talking conspiratorially. The pair of them looked out of place and shifty among my mother's friends. Back in the bedroom, Sam had disappeared. Alf and Susanna were passed out across the bed, and Joseph and Maria were in the dark corner, their arms wrapped around each other, kissing.

♦

We went on holiday in Dorset that summer, to the same campsite we'd been to with the cousins for the last five years. We packed our trailer, fixed it to the car, and off we went in convoy to Osmington Mills, just outside Weymouth. Two weeks on the green cliffs above the sea, barbecues every night or fish and chips, the adults supping beer on benches outside The Smuggler's Arms, us playing on the swings and slides, as the sun went down over the hills.

I had my first bikini that holiday – bright blue with Minnie Mouse's smiling face embossed on the top and bottoms. My mother had found it in a seafront shop in Weymouth. I remember little Alfie running to the campsite pool to tell me I had a present waiting at the tent. I ran back and my mother handed me the bikini. I loved it from that moment and didn't take it off all holiday. Imagine my surprise when, years later, she confessed she'd stolen it. It wasn't only my father whose attitude to the law was flexible. Annoyed at the long queue in the shop, she'd snuck it into her bag and ambled out, making a getaway along the promenade. My father had chased her and grabbed her arm.

'What, you going to call the police on me?' she said incredulously, shrugging his hand off.

'You can't just steal it!' he said. 'You must take it back.' In his view, receiving stolen goods was fine, but stealing them in the first place clearly wasn't.

'Not on your nelly!' she replied.

I nearly drowned that year in the campsite swimming pool. I could just about doggy-paddle, but when Sam told me I should try jumping into the deep end, I did, wanting to impress him. The pool was packed with children leaping and diving in, with rubber rings and lilos. I panicked, flailing, then sinking down, my lungs too full of water when I cleared the surface to call for help. I was only a few feet from the edge and I remember a blonde girl clinging to the side in arm-bands, watching as I sunk and surfaced over and over again, the strange silver-turquoise light of the water and the kicking legs and feet all around me. I knew I was going to die, until an arm was around my neck and pulling me clear as I gasped for air, my eyes fixed on the clear sky above me.

It was Maria, standing on the tips of her flippers, wading through the water from the shallow end where she'd seen me struggling. She dragged me out onto the concrete and held me as I caught my breath and cried into her thin brown shoulder. I was scared and exhausted, shivering in the hot sun, wrapped in my towel. Later we walked across the fields to the tents, and vowed we wouldn't tell anyone what had happened. We both knew it was serious – I was lucky to be alive.

♥

My father was happy on these holidays. Each day we went to the beach, where he would tuck himself behind the windbreaker to read the paper. It was a long, wild beach below the campsite. You had to scramble down. No beach huts, no café, just the high dunes of pale sand and the waves crashing on the shore. My father didn't like the sun and rarely took his jeans and shirt off, but he would get into the spirit of the beach, making sandcastles and burying us. There's a photograph of Sam and me and the cousins sunk into the sand with just our heads visible, my father stood behind us in his anorak, smiling at his handiwork. And he and Auntie Lyn enjoyed each other's company. They would roll their jeans up and walk along the shore together, talking, sometimes gone for hours. *They had an affinity, I suppose you'd say*, my mother said, *because neither felt they fitted in.*

The next year there was no holiday with the cousins because Lyn had gone, and a rupture in our family had started, one that never really healed itself. *She'd had affairs with women before*, my mother told me, *so that part was no surprise.* Lyn had left Uncle Terry and the children, moving out to live with a woman she'd met at work. Where exactly she had gone was kept a secret from us all that year, but I was old enough to understand.

I listened to snatches of my parents' conversation. My father was incensed about Lyn leaving. 'How could she be so stupid? How could she leave the children?' he said to my mother, over and over, an attitude I found odd, another veer in his moral consciousness, since he'd left two marriages and two children himself. Maybe his outrage was because Lyn was a woman. I'd never heard of a mother leaving her children before, but plenty of my school friends' dads were absent. More likely, I suspect, my father, older now, regretted his own behaviour.

I knew very little about his previous lives, only that he had married very young in America and had a daughter, Gloria, whom he'd left when she was a baby. The second marriage was in England, to Elsie, a nurse. They'd had a son, Tom, but my father had left again when Tom was nine, and hadn't seen him much in the years after. They saw each other more when Tom had two children. My father enjoyed his new role as grandfather, but even as a child I could sense his regret that he hadn't been a better father to Tom, a kind, bookish man. I liked Tom when I met him but it was hard to regard him as a brother. We hadn't grown up together. He was twenty-three years older than me – nearer my mother's age than mine.

Instead of Weymouth, we went to Newquay, just the four of us, staying in a run-down B&B that smelt of fried eggs. The week before, my mother had told us there was no money for a holiday this year, and I remember money was a problem all the time around then. My father wasn't winning much. They talked about selling the house and moving somewhere smaller. But money had appeared from somewhere – my father had had a win of sorts, no doubt – and last minute, there was just enough for us to take the coach for seven hours from Victoria to Cornwall, where it rained all week. My father disappeared most afternoons into one of Newquay's betting shops, while my mother remained stoic, taking Sam and me to the Lighthouse Cinema and the Japanese Bonsai

Garden, where we yawned and complained. One afternoon she led us through the drizzle on the seafront with promises of ice cream. The sea was dark and stormy, ominous. Sam hung behind as she marched on. He pulled a marker pen from his coat and 'tagged' a bench and the side of a beach hut in his thick black scrawl. I tried to read what he'd written, but it was indecipherable. I trailed behind him, hoping for the best.

◆

It was soon after we came back that my father was taken into hospital with chest pains. My mother didn't drive, and we didn't have the money for a taxi, so each evening we walked the two miles to St George's Hospital. It was autumn, growing colder, copper leaves piled on the pavements. Our route took us down Glencoe Avenue, where my mother had been born and raised in the Newbury Park house owned by Walter Hart. He came home one evening to find his first wife Stella, Nan's predecessor, had left him, taking every stick of furniture they owned. Stella was a socialite who liked tennis clubs and drinks parties, while my grandfather was more content to walk alone for hours through Epping Forest. He knew all the forest wardens and they left him to himself to sit cross-legged beneath the trees and meditate.

The hospital corridors were jaundiced in the fluorescent strip lights, with a cloying antiseptic smell. My father lay in the ward bed in his paisley pyjamas, his glasses on as he read the newspaper. Illness had made him serious, but then it seemed to be a serious illness – a collapsed lung. They'd pumped it up but he had haemorrhaged, losing lots of blood.

'I was getting colder and colder,' he said. 'I couldn't speak. I thought they hadn't noticed.' He'd needed a transfusion. Tubes ran beneath the blankets and I couldn't see where they plugged into him. 'There's blood in my wee,' he said. 'They say my blood pressure is up.' His face was fixed and grim. He'd come into hospital with one problem but now it seemed that there were others – with his prostate, and the doctor thought the stomach pains he'd had for weeks might be an ulcer. 'I'm not well,' he said, unsmiling.

He came home from the hospital looking grey and weak with a paper bag of pill bottles he carefully stacked in the bathroom cabinet. *He always was a hypochondriac*, my mother said, but now his fears were named. They were conditions to be managed. Tablets for blood pressure, antacids for the stomach ulcer. He worried that the lung problems might be linked to cancer, and tried to give up smoking, but never lasted more than a few days. Cigarettes were swapped for roll-ups, as though they were a healthier choice, but he just smoked more of them, and before too long the black and gold packs of John Player Specials were back on the kitchen window sill where he always kept them.

That was the first time he was very ill, but it was a marker of things to come. It was a shame for my mother – she was much younger, still full of energy. She must have known that a man my father's age, and with his lifestyle, would suffer bad health eventually. She might have known she would end up alone. But of course she looked after him – the hospital visits, trips to the doctor. She listened to his worries, organised his medicine and pills. Other families weren't like ours. My friends had dads who chased them up and down the garden, did ridiculous dad dances in the living room, swung their mothers round. We weren't like other families.

My dad was a liability, my mother stoic and reliable. I felt sorry for my father, but I felt more sorry for her.

♠

We'd had Chloe since I was three or four, since Penny, the dog next door, had a litter of puppies – four mongrels that my cousins and I had marvelled at with their little wrinkled faces and tiny paws. I was allowed to choose a puppy and Chloe had come to live with us. She was a small dog, long-haired, with a dopey face and watery eyes, and she was nervous about everything – the doorbell, strangers, being left alone. My father decided after his illness that for exercise he would walk her every day – the five-minute trot to the newsagent and back – and after years of ignoring each other, my father and Chloe became good friends. When he read the paper in his armchair, she would curl up by his feet or scramble up into his lap.

Much later than my friends, I got a bicycle. It was a birthday present. My father took it upon himself to teach me how to ride. On Saturday afternoons we manoeuvred the bike into the car. I sat in the front seat with Chloe on my lap as he drove us to Goodmayes Park, where I wobbled along on the bike, his hand behind the seat to steady me and Chloe running out in front. As I got better and picked up speed, he'd try to jog behind me, making sure I didn't fall, but often this would end with him bent double in the shadow of a tree, his lungs too tight to breathe or even cough to clear them. He'd recover on the park bench while I whizzed along the path, Chloe behind me, sprinting with her ears pinned back. Yes, I thought, I can ride the bike! When I grew bored, I'd cycle back to him. 'Had enough, Han?' he'd ask

as I dismounted, and we'd put on Chloe's lead, wheel the
bike back to the car and head for home. Sat beside him, I
could hear his laboured breathing, as though he couldn't get
enough air. I glanced over. His face was sad and worried.

6
1940

*T*he boy dealt five cards to each of the men. His movements were quick and precise, making a tidy pile for each player to sweep up and fan in their hands. Outside, the streets jangled with noise – food wagons clattering past and vendors calling, the bark of dogs, calypso lifting from the yard into the night. But the noises were distant in the humid room – only the sound of breathing was loud, and one man tapping his anxious fingers on the table's rim. A bare bulb hung above them, illuminating the cracked wood, the ashtray and glasses, the copper flask of liquor.

The game went on all night. A boy named Felix served drinks, bringing them to the table from behind the bar. The players might change – one man pushing back his chair to leave as another stepped through the door. A man might simply fold his hand and head home with empty pockets, or he might go out into the passageway and climb the stairs to another room where a girl in an orange dress sat waiting on the bed, a bottle of rum beside her. Her name was Zephyr and she was fifteen. He might come down after, to take back his place at the table, or go silently into the alley, quieter inside himself, moving past the stray cats and dogs, his shadow cast on the yard walls.

The boy dealt here two or three nights a week. He took the old yellow bus from Yallahs to Kingston at dusk, swerving on the dim-lit roads into the city, then rode the delivery trucks home at dawn, half asleep, perched on the truck's back step as the red sun rose over the hills.

That first time, he'd jumped off the bus at Half Way Tree, jumped onto another bus downtown and then followed the scrawled map Mr Ho Choy had drawn him, through the grid of roads that led to Barry Street, where the betting shops and card clubs nestled between the bright shop fronts of hardware stores and hairdressers and bakeries. This was Kingston, then, he thought. More people than the boy had ever seen in one place. More dirt, more noise. But these streets had an energy that rose through him. So this was the city his father could not keep away from. It was here that the old shops had been lost.

He walked the length of the street for an hour, the air warm, the sky dark above him and half-bent on a storm. He noted the Chiney shops with their red awnings and slats stacked high with yams and bananas, and the pavement vendors who unrolled their mats to sell all manner of goods – matches, saucepans, clothes, shoes. He was observing what went on here – the mood and movements of the streets, the chatter, how things went and who knew whom. Then, as darkness fell, he went back to the building he'd seen earlier, marked with an X on the crumpled map – two red-brick floors on the corner of King Street in Chinatown. It had dark windows and a blue door he pushed open to find Mr Manny sat alone on a stool at the wooden bar with a cup of coffee, just as Mr Ho Choy said he would be. The boy said his name and why he had come. 'Yes, man,' Mr Manny's voice was deep and hoarse. He stood. 'Charlie tell me to expect you.'

Charlie was Mr Ho Choy's other name but no one in Yallahs used it. The boy took Mr Manny in. He was a tall man with a dark, shiny face, thick creases in the forehead and puckered above his nose, a short deep scar across his cheek. He wore a white shirt, grimy at the cuffs and collar. He was fifty maybe. Some grey in the close cut of his hair. 'So, you want to show me what you can do?' Mr Manny asked.

'Yes, sir,' the boy said, reaching into his pocket and pulling out a deck of cards.

They stood at the round table in the centre of the room, and the boy began to shuffle – simple cuts at first, overlaying the cards in one hand. Tap, tap. Then with both hands, a dovetail, flicking two piles of cards into one. Then a riffle, the cards whispering themselves into place. He flexed their backs into a high arched bridge. Another cut. Tap tap. Every move he made was small and defined. No mistakes. Then he dealt the cards to four imaginary players around the table, and the whole time, Mr Manny stood and watched him, didn't move his eyes from the boy's quick hands. He dealt swiftly, a clear pile for each player, then looked up.

'Go once more,' the older man said, 'with my cards,' reaching behind the bar for another deck and handing it to the boy. 'Six for six hands.' The boy dealt as quickly and tidily as he had before. Then he dealt again, and again. Outside, the rain came down, thrashing the street, sweetening the air.

'You can work tonight?' Mr Manny finally asked. The boy nodded. Mr Manny rubbed his head. 'That Charlie. He say you good.'

Back in Yallahs, his father owned a new shop. The boy still served there, but someone new had come. Her name was

Rhona and she stepped from behind his father's back one day.
James Lowe had come home from Kingston, appearing silent
as a shadow in the shop's doorway as the boy stood behind
the counter. Behind him was a young girl, thirteen or so.
From the boy's position, he could just see her feet. His father
walked straight through the shop into the back room without
a word to the boy, but the girl came right in, her eyes moving
across the chaotic shelves and landing on the boy. She was
small and pretty, with wide eyes in a brown face, the same
colouring as the boy, her plaited hair was just visible below her
little straw hat. She didn't look like the village girls although
her clothes were just as raggedly and poor, and she was as
thin as a stick, her elbow joints wider than the rest of her
arms. She held a bulging satchel. Her eyes dropped down to
the boy's feet. 'Wha', you have no shoes?' she said, looking up
at his face. She had a sing-song voice, strong and sweet. He
looked down at his bare toes, dusty and yellow from the yard.

'I have shoes,' he said, slowly, carefully. 'But mostly I go
barefoot indoors – no need for shoes here.' Then, 'You come
from Kingston?'

'If you *have* shoes, you should wear them!' The girl sang
back. 'He tell me you're my brother, *half*-brother. But looking
at you, I can't believe it. Can't believe I'm related to a boy
so backwater!' She laughed and her pink tongue popped
from between her lips. 'Is *you* I'm talking about,' she added,
widening her eyes at him, tipping her head to one side.

The boy said nothing, taken aback by this girl he had never
seen. His sister, he thought. Another child of his father, who
liked to go with girls who were only children themselves.
He wondered where the girl's mother was, how old she was.

'What's your name, sister?' he asked, in an attempt at
friendship. But just as she was about to answer his father

appeared in the doorway, beckoning to her, and the girl went towards him. Where would she sleep, the boy thought. How long was she staying? There were so many questions – where she was from and why here, why now, and how well did she know her father? How little he knew of his father's life. This was his father's power. The boy was a slave at worst, a servant at best, and why should any master account for himself to a servant?

That was a month ago. It seemed Rhona was here to stay. The boy now slept on sacking below the shop counter, Rhona in his bed. She was around the shop as though she'd always been there, serving the customers in her sweet voice but shirking the hard work – the early-morning scrubbing, the lifting and unpacking of goods. She wanted to know everything about the shop and repeated the same questions again and again about credit, who owed the most, who was the best customer. She made a mess of the ledger book, filling in the wrong columns, doodling in the margins. When the boy saw this he thought his father would explode with anger at her. But James Lowe said nothing, just answered Rhona's questions in his poor English, more words at a time than the boy had ever heard him use. He was surprised by how his father's voice softened when he spoke at length, by the light rhythm of his sentences.

And Rhona was not afraid of their father. When the shop was quiet, she took a book and made herself a nest in the shaded places of the yard, below the orange trees or in the orchid grove. James Lowe, who hated idleness, who had no time for books, said nothing. Or other times, Rhona simply wandered off on her own to the river, where the boy followed her once or twice. He'd been surprised by the quiet plaintiveness with which she sat on the rocks, ducking her feet in the flowing water.

His father didn't care where the boy went in the evenings now, only that he was there in the mornings to open the shop. Rhona served the men at night and the boy saw how she attracted their looks, how she knew her own beauty and met their stares full-on, unblinking. His father stood behind the counter with a paper cigarette between his lips, and watched her.

♦

It was a Thursday when the boy saw his mother from the window of the bus stopping downtown on Darling Street. He knew her face. Hermione. She was standing on the kerb, waiting to cross, one hand on her hat to stop the wind from lifting it. Six years had passed, but the boy hadn't forgotten. He dreamt about her more now, not less, and thoughts of her swam through his head as he lay sleepless on the floor of the shop. He thought about why she'd never tried to find him. Even though she'd sold him, the boy believed she had loved him. He would forgive her. He wondered why he had never tried to find her too. He had travelled all over St Thomas, delivering orders and stock, but never thought to ask for her in the different villages. He knew she had left Hearts Ease, but never thought he would find her in Kingston.

Without thinking, he jumped from the bus and followed her along the street. She walked with a little basket over her arm. Not the poor girl he remembered. She wore a pretty floral dress, neat white shoes with a heel, a small hat perched on her head. He kept close behind as she crossed onto Barry Street, walking to the corner of Gold Street, where she entered the Chiney shop on the corner. The boy followed her in. The shop was like all Chinese grocers, but larger than the one they had in Yallahs, smaller than Mr Ho Choy's. There were aisles of high shelves packed with goods, the salt-fish barrels on one side of the room. The blinds were half drawn, the only light coming from the red paper lanterns hung from the ceiling.

There were no other customers, only his mother standing at the counter talking to the shopkeeper, a man the boy knew by sight from Barry Street. He became suddenly aware of himself, his heart beating hard in his chest. He pretended to choose star apples from a basket by the door, listening to their conversation. Slowly the boy understood his mother wasn't talking in English, but in Chinese, stood with one hand on her hip, facing the shopkeeper. Suddenly she laughed – the giggle of a young girl – and the boy could tell the tone of her talk was flirtatious. The shopkeeper chatted away with her while his hands busied themselves, wrapping fish in wax paper, measuring rice on his scales, then sugar. He took down a jar of pink sweets from the shelf behind the counter, tipped them into a paper bag, rolled the top over and added them to the pile before him. The boy saw one hand go out to squeeze Hermione's waist. She laughed again, like the tinkle of a bell, switching her hands on her hip. Then she leant over the counter and pecked the shopkeeper on the lips before turning with the shopping bag in her arms. It was too late for the boy to move from her path. He looked up as she came towards him, but she didn't even register him. Her face was fixed and grim, no sign of the coquettishness of seconds ago. She walked out the door and down the step.

'You want help?' the shopkeeper called from behind the counter to the boy, eyeing him suspiciously. 'Yes or no? You want help? You want the apples?'

The boy shook his head and placed the apple in his hand back on the pile. He stepped out of the shop into the sun, the street full of people. He looked up and down, but Hermione had gone.

♠

The boy lay on his sack-bed below the counter in the shop. It was nearly midnight. His head was full of Hermione, trying to make sense of what he'd seen the day before. A heavy feeling filled his chest. How could she not have recognised him? Would he see her again? He wanted to, badly. He should have spoken to her. He was angry with himself.

Outside on the veranda the evening customers had gone, but he could hear his father still out there in the night talking to Rhona. He heard her laugh. The boy stood up and went to the front window of the shop, peering through the slats. The oil lamp was burning, lighting the two figures standing entwined. On the table were a liquor flask and glasses, an overflowing ashtray.

Rhona stumbled suddenly but his father's arms were round her and he pulled her up. She threw her head back laughing. 'Oh, I'm spinning!' she laughed, shut-eyed, her arms tightening around his neck. James Lowe pulled Rhona closer to him, bent lower, and led her in a dance, round and round, his face pressed to hers. 'I'm spinning,' she said again weakly, then, 'I want to go to bed.' James Lowe held his daughter tighter and danced her across the wooden floor, his face lost in her hair. Round and round they went, and round and round again.

7

WHITE FLIGHT

But to go to school in a summer morn,
O it drives all joy away!

– William Blake, *The School Boy*

*I*n the summer of 2012 I took the train from London to Norwich to see a friend – reading all the way, oblivious to my surroundings. But on the journey home I stared through the window at the country landscape speeding by, so fresh and green after the endless summer rain. Drawing closer to London, the scenery shifted to factories, scrapyards, backs of houses. Suddenly it looked familiar and I recognised the view – we were on the line that ran behind my childhood home. I hadn't realised the train's route – through Ipswich across the Suffolk border into Colchester, to Romford, Chadwell Heath, Ilford, then on to London. Growing up, I'd caught trains along this line all the time. I strained my neck to see what I might recognise. Soon we were racing through Goodmayes, past the back gardens of Ashgrove Road, a blur at seventy miles per hour. I tried to pick out my house from the others, and I think I saw it flashing past – the skylight in the roof, the weeping willow still cascading onto the lawn.

I felt a strange bewilderment. I've thought so much about that house and what went on there, its existence in my mind so powerful, and yet it's locked in my memory as a place just always out of reach, a history I can't go back to. But of course the physical house, the bricks and mortar, still stand. All houses have their histories, but it's strange to think about the other lives that must now unfold between those walls – another family in the house of my mysteries. There will be different secrets there now.

When I was a child, I was fascinated by those railway tracks. You could clamber on the old stone wall behind our shed and push your way between the pines to reach them. They were so forbidden. I never made it further than the trees, but I'd overheard the other children on our street claim they'd walked along them, or worse, run across the eight steel rails to reach the other side and back again. Sam made those boasts as well. On the other side there was a bus garage, the red double-decker buses parked in tidy rows. I'd driven past that garage with my father a hundred times, but from my bedroom window, with the tracks in-between, it seemed as distant as a foreign land.

I spent many night-time hours, when I was supposed to be asleep, with my face pressed to the glass pane, watching trains run past, the blur of scribbled figures in the windows. Sometimes the train stopped at a signal on the track and those blurred faces came into relief, brought into focus the fact of other people living other lives. 'Where are you going?' I asked them silently, but the real question was, 'Who are you?'

I didn't talk to the other children on Ashgrove Road. All of them had gone to the same school as my brother in

Goodmayes, and they all knew each other. But I had gone to Cotton Lane, 'the other school', which meant we didn't have the common base for friendship. I knew their names, though – Dean and Leila Franklin, next door but one; Bobby and Rami Bent across the road; a family four doors down with seven children. Their dad was Dennis, a wiry Jamaican friend of my father's who appeared at our house all hours of the day and night, always dressed in jeans and a denim jacket, a can of Tennents Super in his hand.

Then there was Michael McCabe, Sam's friend, who lived at number 83. I was often dispatched to his house to fetch my brother home for dinner. I loved Michael. At our house, he would lie on the carpet of our living room playing computer games. I'd lie beside him quietly, pretending to be watching, but really I was sniffing him. He smelt of coconuts. Sometimes, if I was sure he wouldn't notice, I'd nuzzle my face against his jumper and kiss it.

My brother and he were amateur breakdancers, teaching themselves moves from a book called *Breakdance: Mr Fresh and The Supreme Rockers Show You How to Do It!* and from repeat viewings of *Breakdance: The Movie*. Sometimes they were joined by Raminder, a Sikh boy who lived round the corner. The three of them would take my brother's tape recorder into the back garden and stand around a square of lino, swinging their arms in time to the beat of Grandmaster Flash or Run DMC. Raminder's topknot posed problems when he tried to head-spin, but he was the best by far at the other moves – the caterpillar, which involved throwing your torso down and wriggling along the ground, or the windmill, in which the dancer's body rolled around on the ground while his legs rotated at speed in a sort-of windmill motion. I was irked that I could perform all kinds of dexterous manoeuvres at gymnastics club which would have enabled me to breakdance well, but daren't ask to join my brother's garden rehearsals, knowing full well what the answer would be. Instead, when they had finished and disappeared to the ghetto of his room, I would go into the garden alone to practise head-spins.

I wished I had friends my own age on Ashgrove Road to practise breakdancing with, to do anything with. Every day I walked silently past the children on my street – no 'all right?' or 'watcha', no knocking on their doors to see if they could come out. No one knocking for me. I had the feeling that they thought I held myself above them, which I didn't, not one bit, but I was embarrassed, and if I saw a group of them sitting on the low wall outside somebody's house, I crossed the road. Of course, I had my friends at Cotton Lane, and I was sociable, gregarious. But seeing them always had to be arranged – lifts from my father there and back, or sleepovers – because we lived that bit further away. I used to watch the children of Ashgrove Road racing down our street from behind the net curtains in the front room. Summer evenings, games of run-outs. I'd hear their shouts above the piano as I practised, and I always felt left out, somehow forgotten.

That last summer at Cotton Lane, the staff arranged a Leavers Country Dance for the fourth-years, about sixty of us. We'd do-si-doed our way through both Infants and Juniors, and at eleven we had become experts at formation dancing. I promenaded with half the boys that night – our arms folded across each other's bodies, holding clammy hands. I danced with Jitsingh Bansal, who had slammed my fingers in the classroom door two years before, an accident I'd just forgiven him for; with Marvin Pearl, who didn't love me any more and who had a girlfriend in the year below called Mickey – Mickey and Marvin, pah! – with Lucien Festen-Jones, an eccentric boy who'd joined in the middle of the year and was picked on for his funny accent and 1940s clothes. Lucien had replaced Marvin as a potential suitor to me. One day he trailed my father and me as we walked home from school, Lucien declaring his love, much to my father's amusement.

On the night of the country dance, filtered lights were set up in the darkened hall and pools of colour shimmered on the floor. We drank plastic cups of Coke and stuffed ourselves with French Fancies and Wagon Wheels. There was fractious feeling that night, as though we all knew that nothing from now on would be the same. We were on the verge of new lives, whatever they might hold.

Outside, the late evening light fell on the playground's asphalt. I walked across the chalked lines of the tennis court, knowing I'd find Solomon Kallakuri round the corner from the Juniors annexe. He'd become rebellious this year, talked back to the teachers, mucked around in class. He had a fight one weekend with a boy from another school and came to class with a black eye and a split in his lip. Now he was leaning against the wall, where I knew he'd be, smoking a cigarette. This was not the first time I'd seen him smoking. When he saw me, he stubbed it out and came towards me. He was still a few inches smaller than I was. His joined eyebrow seemed to have thickened in the last year. He put his hand on my shoulder and kissed me quickly on the lips. He tasted of smoke. Then he kissed me again, and held it for longer. He tasted of getting older.

◆

I'd like to say that I failed the eleven-plus on purpose, but in fact, I simply failed. I could manage the arithmetic and writing tasks, but I was lacking the ability to *apply logic to simple problems*. I couldn't crack codes or arrange a sequence of numbers. One morning my mother announced that I'd be attending after-school revision sessions for the exam. She was standing in the doorway of her bedroom, half dressed, getting ready for work. My father had just arrived home and was lying in the bed behind her with the newspaper. 'I don't want to take it,' I said. 'I don't want to go to grammar school!' This was Woodford Girls, on the other side of Ilford. I had no interest in going to an all-girl school.

'You're doing it, Hannah, whether you like it or not.' She sounded stern. 'Your dad wants you to.'

I was too surprised to say anything more. My mother sounded unconvincing, trying to assert my father's authority. I peered past her at him. My dad wanted me to? He'd expressed an opinion? I caught his eye, but typically he said nothing, just shook the paper as he turned a page. He had always deferred to my mother in regards to my education – this was the first time I'd ever known him to express an interest.

Then later, after the revision session when I failed to understand most of the questions, I felt angry. What right did he have to interfere now? What did he know about education, for that matter? He wasn't a proper father. He was more like a lodger who came and went as he pleased. He never told me what to do. If anything, it was I who told him what to do – and worse, he would do it. And now he wanted me to take the eleven-plus, because he respected that old-fashioned exam, respected grammar schools, and because if I passed, it would reflect well on him. And my mother supported this decision. So I would have to take it. I was enraged.

And then I failed, as I knew I would. There were twenty or so of us that day in the sweltering gym, the big clock on the wall ticking distractingly – as distracting as my schoolmates' pencils scratching away on their answer books. I answered the questions I could, but half of them made my brain clog, unable to move forward or recall the previous line of thought. Eventually I gave up, staring out to the bright school field instead, where a class of infants were happily running races.

I was only slightly disappointed the morning I opened the letter with the news, even though I knew I wouldn't have gone to Woodford Girls by then. I'd been accepted into Pinners, the school my cousins went to. This was better than a grammar school. I'd had to take a test and attend an interview where the scary headmaster asked about my future plans and ambitions. My mother briefed me thoroughly – *Make sure you talk about the piano*, she said, and somehow I'd been admitted, one of only thirty children from outside the borough, a significant feat, considering my brother had failed the same interview four years previously.

Sam was another reason my secondary school had become a subject of such fuss. My mother didn't want me to go to his school – Hope Park – because of the trouble he'd been in. My mother blamed the school, but I was pretty sure Sam would have rebelled anywhere. His latest misdemeanour had been 'accidentally' setting off a fire extinguisher, covering his Geography teacher in chemical foam. By then he'd been behaving badly for months, staying out later with new friends my mother didn't like. She suspected *something*, but didn't

quite know what. He was short with her and surlier than
ever. Then one day the police phoned to say they'd caught
him in the train yards at Farringdon, with a rucksack full of
spray cans they doubted he'd paid for. They brought him
home in a police car. The following week my mother hid his
trainers to stop him from going out, a strategy I could see
was unwise. They had the most terrible row – my brother,
just fifteen but over six foot tall – squared up to her in the
kitchen, shouting and shouting, bright red in the face. I
thought he might hit her. Finally, she relented, retrieved his
trainers and threw them at his feet. He in turn threw a brick
through our front door on his way out.

He was caught a week later, at the same train yard, spraying
graffiti with two other boys. The police didn't charge him
but he was assigned a social worker, a small black woman
with close-cropped hair and dangly earrings. She came to
our house once a week, sitting in the front room with Sam
and my mother, who laid out bowls of potpourri and doilies
as if these would demonstrate how undysfunctional our
family was. I listened at the door, but was unable to hear
the details of my brother's rehabilitation. My mother had
allowed him to spray the walls of his bedroom in the hope
this would keep him away from public property. The room
smelt constantly toxic, each wall daubed in a thick blear of
red, purple and green paint, dried in thick, globular tears.

♠

There were two ways for me to get to Pinners. On my own,
I could take the train from Goodmayes to Romford, along
the line that ran behind my house, then change for another
train to Upminster. Or if I was up in time, my mother would

drop me round at Uncle Terry's and he would take the three
of us – myself and the girls – to Upney station where we'd
catch the Tube. It was seven stops along the slow end of the
District Line, then a mile's walk to school in our stiff school
uniforms, loaded down with school bags full of folders,
textbooks, our PE kits. Pinners was a sporty school, and
there was no escaping netball, swimming, hockey, rounders,
tennis, high jump, discus and the torturous twice-weekly
cross-country runs.

Soon after I started at school, Maria and I had a strange
encounter on our journey. We were travelling alone one
day as Susanna had an eye test. It was a bright morning but
freezing cold, so we sat in the platform waiting room where
the old-fashioned radiator was turned up high, filling the
small space with the smell of hot paint. A man came in. He
wore bright jogging clothes – tight turquoise tights, a red
tracksuit top with stripes, a woolly hat and gloves. He was
black, forty perhaps, with a short, grey beard. I thought it
strange that a jogger would catch the Tube, and sure enough,
we both soon realised that the man wasn't waiting for a train.
He was in the waiting room for us. He stood facing the
radiator, but slightly angled so he could watch us, making
slow movements with his body, circling his groin against the
hot metal bars. He watched us, and we watched him, and I
had no idea what he was doing. Then the train pulled in,
Maria grabbed my arm and we rushed out.

'Dirty old man!' she exclaimed, slumping into the carriage
seat and pulling a face.

'Was he?' I said, surprised. 'What was he doing?'

'Didn't you see? He had a big hard-on. That's what the
tight clothes were for. What a perv!' But she was laughing.
And then so was I. He'd looked so stupid, gyrating around.

The next day he was there again, and the next. It was the same routine, but we couldn't stop laughing. I laughed so much my stomach hurt, until I could hardly breathe. And on the third day, he smiled coyly at us as though to say *Look, I know I look ridiculous, but it's something I have to do.* Then he laughed. The three of us laughing at a really bad joke.

He wasn't there the next day or the next and he didn't come to the waiting room again, but I used to see him around and about, on buses in Ilford, or in the park. Sometimes with a beard, sometimes without – always in those coloured jogging clothes, but I never saw him jog.

♥

I hated Pinners from the moment I started there – the uniform code with its pedantic requirements for hair accessories to be only brown, box pleat skirts to be two inches below the knee at least, girls' shoes to be chosen from a selection available at Wards of Upminster, the ancient department store which stocked the school's uniform. On the third floor, my mother bought me a pair of ugly buckled sandals called 'Clarissa'. 'They're not *too* bad,' she said, and I agreed, in so far as they were styled more attractively than the lace-up 'Veronica's or 'Lucy's I'd tried on, which made my big feet look like lumps of wood.

I only wanted to go to Pinners because my cousins did. At eleven years old, I didn't care about the school's long tradition of academic excellence, its national reputation for sport. And although the school booklet said I should be proud to wear the Pinners coat of arms embossed on the breast pocket of my blazer, I didn't really give a hoot. I hated that the teachers wore academic gowns and mortar boards as though they were Oxford scholars, marching briskly down the wood-panelled corridors, sweeping dramatically into classrooms, expecting us to stop whatever we were doing and stand up to show them our respect, until they told us we could sit down again. I hated that I was meant to care about the history and reputation of the school, that I was meant to feel myself esteemed in some way, privileged to be there, that I should consider myself somehow above the other children who had not been selected by Pinners, like Sam perhaps, that I was expected to look down on the pupils of other local schools, with whom we had great rivalry. With this as our unofficial ethos, was it any surprise we were hated by the pupils of nearby schools? I didn't blame them.

I made my first friend in Claudia Dean, the only black girl in my class. Her parents were Jamaican but had divorced. She lived with her mother and her white stepfather. I still have a photograph of her and me sat at the dinner table in my house. She has short cropped hair and wears a lime green blouse with a gold brooch at the neck. We are pulling faces at the camera. 'She's a lovely girl, isn't she? Nice mum too,' my mother said when Claudia went home. Our mothers had stood at the doorway discussing the school and work. Her mother was a social worker.

Claudia *was* a really nice girl. Gossipy and excitable. She sort of fizzed. But she had trouble at home, not getting on with her stepfather, and she didn't like Pinners either, had an irreverence similar to mine. My first report said I was *an instigator of low-level classroom disturbance*, meaning I talked when I should have been listening, and did stupid things like flick fountain-pen ink across the classroom, once onto the back of a teacher's shirt. Claudia didn't do the daft things I did, but she was loud and outspoken, refusing to automatically accept the school's authority and its endless, pointless rules.

Then one day she had a fight with a boy, a bully from another form. There were rarely fights at Pinners, and never between a boy and a girl. A rumour went through the classrooms at lunchtime. Someone said the boy had lost a tooth. Good old Claudia, I thought, both excited and repelled by the news. I'd never fought, except with Sam. It seemed a serious thing, something from the adult world. She wasn't in class that afternoon. I phoned her that evening but there was no reply. I phoned the next night and she told me that Rhys had called her names, but she didn't say what. I saw her the next day outside the school office. Then she was gone. Her mother phoned my mother and told her they'd decided Claudia would be better off elsewhere, but we should stay in touch. I had a book of hers, a Judy Blume I knew she'd want back. But I didn't phone, not that week or the next, and somehow we never spoke again.

It was around this time my father gave me a book, an unusual occurrence as he rarely showed an interest in what I was reading. The book was as thick as the Bible with a dark purple cover. Its title was *Atheism: The Case Against God* by George H. Smith. 'I want you to read this,' he said seriously. He was wearing his reading glasses. 'It's well researched and well argued. Everyone should read it.'

I took the book up to my bedroom, but every time I tried to read the introduction, I'd get lost. The words were too complicated, the subject too dry, like all the books my father chose to read – long biographies of socialist politicians or histories of labour movements. His appetite for politics and current affairs was seemingly insatiable. He read the *Guardian* every day from cover to cover and always had a stack of books on his bedside table, while I was still reading Enid Blyton and progressing onto Judy Blumes. Still, I appreciated owning *The Case Against God*. I felt it confirmed my family's creed, rebelling against Pinners, a school so proud of its Church of England ethos. Now, when other people declared their Christianity or Hinduism, I would announce my atheism, as though it were my faith.

A few weeks later my mother gave me a letter to give to Mr Harrington, my head of year. 'What does it say?' I said suspiciously.

'Your dad wants you to be exempted from saying the Lord's Prayer in assembly, which means you'll have to miss assembly altogether.' My mother sighed. 'This is a permission letter.'

Once again, it seemed my father had spoken in regard to my education, but this time it was in my favour. I hated assembly, less because of the Lord's Prayer than because it was half an hour sat cross-legged on the cold, hard gymnasium floor. My fathered hovered in the doorway, avoiding eye contact with my mother. 'No more Lord's Prayer for you, Han!' he said jollily.

'OK,' I said. 'If you say so.' This was all very strange. 'Thanks, Dad.'

♠

If my mother resented my father's part-time parenting, she rarely said so. In fact, she didn't say much about his absences, the petty criminality, his dubious living. Hers was a conflicted position. When he did try to assert himself as a father, she supported him. When he didn't, she tried to fill his shoes. If she begrudged the countless nights he was away from her and us, the solution – that he stay home – meant we'd be poor. It was only years later that she told me how hard it was. *I missed out*, she said. *You children missed out. He knew it too. But what could we do?* Of course, it wasn't just that my father was a part-time parent. He was a part-time husband too.

There was often a tense atmosphere at Ashgrove Road, my father in the proverbial doghouse for reasons unnamed, and occasionally my mother's frustrations spilled over. There were rows. Not cross words that easily erased themselves after an hour or two, but full-on rages. Once, from my bedroom, I heard the sounds of smashing china and crept downstairs to find my mother launching cups at my father, who was ducked behind the kitchen counter.

'You useless bastard!' she shouted.

'Bet!' my father implored. A sea of broken china surrounded him. 'Calm down, will you please? Calm down!' He raised his head above the counter to meet her eye.

'Don't you tell me to calm down!' She lifted another mug from the draining board and launched it at the wall, too angry to aim properly.

'You're bloody mad!' my father shouted. 'Do you want to kill me?'

'Yes!' she cried. Another crash.

Neither of them noticed me, watching from the hall. I had no idea what they were rowing about. I crept upstairs.

Other times, they were the best of friends. My mother loved gardening, and after Nan died she took over the long back garden behind Ashgrove Road. It was a lovely garden, with a pond and a rockery. An old cherry tree stood at the end of the lawn. Behind it, my mother kept a vegetable plot between the shed and Nan's old greenhouse with its rickety frame.

My father helped out in the garden. They spent most Sundays out there – wrapped in big coats when it was cold, gloves and wellies on. My father would dig where my mother told him to, load up the compost, go down on his knees to pull up weeds. It was his job to make the autumn bonfires, a task he relished. I stood between them on those cold evenings, marvelling at the flames, the lovely warmth of the fire. My enthusiasm for bonfires ended abruptly when one of my parents – it was never made clear which, though I suspect my father – threw a cardboard box containing Doug, our hibernating tortoise, onto the pyre – an accident so horrendous no one spoke of it afterwards. We found the remnants of his cremation among the ashes the next day.

My mother ordered a new greenhouse when the great storm of 1987 made the old one keel over. Some of the glass panes cracked, others were loose and threatened to fall out. The new one arrived in twenty different cardboard boxes the delivery men propped on our patio. There was a thick manual of assembly instructions.

'Destructions, more like,' my mother said. 'God knows how we'll put it together.'

She needn't have worried. My father erected it for her the next day while she was at work. It must have taken him hours. She was amazed

'Did you do it on your own?' she said disbelievingly as we all stood in the greenhouse. It was much bigger than the old one, with a small porch and a wooden slatted floor.

'Yes, just me,' he said. 'See what I do for you?'
'I can't believe it,' she said. 'It's like a bloody palace!'
'Oh it wasn't too hard,' he said. 'I knew you'd be pleased.'
He patted her waist as he stepped outside to light his
cigarette.

♥

'Your homework is to write an essay about someone in
your family,' Mr Apricot said, chalking instructions onto
the board, 'and link it with an important event or events
in history.' His yellow moustache was so thick you couldn't
see his mouth. It moved when he spoke. 'Go home and talk
to your mums and dads – you might be surprised.' The bell
rang and the chairs scraped back. We pushed each other
out into the corridor.

I didn't go home and talk to my parents but I did write an
essay about my father. I must have known enough to write
about his Anglocentric education in the colonial system,
which taught him little about the struggles of his own island,
but plenty about the lineages of English royalty – he could
name in order every single king and queen since William the
Conqueror, and all the countries in the Commonwealth. I
wrote about his reverence for the institutions of England and
how he'd taught himself to speak English 'like a gentleman'.
I wrote about his schooling in colonial Jamaica where he'd
learned poems by heart to recite for competitions – always
English poetry about places and things he had never seen,
like 'Composed upon Westminster Bridge' or 'Daffodils'
by Wordsworth. Sometimes he would recite 'If', an ironic
choice, given Kipling's ambiguous association with the
British Empire. He would stand at the dining-room table,

delivering the lines in his best English accent. I wrote about the ship he took from Kingston to Liverpool, believing that England would welcome him, only to be shocked by the hostility and prejudice he encountered, not only in finding a place to live, but also by people shouting racist insults at him in the street.

When I got the essay back, Mr Apricot had circled 'Anglocentric' in red pen with a question mark and a comment: 'Not a proper word.' I stuffed the essay in my bag. Even then I knew there was a heavy irony here – that my dusty, English History teacher pacing to and fro before the blackboard in this dusty, English school would have no need to know a word that just confirmed his position and privilege in the centre.

There was no doubt that Upminster was a whiter place than Ilford, but the racial demographic of Pinners was disproportionate – there were only one or two black faces in each year, and with Claudia gone, there were none in our year. Of course, I looked white, so anyone might wonder why it mattered to me. Was it that I didn't *feel* white? At Cotton Lane, everyone knew my father was black and I was surrounded by people who had origins all over the world. But at Pinners, something told me I'd be better off keeping my background to myself.

The schools were only eleven miles apart but Upminster is further into Essex than Ilford, at the end of the A124 – halfway to Grays and Thurrock. Most of the pupils at Pinners came from Upminster or round about – Hornchurch, Cranham, Emerson Park, relatively well-off neighbourhoods, but still within a stone's throw of poorer places such as Harold Hill and parts of Romford. That whole area of Essex, from Ilford heading east, was sometimes called the Essex Corridor. The term *white flight* was applied here, meaning the migration of the white working classes out of the East End and into Essex, along that corridor, seeking to escape the influx of migrants into London. Lots of the children at Pinners came from such a background, had parents or even grandparents who'd moved out from Aldgate, Bow or Stepney Green. Others had families who'd been in Essex for years and years. But whatever the case, the diversity I'd known before had disappeared, and in its place I found a casual but pervasive racism.

The curriculum at Cotton Lane had been multicultural, responding to the shifts of ethnicities in the area the school served, the high proportion of children whose parents came from India or Pakistan or a country in Africa. The teachers liked the pupils to talk about their backgrounds and we learned about different cultures. I don't think it occurred to me that I was English or white in any self-conscious way, or if it did, it didn't matter. I saw myself as part of a big mix of children and I loved to learn about the way other people lived.

We did projects on the plight of Native Americans and read Jamaican folk stories and poetry. In maths we learned how the number 0 came from India and how the abacus came from China and Egypt. Later, this type of education was nicknamed the 'Sari, Samosa and Steel Band' approach, seen as tokenism, inadequate to address the real inequality between cultures and races. But perhaps what went on at Cotton Lane was a start. There was something in the spirit of that school that was really positive – a tolerance, a notion that difference was good, a disdain of racism and prejudice. At six or seven, the worst thing we could accuse each other of was being a racist, or a *rachist* or *racialist* as most of us mispronounced. 'You're a rachist! I'm telling Miss!' We couldn't always say it right, but we knew what it meant and we knew it was wrong.

At Pinners, that spirit was gone. It was a monocultural school and any efforts to look beyond this were always academic, never real, never lived. I missed the mix of people. I missed the sense that I was part of a world far bigger than Ilford or Upminster. At Cotton Lane I saw outside my own small place, reminded every day that there were other people and far-off places. Perhaps at heart, I missed my friends: Mina, Solomon, Marvin. Even Lucien. They'd all gone to Hope Park, and despite our promises, we hadn't stayed in touch.

After Claudia had left, I became friends for a time with Frankie, who lived in Harold Wood with her mum Viv and three brothers, and their mum's boyfriend Carl, who was twenty years younger than her, and wore black varnish and skinny jeans. I liked Viv. She had peroxide blonde hair and wore skin-tight gothic clothes, always joining in when we gave each other makeovers or backcombed our hair. She used to spray us with her perfume, put her feet up while we watched TV, drinking gin and tonics. She drew us into the adult world with advice about men.

'Let them take you out and treat you nice, girls,' she'd say in front of Carl, 'but never get involved.' I was only eleven, but appreciated her sagacity nonetheless. But after dinner, she might send us to get a bag of sweets or a can of Coke from the *Paki shop*, a term I knew was wrong, but couldn't say so because Viv was an adult. And I was outnumbered

– Frankie and her brothers said it too. Then Viv would curse the 'bloody blacks' who took her parking space in the shopping centre, or held the queue up in the post office, sending packages to 'Zululand no doubt'.

Another time, when I told Kevin Morris in my class that my family lived in Ilford, he said, 'Oh, my dad says Ilford's a right dump – loads of coons and Pakis there, like a bloody jungle!' Those terms and phrases were used so nonchalantly. For half of the second year, the accusation 'Jew-boy!' was in vogue, so if, for example, Mark Parker dropped his lunch money on the floor and bent to pick it up, Tim Sanders might shout out 'Look he's picking up his pennies off the floor – what a Jew-boy!'

Looking back, I can't remember how often I heard this kind of prejudice or to what degree I've let those individual comments stand for the views of the majority. I was sensitive to it. I felt conflicted by it. The norm at that school was white and English, and by anybody's measure, from the outside, I looked normal. But inside, those comments really got to me. They made me feel protective of my father, protective about Solomon and Mina and Marvin. I felt protective about me.

♦

A man called Ray the Pilot was often on the telephone to my father at that time, and the two of them were in cahoots. Ray was from Texas but lived in Durham, near to an airbase from where he flew private jets for wealthy north-easterners. I'd met him once when he'd come to the house in his tan leather jacket and cowboy boots. He was tall and the boots made him taller. He had a suntan and floppy blond hair. He stayed for dinner, directing most of his conversation to my mother, whom he called Betty-Boo. He told stories about women he'd seduced from France to Russia to Thailand. *What a pillock*, she said when he left. *Total sexist pig.*

One evening, my dad put down a small suitcase in the hall. He'd polished his shoes for half an hour that afternoon, and now he had them on with his smart belted mac. 'Where are you going?' I asked him. I'd never seen him with a suitcase before.

'Newcastle,' he said, and winked at me. 'To see a man about a dog.' This was one of his favourite phrases. He was always vague about his evening jaunts, the proverbial dog often cited as a reason for his outings.

'Oh right. If you say so.' I was generally annoyed with my father these days, for reasons I couldn't specify, and I wasn't going to let him think I cared what he was up to.

'See you, then,' he said, picking up the suitcase. 'Tell your mum I'll be back on Thursday.' It was Tuesday and my mother was at Keep Fit, bounding around in her new leotard and legwarmers.

'Hmmm,' I grunted as he shut the front door.

There would many more trips in the coming months. Newcastle again. Guernsey. Then Paris, then Berlin. No more explanation from him. My mother said he was 'doing a bit of business', whatever that might mean. Each time, I'd watch him straightening his coat in the hall mirror, the little suitcase at his feet. Then he was gone, just like that, just like a lodger.

The last time he went abroad it was to Prague. It must have been the one time my father's preparations were not concealed from me. I remember he stayed up very late the night before, sitting at the dining table doctoring the cards, the overhead light supplemented by two bright lamps on either side. He was there after dinner and still there when I went to bed. Nothing was said. There were glass pots of ink on the table, the little guillotine from the hall cupboard. In the morning I watched him climb into the big black car waiting at our gate. There were three others – two I didn't recognise, but driving the car was Sylvester, one of the men who made dice tables with him.

I watched them pull away and, for the first time, had a pang of worry about my father. From snatches of overheard phone conversations I had gathered there was a dealer in a big casino there who was willing to swap a deck of marked cards into a poker game for a share of the winnings. Surely my father was too old to be doing that sort of thing?

He was supposed to be gone a few days, but he was back the next afternoon when I came home from school, and in a stinking mood. 'The guy lost his nerve!' he was telling my mother in the kitchen. 'He was blind drunk! Stumbling round the place, security guards everywhere. Oh, it was a posh place. Top notch. We could have cleaned up.' He took a long drag on his cigarette. 'But as soon as we saw him, it was game over. We were in bed by nine. And here I am now,' he said, leaning back on the counter. 'What a waste of time. And the fool man still has my cards. They could make him a bit of money, I can tell you.'

'Well, what can you do?' my mother said, pulling on the washing-up gloves. 'Ring the casino and complain?'

'Hello, Dad,' I said, making myself an orange squash. 'Thought you were gone until Sunday.'

'Hmmm,' he said. 'The dog I went to see was dead.'

♠

There was a swimming pool in Romford called the Dolphin – not just any swimming pool, but a special one

– hexagon-shaped and surrounded by tropical plants and rockeries. You could walk into the water on the sloped floor of shell-coloured tiles as if it were the ocean. The showers at the side of the pool flowed like waterfalls, cascading out of fake rock. There was a high slide to slip down and splash into the deep end, and it had a wave machine. I'd had my tenth birthday party there with eight friends from Cotton Lane. We'd swum and played, then changed into our party dresses, heading upstairs to the café where coloured balloons floated above the table spread with sandwiches and birthday cake.

At twelve, I still loved the Dolphin. I had another new friend, Kim, and she and I spent most Saturdays wading and flopping through the turquoise water. The wave machine began every hour, creating huge surges as the water rose high and dipped low on the pool's sides. I was just playing around when the accident happened. It didn't occur to me that the depths of the water shifted so dramatically when the wave machine was on, and so I dove deep into what should have been five feet of water, but was actually much shallower. My chin hit the tiled floor hard. At first I couldn't right myself. Then I was standing and all the lights above were wobbly. Someone gasped and someone else put their hand on my shoulder, and suddenly the lifeguard was there. I put my hand across my mouth. Where my front teeth should have been was a hard, jagged ridge. I had a palm full of blood.

The lifeguard walked me out of the water, wrapped a towel around me and led me to the first-aid room, where a young woman in sports clothes tried her best to fix me up. I couldn't stop crying. All I had left were two stumps of front teeth. They had punctured my lip. I looked in the mirror and cried harder. I'd liked my front teeth. Half an hour later my father was there, car keys in hand. I was still crying, but as soon as I saw him I pulled myself together. I didn't want him to hug me.

'Oh dear, Han,' he said in the car. 'You've ruined your teeth.' This was the last thing I wanted to hear. I knew it was bad. I held back the tears as we drove silently home.

♥

The South African dentist made me a pair of veneers to match the size and shape of my old teeth, and fixed them on with ultra-violet rays. This was not before I had to spend two weeks at Pinners with a dull ache in my jaw and my smashed teeth on view to everyone. 'You look well ugly,' Simon Porter told me, and I spent lunchtime locked in the sports changing rooms, where no one would find me.

'Make sure you say thanks to your dad,' my mother told me on the drive back from the dentist. She wanted me to respect him. The veneers had cost £300, money he had spare since he'd been taking his various trips. The new teeth were really good. I looked normal again.

'Thanks for my teeth, Dad,' I said, hovering in the living-room doorway.

'You'll have to be careful with sports,' my father said, looking over his newspaper. 'I need to protect my investment.' He laughed. I could see that he was pleased to be acknowledged.

It was a year of accidents. Sam had broken his collar bone three months before, falling from a wall behind his school. I wondered what he'd been doing on that wall. There was a rucksack hidden below his bed, stuffed with cans of spray paint. My father had an accident too, one Sunday after lunch. He was outside, up a ladder, painting the window frames. My mother was in the back garden, Sam was in his room, and I was practising the piano. Suddenly the doorbell rang, and rang, and rang, shrill and intrusive, as though someone was holding it down. But in the hall I saw a pane of the front-door glass was smashed and protruding through the gap was the end of a ladder. I opened the door to see the ladder had fallen, one of its legs breaking the frosted glass. The other leg had wedged against the doorbell. I pushed the leg to the side to stop the bell ringing, and at the same time saw my father, lying across the garden path, half in the flower bed, surrounded by red rose petals. His arms were tidily folded over his body, as though he was asleep. One petal on his cheek looked like a tear.

'Dear God!' shouted Irish Bridget, our next-door neighbour, rushing up our path in her apron. She crouched down by my father.

'Ralph, Ralph, can you hear me? Don't worry, my darling. Oh dear God, dear God!' There was no response. My father looked very peaceful. 'Dick, I think he's dead!' Bridget cried, looking up to her husband, who was coming up the path looking perplexed. 'Call an ambulance!'

Then my mother appeared. 'Oh no,' she said. 'What's he done now?' She knelt down beside my father and lifted the rose petal from his face. 'You silly old fool,' she said, and stayed there holding his hand as the other neighbours came. A siren sounded in our street. The medics lifted my unconscious father into the back of the ambulance and my mother climbed in. I watched them disappearing down Ashgrove Road, the blue light flashing.

Joshua from Trinidad, our neighbour on the other side, came up behind me. I was scared of him. His clothes were always stained, he smelt of ale and something sour. He put his arm around me, bent down close, his face on my neck. 'Don't fear, don't fear about your daddy,' he whispered hotly in my ear.

◆

There was the sensible way, my mother said, *and your father's way. And the two were not the same.* The ladder had been uneven and my father thought to prop it in the flower beds on a piece of Contiboard to even up the legs. Contiboard is both shiny and slippery, so it was surprising he'd even reached the top of the ladder before it slid from under him and he toppled ten feet into the roses. He was lucky. He'd only cricked his neck, bruised his coccyx, banged his head. He had mild concussion and had to stay in hospital overnight.

My mother took me to the ward the next day. He was sitting up in bed, tearful and glum. 'I do everything wrong,' he said. His head was held rigid by a thick white neck brace. 'Don't make the mistakes I make, Han,' he said to me, a statement I understood had a far wider resonance about his life in general.

'I'm more concerned about the roses,' my mother said gently, repeating what she'd said the day before, her hand over his hand: 'You silly old fool.' I was surprised to see her gesture. I'd never heard my parents say they loved each other, never seen them kiss.

As soon as my father's neck got better, the trips to Newcastle recommenced, once a fortnight. He took the train from King's Cross, returning the next day or the one after, appearing in the kitchen with his little suitcase. We were noticeably better off. My mother was redecorating. There were new things in the house. Something was going very well up north.

♠

Now I can look back on life at Ashgrove Road with more clarity. The illegal goings-on were interwoven with the everyday domestic. My father often did the ironing, standing with a pile of clothes, watching the television as he worked his way through them. But now and then, instead of clothes, he'd be ironing a square of cellophane around a deck of cards he'd marked, to make them appear brand new and still wrapped. When Sam and I were very young, everything was kept secret, so if we were playing in the garden he'd be upstairs loading dice in the back bedroom, or he'd wait until we were out to mark a deck of cards for the next night's game. As I grew older I saw more, perhaps because I was more observant, or perhaps he was just less concerned. Perhaps he had worried that a younger child might accidentally blab about what they'd seen.

I remember another failed mission, like the one to Prague, when my father was supposed to fly to New York. I didn't know it then, but he was planning to carry back a suitcase full of cannabis. I assumed he was going to play cards. All I saw was my mother's fury. 'What good are you to me locked up?' she shouted at him, tears springing to her eyes. And late in the night, I heard him knocking around downstairs. I came down to find him at the table, smoking a roll-up, the ashtray brimming with his crumpled butts.

In the morning, he stood at the front door. 'See you in a few days,' he said.

'If I'm unlucky,' my mother said.

It was a Saturday and I had ballet. She dropped me off and picked me up. When we came home, he was making tea in the kitchen.

'How far did you get?' she asked.

'Halfway to Heathrow.' He laughed, and put his arm around her. 'Your old man lost his nerve.'

Then there was the time the two Americans came to stay. They dealt in emeralds, they said. *Emerald dealers? Bloody emerald thieves, more like*, my mother said. Their names were Jed and Spike. I was small, but I remember them hazily. Jed was tall with a big Afro. They wore flash clothes – flared suits, thick gold rings and heavy chains at their necks. Spike had a fur waistcoat. The house was full of the scent of strong cologne.

My father had met them at a poker game in Paris. Six months later they were on the phone, coming to stay. *It was meant to be three days*, my mother said, *not three bloody weeks*. According to her they were lazy, expecting her to cook them dinner, clean up after them and make their beds. Jed lingered too long in whichever room she was in, constantly asking her questions – what were her favourite flowers, her favourite food, her favourite perfume? 'They've got to go,' she told my father. 'As soon as possible. Like today!'

But nothing was that simple. Apparently my father had set a job up for them, to earn them some money to move on – delivering an important package for an Indian friend of his, but something had gone wrong. My mother and I came home one day to find the Americans gone, but there was a big hole in the garden, right in the middle of the lawn. It was deep and narrow, the size of a grave. My father was filling it in. 'What on earth's been going on?' my mother asked.

It turned out that the important package was a Mini, the panels of which were packed with top-quality hashish. It was parked on a side street in Hamburg, waiting to be driven to London. The Indian had been keen when my father had suggested the two Americans for the job, but had been put off when he met them. He didn't trust them. He was meant to come to our house a week later to give them plane tickets and directions, but arrived an hour late, full of excuses and without the tickets. Jed disappeared from the room, gone for ages as the chat became more stilted, the excuses running out. Finally, my father went to see where Jed was, and found him in the back garden, digging the earth up with my mother's spade.

'What are you doing?' he asked, and Jed had leant conspiratorially towards him, a sheen of sweat on his brow.

'Keep that fucker there,' he whispered. 'I'm going to shoot him dead and bury him.' He patted a gun-size lump in his jacket.

My father relayed the story with great relish as my mother's eyes bulged.

'I had to stall him,' he said. 'And thankfully Mr Singh had let himself out. Anyway, they've gone to Manchester. Probably to rob a bank. We're lucky no one's dead.'

'Just fill this bloody hole in,' my mother said. 'And never again, you hear me?'

♥

I came downstairs in my school uniform one morning to find a commotion in front of the house. My father had just arrived home from Newcastle, driving all night in a bright yellow Triumph with a black roof. It was a gift for my mother. She had taken her test years ago, but hadn't driven in decades. Now she was going to have to, and no one was going to miss her in that car. She was standing on the path with a tea towel in her hands while my father showed the car off to Irish Bridget. 'Well she's a beaut for sure,' Bridget said, nodding. 'What do you think, Betty? I wish Dick would buy me a car. No chance of that!' Her laugh turned into a hacking smoker's cough.

'It's only done ten thousand,' my father said to my mother. 'She drives beautifully.' He looked pleased with himself. 'I drove all night to wake you up with a surprise.'

'It's lovely,' my mother said. 'A real surprise.' She opened the driver's door and shut it again. 'I better go in and get the kids off.'

She passed me in the hall. 'What do I want with a bloody car?' she said. She didn't require an answer. 'Oh I could bloody kill him.' I could hear my father outside, still talking to Bridget.

'Bright yellow,' he was saying. 'I knew she'd love it.'

♣

The next time he came back from Newcastle, my mother, Sam and I were eating dinner in front of the television. It was a documentary about death row. He popped his head round the door. 'Evening,' he said cheerfully.

'Oh, hello,' my mother said. 'Didn't think you'd be back tonight.' The yellow Triumph was still parked on the drive, waiting to be driven.

He rummaged in the pocket of his suede jacket, pulling out an envelope and dramatically slapping it on the coffee table. 'Who's going to open it?' he asked, looking from one to the other. Sam was slouched in his armchair, his legs spread. He craned his neck to look past my father at the TV. My mother looked worried. Suddenly I felt sorry for my father. 'I will!' I said brightly, leaning over for the envelope. I picked it up, unpeeled the flap and pulled the papers inside out. It took me a while to realise what I was looking at. 'It's tickets to Jamaica!' I said. I was holding four plane tickets. The summer holidays were only two weeks away.

'It's bloody not,' my mother said. 'Is it?' Her eyebrows were raised.

'We going to Jamaica?' Sam looked up.

'Yes we are,' my father said emphatically. 'For the whole of August. What do you think?' None of us said anything. We were shocked. He rubbed his hand through his hair. He looked sad.

'I need to go home,' he said.

8
1941

'The only way forward is for the workers to organise!' The man's voice was loud on the stage. The spotlight shone on him. He had a hollow face, light skin, a thin moustache. The rest of the hall was in half-darkness, humid and thick with cigarette smoke. 'We must throw off the shackles of the colonial rule that has divided Jamaica for too long,' he continued. 'We must raise confidence. We must engage in the great task of persuading our fellow Jamaicans that we are not preordained to perpetual inferiority. We are a nation capable of administering our *own* affairs!' There were murmurs of agreement all around. Then he spoke more slowly, emphasising each word, moving his hands with his speech. 'We must organise. We must work together. We must find the self-determination to build a more prosperous future for *all* the people.'

'Yes!' someone called out from the back. 'Yes!' Loud applause. The lights came on overhead. There was a big crowd in the theatre – students, union members, representatives of workers' groups. The boy sat at the back. They'd listened for an hour to speeches on the need for Jamaica to govern itself, universal suffrage and the increasing power of the People's

National Party and BITU, the trade union led by Alexander Bustamante.

As the audience dispersed, the boy made his way to the front, where the speaker stood near to the stage with the three other party men. His name was Thomas Reid. He was a leading trade unionist and Marxist and the boy admired him greatly, had come to hear him speak for weeks now, in awe of his convictions and the articulacy with which he expressed them. The group turned towards the boy as he held out his hand to Reid, nervous as he spoke: 'That was a brilliant speech,' he said. 'I'm from Yallahs, St Thomas. I want to get involved. What can I do?' The men took the boy in. He was sixteen now. Tall. A handsome, determined face.

'Welcome, comrade,' Thomas Reid replied. 'I've seen your face before. Good to see you again.' He introduced the other men, who nodded to the boy. 'What can you do?' he continued, lighting a cigarette, exhaling. 'Keep coming to these gatherings. That's the first thing. There's a big meeting coming up at the racecourse. Bustamante will be speaking. Spread the word about it. What else?' he looked to the other men.

'The union groups need people to go door to door,' said the smallest of them, 'to get the workers on board, politicise the people. Whose children are at school? Who has water? Who has light? The war is making things worse. People must realise we need change.'

'That's right,' said Reid. 'Any of the workers' groups would welcome help. How old are you?'

'Sixteen,' said the boy.

'The party has a youth commission,' said Reid. 'You should join. There's a big membership already and it's growing. The party depends on our young members.'

Another of the men held out a leaflet. 'Read this,' he said. 'This is the way we want to get people thinking.' The boy took the leaflet. 'There are classes, too.' He had an intensity about him, accentuated by his close-cropped hair and glasses. 'At one of our houses on Monday nights. You should come. We're reading Karl Marx. There's a lot to learn.'

That had been six months ago and since then the boy had attended meetings as regularly as he could. He went to rallies where Bustamante and the PNP leader, Norman Manley, spoke. He talked to everyone he could about what was happening – back in Yallahs, and in Kingston. So many of the village folk had been driven to the city for work, living in squalid tenement yards, toiling long hours to send money back to the country. The boy urged them to support the party.

He went to the reading groups of the Youth Commission and saw other young people had found their way there as well. There was a feeling that change could happen, a hopeful atmosphere in rooms made hot by the close bodies and the energy of the debate. The boy was reading books about revolutions, and every day the newspapers told of a Caribbean on strike. Not just in Jamaica, but across the islands, dockers and miners and factory workers were rising up in protest, demanding better pay and better conditions. They discussed these events, and the boy loved to be part of the discussions, loved the way the focus moved from the whole crowd to small groups talking about change. Often it was past midnight when he stepped away, strolling the mile back to Barry Street to deal the late-night game.

The boy dealt five nights a week now and had a little money saved. The men at the card table left him tips when they won, and Mr Manny paid him two shillings a night. It was something. And early evenings on the hot cement of the Kingston waterfront, in the shadow of the tall warships, he rolled out the felt for Crown and Anchor, playing banker to the RAF fellows and the soldiers milling around, waiting for the ships to take them off. It was fool's odds: the boy won nine times out of ten, and the one time a fellow won against the boy was always enough to make him roll the dice again. Crown. Anchor. Heart. Spade, Diamond, Club. Again, again. He was making money.

And he was playing cards himself, in the small clubs or back rooms of laundries on Barry Street. He and Felix, betting their wages on kalooki and poker and rummy, the boy's favourite. He had a photographic memory, his mind's eye remembering every card discarded. And every now and then, not often, but here and there, he'd swap a card in from his pocket, hold it curved into his palm then slip it into play, swinging the game the way he wanted. Yes, he was making money.

♦

'You want to stay in my room tonight?' Felix asked. They were standing in the early light on Barry Street, the game finished, the players dawdling home. It was eerily quiet. Felix had a place in the district above a liquor store. The strange boy Felix, with his one blind eye nearly shut, giving his face a lopsided look. He had a losing streak at cards but couldn't stop playing. The boy lent him money, gave it when he could.

'No, I need to go home,' he answered. Most nights now they played until the sun appeared in the sky, then the boy ran for the trucks that lit out from Kingston at dawn, arriving back in Yallahs to open the shop.

They parted, the boy heading for the trucks. In truth, he didn't know why he always rode home. His father had Rhona. He didn't care what the boy did now, but the boy was like a trained dog, always running back to his master.

♠

The next time he saw Hermione he followed her home, speaking to her back as she put her key in the front door of the whitewashed duplex. 'Ma?' he said. She spun round. This time she recognised him.

'So you found me,' she said. 'Well, well.' A smile of pretty teeth. The boy couldn't think what to say, standing silently, racking his brain until she spoke again. 'You coming in?' she said. 'Can't stand here all day.'

He came up the steps and looked down at her. She was small, bird-like. Suddenly she reached her arms up around him, a quick, fierce hug. The boy smelt oranges and frangipani, those scents lodged deep in his memory. Hermione held him away from her to look up at his face. 'What a handsome boy,' she said. 'I knew you gon' come find me one day.' She smiled again, took the boy's hand and led him inside.

The house was neat and dainty. Two rooms on two floors and everything in its place. The boy looked around at the glass figurines on the mantelpiece, the peach satin cushions placed upright at each end of the cream settee, lace portières moving in the breeze at the window. Hermione did not stop moving, back and forth to the kitchen, bringing more tea, then cake, wiping the surface of the end tables, shifting doilies. The boy felt big and clumsy perched on the narrow armchair, balancing a porcelain cup on a floral saucer. She chattered constantly. 'I live on this street for three years, and next door is Mr Simmons. His wife has passed, but he has a daughter name of Pamela, and she live at the end of this street, where it crosses with Tide Street. Opposite the Baptist church. You know it?' She didn't let him answer. 'She's very educated. A teacher of English. But she can't find a job. Can you believe it? All that training and education and then no job?'

On and on she went about neighbours, who did what, who had married whom. She was not the girl he remembered from Hearts Ease. The same sweet face, yes, the wide eyes, but something had shifted in her – the sorrow was gone, replaced by a self-styled lightness. She smiled at everything, talked on and on, not pausing to let the boy speak, not asking a question. Then suddenly she stopped, looking dramatically at the slender gold watch on her wrist. 'Oh dear! I have to go. I have an appointment. At the hairdresser's. I mustn't miss it!' She stood. 'Could you come again another time? Would you mind?'

'Yes, Ma,' the boy said awkwardly, handing her his empty cup. He couldn't believe he was standing in his mother's house. Would he see her again? Of course he would, he told himself.

'And best not to call me Ma,' she said, her hand on his arm at the screen door. 'It makes me feel so old, you know?' She hesitated, her face serious. 'And nobody knows I have a son, you see?' She couldn't meet his eye. 'You *do* see, don't you?' Her grip tightened. But you could call me Ida. That's what they call me around here. Call me Auntie Ida, if you want?'

The boy had no time to reply as she kissed him lightly on the cheek, stepped backwards and disappeared behind the gauze screen. The boy's feet carried him back down the road, the way he had come, past the Baptist church. Ida. Hermione. She wasn't the same, but walking back to Barry Street, he felt happy and dazed. Ida. Auntie Ida. Ma.

♥

The next week they sat on the little porch at the back of her house. There were shells arranged on the rim of the white railings, the neat garden blooming with pink and purple bougainvillea. Hermione carried a jug of home-made lemonade from the kitchen, filling the boy's glass. 'I'm an independent woman,' she told him. 'I don't rely on anyone, and nobody relies on me.' She had lived alone since leaving St Thomas. There was no husband, no gentlemen friend. 'Everything I have I pay for myself,' she said, sitting down. She wore a flowing peach-coloured dress, her bare feet resting on a stool, and in one hand an ornate Chinese fan to cool herself.

The boy remembered the first time he'd seen her on Barry Street, laughing with the Chinese shopkeeper, her head thrown back, a coquettish hand on hip. He wondered where she got her money, but he didn't ask. Instead, he told her about the Chiney shop in Yallahs, how they were losing business, so many people leaving, crops failing, prices slashed so low people couldn't live. There were families starving in Yallahs. His father had stopped giving credit, knowing it couldn't be paid back. 'Oh it's a sad story,' Hermione said, sipping her lemonade, as though it were only a story. She said nothing about the boy's father. Then she announced an appointment at the dressmaker, and as she had before, asked the boy to leave, making him promise to come again soon.

The next time, Hermione had just returned from a trip to the shops. She unwrapped the packages on the table, lifting her purchases to show the boy – a chiffon blouse held up against herself admiringly, stockings he blushed to look at, sweet soaps she insisted he smell. 'Lovely, aren't they?' she said, holding a bar to her nose. The boy thought how the island poverty had not affected her. 'They're gifts,' she said, slightly defensively, as though she could read his mind. 'What, you think all these things are for me?' She laughed. 'No, gifts. I'm going to Golden River by Above Rocks to see my sister, your Auntie Fay. She just had another baby. Dolores. You remember her other children? This is for Angela.' She held up the blouse, then a handful of coloured ribbons. 'These are for Laura.'

The boy searched his mind, but had no recollection. 'Oh yes,' said Hermione. 'You used to love to play with Angela when you were a baby. You don't remember?' She looked surprised, and the boy thought, how can I remember a lifetime ago?

'Do you want to come with me?' she said suddenly. 'I can show off my handsome grown-up son.' The tinkle of her laugh. 'We can stay a night, come back the next morning. They'd like to see you. Will you?'

And so the boy came back the next morning, and carried his mother's white valise to the bus station, and the two of them caught the yellow bus high up into the hills.

Rhona disappeared. As quickly as she had arrived, she had gone. Gone back to her mother, his father said, but the boy felt uneasy about her. He walked through the village, where old men sat on their porches and the women carried baskets of laundry down to the river. He asked if anyone had seen Rhona, but no one had.

Down on the beach he found his old friend Rufus wandering along the shore, a bucket in his hand. 'Long time no see, Rufus,' the boy said, and the two of them sat in one of the old blue fishing boats, catching up. Things were hard for Rufus – he hadn't been home in a few days, avoiding the drunken rage of his father. 'I keep thinking to go to Kingston,' he said. 'Think I'd be better on my own. If I can find work.'

'Maybe,' said the boy. 'But things are tough there, man. A lot of people without jobs. The war makes everything expensive.'

'I know, I know. But I can't let my dad beat me once more, you know? Once more and I might kill him.'

'I know what you mean,' the boy said. 'I know.'

◆

Back at the shop, it was quiet. The boy read the newspaper in between serving customers. The government had announced that any man convicted of stealing fruit or vegetables would be punished by public flogging. It was cruel and wrong, the boy thought. What next? There were mounds of rotting bananas by the roadside at Yallahs. Clouds of flies juddered in the air above them. The boy could smell them from the shop, a sweet reek. The war had stopped all commercial shipping. No export, no money coming in for produce. People couldn't afford food, but there were fields of rotting bananas. It was madness.

Later that evening, his father caught him by the arm in the back room. 'Don't think I don't see you,' he hissed. 'I see you with the scales!' Earlier the boy had served customers, making sure the measurements were accurate, sometimes giving a little over. He knew his father mixed new flour with old, scooped extra salt onto cod-fish to raise its weight. The boy hated this.

'You don't need to take from them,' he said. There was so little to go round. 'You shouldn't do it, Dad.'

He felt his father's hand swing into his face before he saw it. 'You do as I say!'

The boy's eyes smarted. Suddenly he flung himself at his father, threw both arms around his neck and dragged him down to the floor. The two of them rolled back and forth, the boy closing his hands tighter on his father's throat. He raised himself and brought his fist down on the side of his head. But James Lowe was stronger than the boy and, in truth, the boy was always, always scared of him. He pushed the boy off and came to his knees, then onto his feet, landing a kick in the boy's ribs that knocked the breath from him and made him retch. Then he lay there, retching again and again with every kick, curled in the shadows of the counter, retching and sobbing as his father kicked, and kicked again.

♠

It was midnight, the blue light of the moon filling the room where James Lowe lay sleeping, his face pale and solemn as the boy limped around, slipping his clothes into a cloth bag. He didn't have much. Bile filled his mouth. The pain in his ribs was excruciating.

How he hated his father. How he wished him dead. The sight of the peaceful face enraged the boy – a black anger he felt in his chest, in his feet and hands. He moved silently round the bed to the cabinet by his father's bedside, slipped open the bottom drawer.

Was it a minute or an hour he stood there? In his hand was a gun and the gun was pointed at his father's head. He willed him to wake and see the black eye of the barrel looking straight at him, the bullet waiting for him. The boy's finger resting on the trigger – cold metal on his skin. His tears ran a salt trail onto his tongue, dropping from his jaw.

He could do it. He couldn't do it. He could do it. He couldn't.

He laid the gun down on the bed, picked up his bag. Out of the door into the hot night – stumbling, running.

Dawn on Barry Street. He'd hitched a ride from Yallahs, holding his battered body to the back of a truck as it bumped and swerved along the road to Kingston. 'Felix?' the boy knocked on the peeling door. His voice was weak. 'Felix? You there?'

There was a ruffling behind the door and Felix appeared, rubbing his face. 'Chick!' It was a name he had given the boy. 'Come in, man, come in.' And the boy went in and asked could he sleep there. He lifted his shirt to show his bruises. Felix sucked in his teeth.

'Your daddy a sadist, so?' he asked. Then, 'Sleep in my bed. I'm on the floor, Chick, I'm on the floor.'

The first light shone through the slats of the room's window, a pale beam across the dusty boards. The boy lay under the thin sheet, Felix curled down at the wall. Noises from the street rose up – the clattering of hooves from the coal man's horse, the vendors wheeling their barrows to market. The boy was exhausted, on the verge of sleep when he felt a movement, a body coming into the bed. A slow shuffling towards him. Then nothing. Then warmth on the back of his neck. Felix's lips? Not kissing, but lips resting on his skin. 'No, Felix,' the boy said softly. He shrugged him off. 'That's not for me, man.'

Felix said nothing, only stopped in his movements, his body gone rigid. Then a moment later, he softened and reached a tentative arm over the boy's body, let it rest lightly on his shoulder. Paused. Shuffled a little closer. The boy lay with his eyes open. Felix's chest on his back felt like a warm blanket.

The pink sun rose up over Kingston. It was beautiful. He slept.

9
DISCOVERY BAY

This is my island in the sun
Where my people have toiled since toil begun
I may sail on many a sea
Her shores will always be home to me

– Harry Belafonte and Irving Burgie,
Island in the Sun

My father hadn't been back to Jamaica since 1973, and before that, not since 1962, when Ray the Pilot suggested flying his brand-new two-man aircraft from Oklahoma to Kingston. The new plane needed to be picked up from Oklahoma City, so the pair of them had flown there together and taken a cab to the airfield, where Ray had handed over a briefcase of cash. They fuelled up and took off, flying east over Mississippi, Alabama, Georgia, refuelling in Florida and then continuing out across the ocean to Jamaica, landing at Port Antonio. The plane was shaken and rocked by the wind the whole way and, shortly after landing, Ray took a photo of my father at the airfield to evidence that he had turned white with fear during the flight. In the picture, my father is hunched a few feet away from the little plane looking pale and shocked, his hair standing on end. Ray was used to the bumpy conditions, but my father hadn't been prepared. *He phoned me from the airport,* my mother said. *His voice was shaking. He thought he was going to die.* That experience gave my father a lifelong fear of flying. On our way to Jamaica he sat in the smoking section of the plane and smoked the whole way there.

It was my first time in an aeroplane and I was excited. I remember watching the shelves of cloud from the window, miles below, and an island my mother said was Cuba swirling in the turquoise sea. We landed in Montego Bay, where my father's half-brother Ken – or Honey, as they called him – waited at the arrival gates. He and my father hadn't seen each other in twenty years. 'Long time no see,' Ken said, smiling as they shook hands then hugged then shook again. Suddenly, standing side by side with Ken to introduce us, my father shifted position in my perception – from *outsider,* marked visibly by his racial difference from us, to *insider.* Ken and my father were a pair – two black men who strongly resembled each other – and then, looking around the airport at the travellers, the airport staff, the cab drivers, it dawned on me that in Jamaica, my father fitted in, and it was *we,* my mother and Sam and I, who stood out. I wondered what Ken made of my father's shiny white family.

We knew only that Ken had a house in Discovery Bay, and that it was big enough for us all to stay. Years ago, I'd seen his letter. *Dear Ralph,* it said, *Your family is welcome with me. Come anytime. Come home.* Now we were on our way, following Ken in the hire car he'd arranged for us. I rolled down the window. So this was Jamaica, my father's island. My memory holds some details so strongly – I can still smell the humid air that night – sweet and heavy, and the sea flashing in the black night.

When after an hour a sign flashed by for Discovery Bay, we began to climb a steep, bumpy hill. 'Oh Lord, is this safe?' my mother asked as we curled around the hairpin bends, my father focusing hard on the road in front, lit brightly in the headlights. I couldn't see how high the hill stood in the darkness, only a yellow light shining above us, so far up it looked like a star. 'I hope his place isn't up there,' she said, and of course it was. The house on top of the hill – grand and white behind iron gates. The light I'd seen below was a lantern hung from the veranda, swinging in the breeze above a sheer drop.

Inside, Ken showed us round. 'He's not a talker,' my dad had said, and he was right. 'You sleep here,' Ken said opening a door for Sam. 'And you sleep here,' he said, opening a different door for me. It was a big room – turquoise walls, a stone floor, a huge bed. But for a long time that first night I couldn't sleep – overwhelmed by the change in time, tiredness, the strangeness of everything – a gecko running on the wall, mosquito nets rising ghost-like above me where I lay. The moon in the window was bigger than the Ilford moon.

The world was colourful in the morning, the sun already high when I woke. I could see orange trees and lemon trees outside. Ken had gone to work; my father and Sam were still asleep. Slurping on a mango, I followed my mother around the garden as she admired what grew there – tall, spiky plants, vines of purple flowers, green-orange mangos drooping in clusters from the trees.

But at the front of the house, a low, ramshackle kennel of nailed-together tin and wood stood in the scorching sun. Inside, two Alsatian puppies whimpered and panted. I had woken in the night to their cries, not knowing where they were or what to do. They were being 'broken in', my father said nonchalantly when he finally awoke. The dogs' suffering would make them tough. In Ilford, he fawned over Chloe, tearful when a thorn stuck in her paw had turned septic and made her whimper. Here he was unsympathetic to the dogs. 'But they're crying,' I said. 'It's torture.'

'Things are different in Jamaica,' he said. 'No point in getting upset.'

Miss Rose arrived as I was standing on the veranda, taking in the view of the bay in the bright morning haze. She was Ken's girlfriend, a large woman in a billowing white dress, flapping an enormous white fan. She was to be our host when he worked. 'Greetings, darlin',' she said, wrapping me in her chunky arms. 'Welcome home.' Home? My father's home perhaps, but perched on the hilltop in the burning sun, this place felt a million miles from Ilford. 'Follow me,' she said, climbing into her car, and we retraced the route from last night, a half-hour drive down the stony hill past other houses tucked away behind iron gates, still others unfinished, their skeleton frames abandoned in the overgrowth. Old goats chewed rubbish at the roadside, and now and then men tending land stood to watch our shiny procession.

On the corner of the main street downtown was Miss Rose's restaurant and bar. It was opposite the beach – 'Beach! Can I swim after, Mum? *Plea-se.*' Inside, it was a simple room of red-check-clothed tables, a kitchen at the back, a whirring ceiling fan. The cook, another plump woman in white overalls and a white hat, sat on a table by the counter, while a few men tucked into their lunches. They looked up as we came in.

'Everyone,' Miss Rose announced grandly, 'this is Honey's brother, all the way from England. And this is Miss Bet, his wife, and these are his children.'

I shifted uncomfortably from foot to foot as the diners nodded to acknowledge us in turn. 'This is Cook,' Miss Rose continued, and then, pointing to each of the men, 'Linton, Lowell, Ronny and Walksy.'

'Welcome home,' Cook said, smiling, coming forward to take my father's hand. On the table by the door, a feast was laid out for us: plate after plate of food.

'There's lobster here,' Miss Rose said, lifting the fly covers. 'Red snapper. Shrimp curry. Crab. Eat, eat, eat!'

My father stared round, looking at the spread. I could tell he was surprised, and proud.

◆

I'd never swum in sea like that. Perfect white sand and coral shells, warm water. Tiny coloured fishes dashed around my feet. I swam to a wooden launch moored half a mile from the shore, and back again, the sea empty except for me and a black man floating on his back, singing 'Wind Beneath My Wings' to the sky.

I trod water, trying not to look at him. 'I love Bette Midler,' he announced, as he floated past.

'So does my mum,' I said.

'What about you?' he asked, making a circle around me. He was young, a year or two older than Sam, I guessed.

'I like Kylie Minogue,' I said, flicking the water with my hands. 'I don't suppose you have her in Jamaica?'

'Kylie Minogue?' he said. 'I don't know her. Any good?'

'Not bad.'

His name was Owen. My new friend. Or our new friend, I should say, since he followed me out of the water to meet us all. Owen was a flatterer. 'Miss Bet,' he said later, sprawled on the sand next to her, beads of sweat glittering on his skin, 'you are a schoolteacher. What a noble job. Do the children love you?' and, 'Mr Ralph, I can't believe you are sixty-five. Is it true?' He and Sam wandered off up the beach together, returning with bags of chopped pineapple. 'You are beautiful, Miss Hannah,' he declared to me as I ate. 'I wonder if your mummy will let me marry you?' I laughed too loudly, conscious of my thin body in my new swimsuit, which turned see-through when wet; aware that my body was changing, that I was changing, and ever since the incident with the jogger in the station waiting room, wary of the way men looked at me. I didn't want to be taken advantage of again, although I didn't know how to stop it.

But there was something innocent about Owen. A sadness hung over him, even as we lay there laughing and talking in the bright sun. His own parents were dead, he told us. He lived on his own, working evenings as a hotel waiter at Runaway Bay. I think he was lonely on the beach that day, intrigued by the look of us – there weren't many tourists at Discovery Bay. Maybe he thought we were rich, but I don't think it was that. Every time we came to the beach, he was there, floating on his back in the turquoise sea, singing to the sky.

♠

No one would tell me why Ken was called Honey, a name too sweet for my silent uncle. He was friendly but inscrutable. He had built his house himself, high up, away from everyone

– Miss Rose had her own house – and this was his palace, the big rooms with their grandiose touches – marble floors and chandeliers, a sunken bath with gold taps. He worked hard, six or seven days of the week, then came home to drink beer on his settee. 'He did all right, Honey,' my father said one morning over breakfast. 'When you think where he came from.'

'Where did he come from?' I asked.

'From the same place as me,' my father said. 'When Honey's mother died, he lived with my dad for a time, after I had left. But my father liked a woman who didn't like Honey. So when he was twelve, he gave him a dollar and sent him off.'

'What a bastard,' my mother said.

'Where did he send him?' I said.

'Off,' he repeated. 'Who knows? He went to the army at some point. Never saw my father again. And look at Honey now, eh?'

That night, Ken's daughter, Cora, arrived from New York, where she lived with her mother. I didn't know the history surrounding this arrangement and no one thought to enlighten me. With my family in residence, she and I had to share a bed, an idea everyone seemed to think a good one. 'It'll be nice to have a friend your own age,' my mother said, but alone in the bedroom Cora ignored me, keeping to her side, rubbing coconut oil into her skin, painting her nails. She was very pretty. '*How* long are you staying for?' she finally asked.

'Three weeks,' I said, pretending to read my book, ignoring her dirty looks. I was unfazed. Thirteen-year-old girls are not nice. I was one, and I knew. At worst, they are a nasty combination of insecurity, self-obsession and spite. Forced together and expected to be friends, Cora and I bucked.

That night and for more nights to come, she claimed the territory of the bed, wriggling stealthily across the moonlit sheets until I teetered on the edge. I put up little resistance.

In the morning, she greeted my parents like they were long-lost friends. And if Sam – who had suddenly become handsome – was in the room, she transformed absolutely, laughing gusty laughs and clapping her hands, finding secret ways to touch him.

♥

Despite Owen's feigned amazement, my father *was* sixty-five, and worried about his health for good reason. He must have known this would be his last trip home, if Jamaica still meant home to him. He wanted to show us where he came from, and he wanted to search for his past. His mother and father were dead, but there were places and family he wanted to see again – people I couldn't remember him ever mentioning before. He had an itinerary that took us all over the island, and as we drove it was apparent something strange had happened: he was in control. This was his world to navigate, and away from Ilford my mother deferred to him as our driver and guide as we criss-crossed the island, over mountains, along dust tracks, down the winding coast roads. He introduced us to people all over the place, and I could tell my mother was proud to be with him. I was almost proud too.

Jamaica was beautiful and poor. I knew the country was more than picture-postcard beaches and coconut palms, but I hadn't expected poverty so extreme. The north coast's beaches were tourist idylls – long stretches lined with shiny palm trees and gleaming hotels. But ramshackle shanty towns gripped the hills outside Kingston and Montego Bay, whole neighbourhoods of plywood and corrugated metal, like the kennel Ken had nailed together for his poor puppies. I couldn't believe people lived beneath those metal roofs in the burning sun. As our car sped past, I saw old women struggling with pots and plastic bags in the alleyways, skinny children chasing dogs along the tin boundary fence. Even from the car I could hear the noise, smell the stench of human waste, feel the heat and pressure of overcrowding. 'It was the same when I was young,' my father said. 'But worse now, you know. There's more of it, and it looks worse.'

We were wealthy by Jamaican standards then, and my father was a rich man returning – that's what people thought, though it was a strange notion since things were so often tight at home. But I could see poverty was relative. 'The right thing here is to spend money,' my father said, and spend is what we did, stopping at roadside stalls for sugar cane and pineapple and the amazing guineps, their tangy pulp hidden in a thin skin you broke with your teeth; buying small carvings of painted parrots and kissing fish from the beach higglers who wandered the shore, and in the market, haggling for lignum vitae busts of Rastafarians, so heavy it took my father and Sam to carry them. We would bring a little of Jamaica back to Ilford – their gleaming faces and polished dreadlocks sat for years in our home.

That first week our car climbed Old Stony Hill Road, twisting and turning past wide ravines that ran down to a spring, past Long Coconut Tree, where the parish of St Catherine's begins, to find Above Rocks and Golden River, the small place where my father came as a boy to stay with his aunt. 'Nothing's changed here,' he said. Up in the cool hills, the trees bent ominously over the road and creepers hung from their branches, making a green, eerie canopy like something from a fairy tale. And it was like a fairy tale, the way we found his Auntie Fay – the old woman in the woods – living by herself in a one-room shack. But Auntie Fay wasn't a witch, just an old, old lady with hollow cheeks and deep lines in her face. She was child-size, her small hand in my father's as they sat on the bed in her room, the bed in one corner, a stove in the other. It had been years and years since they'd seen each other. Perhaps to come without warning was too much – Auntie Fay didn't speak, just laid her head against my father's shoulder and smiled for a photograph it seemed garish to take. As we were leaving she took my hand too, her fingers like tiny, gnarled twigs.

'Were you close when you were young, then?' I asked in the car as we pulled away.

'Yes,' my father answered. 'My mother brought me here when I was small, and again when I was a teenager. My last years in Jamaica, I used to come up here to escape my dad.'

Auntie Fay. My great-aunt. I knew I'd never see her again. In the front, my mother passed my father a tissue. I could see his tears on his face in the mirror as we drove back through the green shadows.

Next was Aretha. Perhaps I did know my father had a sister in Jamaica. I can't remember. My father's recollections of family were always hazy or evasive. Was it six brothers and sisters he had, or seven? And none of them siblings like I was to Sam, not people he'd fought and played and grown up with. They were names I heard fluttered through conversation – Aretha, Vic, Rhona. Sister Louise in Peckham, whom my middle name is for. All had the same father, some shared a mother. Now they were flung across continents – Canada, America, Europe – a Jamaican story, families scattered to the wind.

'Welcome to Jamaica,' Aretha said, kissing us all at the driveway to her house. 'Welcome home,' she said to my father, her thin arms reaching around him. This was Red Hill, a wealthy hill suburb of Kingston, Aretha's house built into the side of a cliff among sculpted gardens. Not everyone in Jamaica was poor, then. It seemed to me there was a clear divide – the big gated houses like Ken's and Aretha's, and the shanty towns. We followed her inside where Albert, her husband, laid a table for lunch. He was white with a shock of white hair and white rimmed glasses. In a thick Jamaican accent he told us he'd been born in Red Hill and lived there all his life. I must have looked surprised at the way he spoke.

'Wha', you think everyone in Jamaica is black?' he said, turning his palms up. 'We have Lebanese here, you know. Syrians, Indians, Chinese, Jews. My grandfather was Syrian. Scandalously married an English woman, had three children, my father the youngest. He married a French woman from Trinidad, my mother. Brought her to Red Hill.' He pointed to himself. 'And here I am!' Everyone laughed. I suppose I had believed Jamaica was an island of black people. Even my Chinese grandfather I'd thought of as the *only* Chinese man in Jamaica – lost on his way to somewhere else or washed up in a shipwreck. But in the week we'd been there, I'd seen Chinese restaurants and laundries. I'd seen people of all shades and mixes, so I knew Albert must be right.

We ate on the terrace, watching a storm come in from the west, heading east. Twenty minutes of torrential rain that shook and battered the plants and trees, splashing up onto the marble floor, the damp smell rising from their shaded garden. Side by side, my father and Aretha were very alike in both looks and manner, reminding me again that this was a place he fitted in. 'When I was a child, I knew I had a brother named Ralph,' Aretha told us all. 'But I never met him. Never knew him until he come back here in 1962.' She lit a white-tipped cigarette. 'My mother was Bernella, but that's a sad story. I never knew my father, only he was Chinese. My grandmother brought me up. Mary McCormack. She was a good woman.'

My father crossed his legs in the chair, inhabiting his storytelling role. 'I knew I had another sister too,' he said. 'But didn't know where. You were a baby when I was grown.' He turned to Aretha. 'I was already leaving and you were still in nappies.'

Aretha laughed. 'My grandmother used to sing hymns to me. That's my earliest memory. The only time I ever heard of my father was when Mr Ho Choy would come to our house and give us a little money. He used to shame my father into paying something for me. And I thought to myself, what sort of man is this, that needs to be shamed into providing? I never had a thing to do with him.' Aretha exhaled smoke. 'It's true. Then when Ralph came back my sister Cherry phoned me up and said you have to meet our brother. I said, what brother? She said, our brother Ralph. All the way from England. Same daddy as us.'

'I tried to see them all,' my father said. 'Cherry, Vic and Rhona. All my father's children, or the ones I knew about.' He laughed and shook his head.

'How many of them did you meet?' I asked.

'Well, Cherry was here already. So was Honey. But Vic was living in America by then. Or was he in Canada? I can't remember.' He rubbed his head.

'And what about Rhona?' I asked.

Aretha spoke. 'Well, Rhona went to New York when she was young. Sixteen or so. She was married, then divorced, then married again.'

My father sighed. 'She always had a bad time of it. All those different men. She had a bad thing for men.' They were silent.

'Rhona killed herself in 1975,' Aretha said. 'They found her in her garage in New York. She'd suffocated on her car exhaust. Our poor sister, eh?' She looked at my father, who shook his head as though he still didn't believe it.

♦

Back at Ken's house, a drama was unfolding, since Ken had mysteriously disappeared on a business trip and reappeared with another pretty daughter. She was Sharon, the same age as me and Cora, another cousin I didn't know I had. 'I gon' kill that man,' Miss Rose said to my mother. 'Six years together and he never mention the girl!' It wasn't hard to work out what had gone on, and Honey's name began to make sense. It struck me that family was an amorphous thing in Jamaica, thinking of my father's scattered siblings, his own scattered children, Aretha's story, Ken's children. Sharon was funny and friendly, much more so than Cora, but that didn't mean I wanted her to join us in the big bed in the turquoise room where more territorial conflict would ensue. Cora was surely more threatened by her than me.

That night, uncertain of where her loyalties lay, Cora took the middle of the bed and spread herself like a starfish, kicking her legs and arms throughout the night. There was little sleep on the outposts, and after hours of small retaliations, Sharon stood, grabbed Cora's leg and dragged her to the floor, where they wrestled and brawled. 'Don't vex me, huh?' Sharon whispered menacingly, as she held Cora to the ground.

'Get off me! Get off me!' Cora cried. She looked at me for help. No way, I thought. I went to the sofa in the lounge, returning only when it fell quiet in the bedroom. On one side of the bed, Cora was curled and snoring, on the other Sharon lay peacefully on her back, one arm flung above her head. Half-sisters asleep, beautiful in the moonlight.

♠

The storms came in across the sky at Discovery Bay like a set change, the blue sky dissolving into dark grey, the clouds churning ominously. One fat drop of rain hit the ground, then another. The sky drummed with thunder, throwing down a sheet of rain. From Ken's living room, only the veranda was visible in these tropical storms. Beyond, the landscape disappeared, replaced by grey haze and rain so loud you had to shout to be heard. Wind dragged at the trees as insects piled up against the veranda doors – big spiders and moths the size of small birds that Ken would sweep away with a broom. My father and I played cards through these storms – a new game he taught me there, a variant of rummy with two decks and both jokers in play. I can't remember the name, only that it hurt my brain to think out each move – it had more of the strategy of chess than any card game I'd played before. We lost hours to it, while my mother napped and Sam read. 'Oh no! You beat me again, Han!' my father laughed, each time I won. We were having a good time, but even as I enjoyed it, it felt strangely intimate, uncomfortable even, to be alone with my father like that. We didn't do this in Ilford.

Then, in the evenings, we drove to Miss Rose's to eat – thick, earthy Jamaican food: chicken and stewed peas, curried goat, red pea soup – the same food I ate in England. After dinner, Sam would slip outside, where the younger men hung against the wall, reggae crackling loudly from a battered speaker. He wanted to go to the sound system parties in Kingston, but my mother wouldn't let him. My father joined the men in the bar for heated political discussions, a game of cards, or both. 'Listen here, me friend,' he'd say in his best Jamaican accent, launching into a polemic about the power of the old labour movements in Jamaica. Michael Manley had just been elected again, and my father, like many Jamaicans, was disappointed that the socialist reforms he'd introduced when he was leader in the 1970s were no longer part of his agenda. Those discussions went on for half the night, while we sat in the restaurant with Miss Rose and the other locals. 'Family from Englan',' Miss Rose would say again, by way of explanation anytime anyone wondered who we were – 'Honey's brother's children.' But her answer sometimes prompted more quizzical looks, echoing the way of things at home – people wondering if we really were my father's children.

♥

One day we drove east from Discovery Bay towards Port Antonio. We stopped for lunch in a restaurant on a busy road by the port and sat upstairs overlooking the street as a quick, heavy storm broke. The shoppers and street vendors scattered, but a moment later two men with long dreadlocks came jogging down the road in their shorts, bare-chested, bottles in their hands, stopping opposite, where two storm pipes overflowed. In the gush of rainwater, they shampooed and rinsed the ropes of their dreadlocks, a spectacle for the diners above. One looked up and waved at his audience. I waved back.

I was intrigued by Rastafarians. I saw them all over Jamaica, often wandering alone on the roadside, their dreadlocks swaying down their backs or bulging in their tam hats. I didn't know what they believed in, but they seemed like peaceful people to me, and I had liked the Rastafarian boy at Cotton Lane – Malachi Paul, whose little sister had dreadlocks too, and whose mother looked serene at the school gates in a white headdress. We'd visited a museum in Kingston where photographs of Rastafarians lined the walls – one from the 1960s showed a thousand Rastafarians on the asphalt of Kingston airport, waiting for Haile Selassie to disembark from his plane. In another, Rasta men and women lined a railway track as his train went past, holding their babies in the air to be blessed. Now I wondered aloud about the hair-washing we had witnessed – did Rastas only wash their hair in rainwater? None of us knew.

We drove on. We were looking for Mr Picketts – a Jamaican man my father had played cards with in England, who'd moved back five years ago. He'd been to the house in Ilford once or twice, smelling of rum or beer. It didn't take us long to find his house. A private gate marked 'Picketts' led down a long gravel drive towards the sea. At the end, a wide white villa faced the ocean, surrounded by a grove of orange trees, bright bougainvillea spilling down the walls. 'I never guessed Mr Picketts had money,' my father said, taking in the house. 'In England, he lived in a bedsit at Clapton

Pond. He must have been saving.' He climbed out of the car and went to knock on the door. 'You never guess it,' he said, returning a minute later. 'The maid says Mr Picketts went to England for a holiday this morning. This morning! What bad timing. He'll be in Corals by tonight, I bet.' Mr Picketts had lived in Clapton for thirty-five years, my father told us – married, had children, divorced, played cards. 'But Jamaica was in his heart,' he said. 'He spent thirty-five years waiting to come home.'

We carried on, towards St Thomas, for hours it seemed, the sky darkening as my father told a story about Mr Picketts's mad English wife, and a long tale about his childhood friends Luther Bogle and Haggai Tucker. He'd told stories about those two when I was small, so many I doubted they could all be true – but the characters of Luther and Haggai were always real to me, alive in the Jamaica of my mind. Haggai was thin and lithe and stupid, while Luther made up for his heavy body with a quick wit.

Outside, the landscape changed, becoming more mountainous and rural, much less built-up than the north coast. My father continued this particular story, which involved a catapult, a robbery and an improbable near death by falling mangos. 'There's a reason I told you this tale,' he said when he'd finished. 'Because we're just pulling into Morant Bay, which is where the Morant Bay Uprising took place. You know what that was?'

'No,' I said, 'but I expect you're going to tell us.' Jamaica had made my father garrulous in a way he'd never been before.

'Yes, you're right,' he said. 'It was the uprising of former slaves against their white oppressors, led by Paul Bogle. Courageous man! Caused the English to quake in their boots!

In Jamaica *and* England. No one could believe we could stand up for ourselves.'

'Ourselves?' I questioned.

'If I'd been alive then, I'd have been on the front line,' he said, lighting a cigarette from the car lighter. 'Anyway, the English came down hard on the revolutionaries. They caught Paul Bogle. Hanged him outside the courthouse. Let him swing. But his name lives on.' He flicked his ash from the window. 'There he is,' he nodded in the direction of an iron statue, lit up outside the Morant Bay courthouse. We all turned to see. 'One of my friends from boyhood was Luther Bogle, Paul Bogle's grandson,' he continued. 'So I was keeping good company back then, you understand.'

'What went wrong?' my mother said as we rolled on out of town. We drove into a dark, green valley where the yellow moon hung in the sky. St Thomas didn't look like anywhere else we'd been in Jamaica. They called it 'the forgotten parish', because industry and the tourist trade had largely passed it by, and more people had migrated from St Thomas, escaping its poverty, than from anywhere else on the island. I heard Ken called St Thomas 'the balm yard', and my father explained that the name referred to the spiritual practices that still went on there – Kumina, Revivalism, even Obeah. In the museum in Kingston I'd seen a black and white photograph of the Revivalists dancing at the river at Hearts Ease, dressed in long robes and headdresses, a man's hand frozen over a big drum. St Thomas had the 'rebel spirit', everyone said, keeping Africa alive, resisting the imposition of the British and the Anglican church. The Kumina followers believed in duppies – malevolent ghosts haunting the towns and roads at night. I knew that word well – it was another of my father's jokey threats: 'Be good or the duppy will get you!' Now he laughed, 'Look out for the Rolling Calf!' as we followed the winding country road, the shadowy foliage bent over the road, lit ominously in our headlights.

I knew about the Rolling Calf from a poem my father would recite when I was a child. It was a red-eyed beast – cow, dog or even a cat – roaming the rural roads at night to do the devil's work:

> Me deh pon has'e me kean tap now
> For Tahta John a-dead
> De oda nite one rollin'-calf
> Lick him eena him head

For all my father's claims of atheism, growing up in St Thomas must have touched him. As a young boy he'd been given a 'bush bath' by local women when he'd fallen very ill. They bathed him and rubbed strange oils into his skin, dressed him in red flannels and put him to bed for three days – a ritual he believed had cured him. And years later, I found his writing on notepaper, tucked into a book of Caribbean verse. He'd copied out the lines of the *Rollin' Calf* poem and hidden them. *Be warned*, he'd written in big letters at the bottom.

At last, we pulled up at the Whispering Bamboo hotel, but it was so late all the rooms were gone. Only the Honeymoon Suite was available, the manager assuring us it would comfortably accommodate us all. And so it was that we spent the night in an enormous floral love-nest, my parents sleeping on a padded peach circular bed below a mirrored ceiling, Sam and I on children's put-up beds. Outside the window, the palm trees swayed dramatically in the wind. I lay awake listening for duppies, the cry of the Rolling Calf.

Hannah Lowe

♣

In the morning we drove on to Yallahs. It was strange to finally see the town, after having known its name so long. The main street was lined with battered duplexes, jerk shacks and shabby shops, behind which lay a narrow beach lined with peeling fishing boats, silvery waves crashing on the shore. A stench hung over the town that made me wince. 'It's the salt ponds,' my father said. 'You get used to it.' We traipsed behind him in the blistering midday sun – down one street and up another, all tired from the surreal night in the Honeymoon Suite, where the air conditioner rattled loudly and couldn't be turned off.

Yallahs was a scrappy place, I thought, but my father strode through the town as though he couldn't see the rubbish on the ground, the half-finished houses, weeds growing between the grey breeze blocks. 'The police station was here,' he said, standing on the corner by a plot of rubble and long grass. 'Spring Pass was here. It ran down to Catholic Lane.' He stopped and turned, walking back in the direction we had come from. 'Ah, I know where we are now,' he said. 'This is where they had the market.' We had emerged in a square of sorts, eerily quiet. He stood silently, staring around as though he could see something we couldn't. 'Nothing looks the same,' he said. 'It doesn't look like Yallahs any more.' Men sat on a low wall on the other side of the road watching us – an old black man leading his white family, looking for ghost streets, a ghost market, ghost people. Whatever Yallahs was, it was far from the tourist trail, and we looked out of place.

'You people lost?' called a young man from a car workshop. He came towards us, dressed in mechanic's overalls, wiping his hands on a rag.

'Good afternoon to you, sir,' my father said. 'I used to live near here, many years ago. I'm just showing my family around. But everything seems to have moved.'

'A little history tour?' the man said, smiling to show a row of gold teeth. 'Everything changed, huh? You're right about that, man. My granny says the same.' He gestured vaguely in the direction of the city. 'A lot of people leave, you know. A lot of people scared. We have murders around here, you know.'

'I read about them,' my father said distractedly, still looking around. 'It seems to have grown here, though, since I was a boy. Is there still a market here?'

'Listen to me, old man,' the mechanic said softly, ignoring his question, suddenly serious. 'You should get going. It's not safe here.' He looked at the men on the wall then back at us. 'The way you people carrying on, you looking to get robbed.'

'Oh, let's go, Ralph,' said my mother. 'I don't like it round here.'

'Thanks for the advice, my friend,' my father told him, 'but we're OK, I know where we are.'

'OK, man, have it your way.' The mechanic shielded his eyes from the sun. 'But if I were you, I'd see what you need from inside your car.' He went back into the shop.

'I don't want to get robbed,' I said.

And so we walked back to the car. I remember my father stopping every now and again as though something he recognised had flashed to mind. We drove out onto the highway around the town. 'See that road?' he said, pointing to a junction where a dirt track split from the highway. 'That road takes you to the village where my dad's shop was.'

'Are we going there?' Sam asked from the back seat.

'No, no,' my father said. 'We haven't got time. Remember how long it took to drive yesterday. We need to get back by tonight.'

'No time to look?' my mother asked. 'Are you sure?'

'Not this time,' he said. 'Not this time.'

♦

Our last day in Jamaica was Independence Day, a celebration my father had to explain to me. I knew Jamaica had been a British colony once, but not much more. The Jamaican flag hung in rows of bunting along the beach above stalls selling sugar cane, fresh fruit, ice cream. A big sound system blared music from a stack of speakers piled precariously. They wheeled the oil-drum grill over from the restaurant, and cooked up chicken and pork in a cloud of spicy smoke, the cook dramatically chopping the meat with his machete. We sat on the beach among all the other families, eating, chatting, children playing in the sand and sea. This was the only day my father came to the beach – he hated the sun, even the Jamaican one. Now he sat in his polyester swimming trunks with his newspaper, his scrawny legs on show, his moles visible to all. But I'd seen other men and women in Jamaica with moles like his, and somehow they'd lost their potency. They were just moles, after all.

After a month in Jamaica, my skin had turned a dark nut brown. Sam was the same colour. 'Nice touch of the tar-brush,' my father said on the beach, pretending to rub at my skin with his finger to see if the tan would come off.

'Oh, stop it, Dad!' I moaned, clambering up and away from him, towards the shore. I saw Owen, singing in the water. 'Big celebration today, Miss Hannah,' he said, sitting down beside me when he emerged. 'How you good people enjoying the island?'

My father told him about our travels to see Auntie Fay, Aretha, Yallahs Bay. 'Family is important to you, is so, Mr Ralph?' Owen said. 'You a family man for sure.' He told us he had to work soon, and said goodbye, but later I saw him further along the beach, lying on the sand, staring out to sea.

When we came home to Ilford, a letter arrived from Owen, thanking us for our friendship, saying he missed us. 'Poor boy,' my mother said. 'We must write back.' She wrote him a letter, but we didn't ever hear from him again.

That final night, before bed, my mother gathered the 'children' together for photographs – my brother and my new cousins – knowing we'd not see each other again for years, if at all. Cora was heading back to New York the next week, Sharon back to her home and school in Negril. Dressed already in their nightshirts, my pretty cousins flirted with Sam, slipping their arm through his as we smiled for the camera, laughing too hard at his jokes. 'Say "cheese",' my mother instructed, and we posed, but I look foolish in these photographs, wearing a rainbow-coloured T-shirt saying *Irie*, Cora sticking her fingers up behind my head.

Later, I slipped from the crowded bed to feel the warm night breeze on the veranda, but my father and Ken were out there, talking. I stood in the dark and listened. 'You can get land here,' Ken said. 'Not difficult now. Not expensive either. You buy the plot, make sure it's plumbed for water and the electricity laid first. I can help you with that, and with someone to build your house for you. Same man who design this one can design you a house.'

'How much you think you need?' my father said. I could see the red glint of his cigarette.

'Maybe fifty thousand dollars US. Maybe less. I can find out for you. You have money free? I can help you.'

'We have the house in England.' He paused. 'But no way Bet will go for it. And the children are still at school. How can they adapt to it here?'

I stayed in the shadows, holding my breath. How could we adapt to it here? I liked Jamaica, but I didn't want to live there. It didn't matter, though. I already knew it was just talk, dream talk. Jamaica had got to my father. He was two people here – the man who belonged, and the man who was lost – of and not of this place. I remembered Mr Picketts. Perhaps my father thought coming home would resolve his crisis of identity.

'Maybe they'll be fine you know,' Ken said. 'People come back, bring their people.' Like Mr Picketts, I thought again, waiting his whole life to return, but missing England enough to go back on holiday there.

'Perhaps,' my father said. 'Oh, I don't know. I'll mention it. I left so long ago, but I miss it, you know. I dream about it here.'

He stood up, stubbing his cigarette out in the ashtray. I stepped silently across the floor, down the hall, back into the bedroom where my cousins slept. I could hear the puppies whining in the night.

10

1943

*T*here was a crush on the dock as the men strode forward, clutching their suitcases and permits. They were well dressed for America in smart slacks with braces, trilby hats and two-tone shoes. The boy was among them in his best clothes too, nudging his way along the dock, the gangplank almost in sight.

Four thousand were climbing aboard the SS *Shank* that day, although the capacity of the ship was less than half that number. No women were allowed, so sweethearts and mothers waved the men off from the dock. Hundreds of people were waving, but not one among them had come for the boy. He'd sent word to his father he was leaving, but nothing came back. He had been to see his Auntie Fay again to say goodbye, and he had told Hermione. She told him she would come to see him off, but he couldn't find her in the crowd.

The boy stood on the middle deck, looking out at Kingston sprawled before him, the sky a blinding bright blue above the proud white colonial buildings and the crumbling slums. People were dying in the country and men were getting out – not abandoning the island, they told themselves, but leaving to earn money, send money home, come back with money – then make a change. They'd make more in America than they could ever dream of in Jamaica.

Like the others, the boy had read the advertisement in the paper, read it again, torn it out and slipped it in his pocket: *US Farm Worker Program – Jamaican Men Needed for Three-Year Contracts. Good Rates of Pay.* By then he'd been in Kingston eighteen months, dealing at the club on Barry Street. He had saved money, but not enough after rent and food and a losing streak on the horses. The last of it had greased an official's palm to be among the passengers on the *Shank*.

Everyone wanted a permit. Adult suffrage had finally been granted, an election loomed, and the permits were in the hands of a government desperate to keep their power and keep out the People's National Party. They distributed permits in the hope of votes, for favours and for bribes – so most of the men were educated and had trades. Most came from decent homes. The real farm workers – the cane cutters and banana farmers – would stay poor and left behind.

No work below the Mason–Dixon Line. That's what the government agreed for them. Everyone knew and obeyed the island's own informal hierarchy of shade, but formal segregation was another thing. They would not be sent to the Deep South. The Jamaicans did not know Jim Crow law and would not respond well to it. Instead, the sprawling farms of the north – New Jersey, New York and Maine – awaited them.

On board, they swiftly organised themselves in shifts for meals, to wash, to sleep in the bunks. Ten days at sea and then, despite the government's vows, they docked at New Orleans, the men steered through the port and onto trucks that drove them to Camp Pontchartrain, a military camp for black US soldiers, a holding pen for the Jamaicans. Not a white face in sight. The black soldiers milled around, waiting to be sent to war, eyeing the Jamaicans with curiosity through a partition fence. The Jamaican men watched them back.

Each day the men were issued with paperwork and fingerprinted and dispatched in batches to the night train north. 'How big *is* America?' they asked each other as the train rattled past endless fields and hills, through cities and small towns. How was it possible to fall asleep and wake up, and still be travelling in the same country? They had thought Jamaica a big island until then.

On the first farm, the boy and a hundred other Jamaicans picked beetroot, nine hours a day, bent in the scorching sun, working up one line, down another. Two weeks with their hands stained bright purple. Then the boy and half the rest were moved further north, standing in the backs of trucks, riding across the flat land at dawn to Cranthorn Farm, Smithfield, New Jersey, a vast estate the size of a small town with a processing plant, huge ice houses for freezing vegetables, a fleet of trucks. To the Jamaicans' surprise, they weren't the only imported labourers – two thousand Japanese-Americans resided there already, sent from the internment camps to work through the war. On their way to their barracks, a handful of Japanese children ran after them, pulling at their clothes.

But the Jamaicans were a new curiosity to the people of Smithfield, who sent a marching band to the gates of the farm to welcome them on the day of their arrival. The sun was high in the sky as schoolchildren with horns and trombones played jaunty tunes, marching back and forth before the men, who regarded them with curiosity. Behind the band, the town's men and women stood smiling and waving at the Jamaicans. Some held baskets of food and cloth-covered pies. 'They playing this stuff for us?' George McLean asked the boy. He was the youngest of the Jamaican men, his face still round with puppy fat.

'Looks that way,' the boy replied.

'You think that food's for us?'

'Who knows? It might well be.'

'It might be poisoned,' George whispered. 'But if it's not, I'd love some pie.'

'This is strange,' said the boy. 'I didn't think we'd be rubbing shoulders with white folk, you know.' He whistled under his breath. The Jamaicans had heard much about the racial divisions of this country, none of it good.

A middle-aged man with a red face and white hair came forward as the music stopped, and stood before the Jamaicans, his hat in hand. He spoke slowly and loudly, as though they might not understand English. 'My name is John Bentleman. On behalf of the people of Upper Deerfield I would like to welcome you boys here to America, to New Jersey.' He spread his hands to indicate the land around them. 'You will be picking peas on the fairways and greens of the Gehret Country Club, an institution of which I am president. I would like to formally invite you to make full use of the club during your time here. The club is at your disposal, and we, the townsfolk of Smithfield, will do all we can to assist your stay with us.'

He made a small bow and the townspeople began to clap. Some came forward to present their gifts. The boy wondered why they were clapping, but before he knew it, a few of the Jamaican men around him were clapping too. Then more of them were clapping. Then George beside him was clapping. The black men and the white folk stood applauding each other, across the rows of children still holding their instruments. Soon they lifted them and began another rollicking tune. The sun was baking the ground. A few of the Jamaicans stepped forward and gave a little dance.

♠

The Jamaicans were housed on the other side of the farm from the Japanese in a one-storey wooden barracks that slept twenty men. There was a camp store, showers, comfortable bunks and blankets. It was more than they had expected. They felt welcomed.

In the weeks to follow, the townsfolk became more fascinated by the men. Their generous offers became a source of bemusement. 'Mr Hoffman's daughter is coming to drive me to church tomorrow,' Enoch Leaford declared from his place on a top bunk, cleaning his glasses. 'Asked if anyone else needs a ride? Any of you?'

'No, I'm fine,' replied Ronald Chin. 'Dora Green, that nice girl from the camp store, already offered me a lift.' He laughed. 'These people like us, man. The girls especially.'

'The Americans like a sophisticated Negro,' Enoch said. 'They use that word. I read it in the leaflet they gave us. Listen to this.' He unfolded the crumpled paper, perched his reading glasses on the end of his nose. 'The Americans' use of the word "Negro" is not meant to offend you Jamaican men,' he read. 'It has the same meaning as coloured in Jamaica.' He put the leaflet down. 'I'm not sure about that.'

'I bet some of them can make it sound offensive,' said the boy. 'Especially in the South. They like us because we sound British and behave ourselves, so far. They think we're a notch above the American "Negroes", whom they treat like dogs.'

'You might be right,' said Ronald Chin. 'I'm being careful. We're so far from home. Who knows what the rules are?'

♥

The Jamaicans played dominoes in a booth at Marnie's, a late-night diner half a mile from the farm. Green leather seats, red lamps hung low over the table. One night, the boy and his friends were lost in a game, not noticing the three white men edging closer to them, beer bottles in their hands, all of them wearing denims, the uniform of local labourers.

'I'm sorry,' said one of them, smiling to show a mouth of broken teeth. 'Don't think us rude. We wondered if one of you fellows might say something for us?' He looked at his two companions – one much smaller than him, the other with a slick moustache in the style of Errol Flynn. 'It's just that you boys sound so British – my friends here don't believe me.'

The Jamaicans looked between each other. This wasn't the first time they'd been asked this. Ronald Chin cleared his throat. 'We *are* British,' he said, in his best British accent. 'We are part of the war effort, and Jamaica, as you know, is part of the British Empire.'

'Hot damn, you're right!' exclaimed the small one. 'They *do* sound British!'

The moustached one shook his head in disbelief, his mouth open. 'Can you say something else?' he asked the Jamaicans.

'Perhaps I could draw you a map to show you where Jamaica is?' offered Enoch politely, lifting a napkin, pulling a pen from his jacket. They had not met one American yet who'd known where the island was with any certainty.

'Please do,' said broken teeth. 'I have no idea.' He looked again at his friends. 'Can you believe it?' he said to them. 'I close my eyes and I swear I'm in a British film or Buckingham Palace.'

'You boys don't sound a bit like American Negros, that's for sure,' Errol Flynn told them. 'Well, well. Hope you all are settling in and enjoying your time?'

'Oh yes,' said the boy, and the Jamaicans agreed. 'We've been made very welcome.' They all introduced themselves, shook hands, and the Jamaicans shoved up, allowing the three to squeeze into the booth. Enoch presented his map, pointing out the Caribbean's proximity to Florida, the location of Cuba and Jamaica.

'Well, I surely didn't know that before,' the small one said. 'Did you fellows?'

And Errol Flynn replied, 'I never even heard of Jamaica until these guys showed up, and that's the truth. But pleased to meet you all.'

♣

The Jamaicans worked hard at Cranthorn's, but conditions were fair. There was a sense of hope among them. They were earning fifty cents an hour, a day's wages in Jamaica, and sending money back to wives, children, parents. The boy thought about Hermione. However she was earning money, he didn't like it. He would rather send her a wire than have her go flirting and eyeing the shopkeepers on Barry Street. He sent a little to Felix too. Each time he went to Western Union he thought of his father, but he couldn't bring himself to send a penny to him. Times were tight, but James Lowe always survived.

'Working overseas is what we Jamaicans do,' Enoch said in the barracks one night. He was sitting at the table with a tin mug of coffee, his long legs crossed. Enoch was like a gangly professor, prone to outbursts of analysis. 'We've been working abroad for ever. Who you think build the Panama Canal?' He looked around at the blank faces in the room. 'We did! And we've been travelling to America and Cuba for years.'

'Well, that's true,' said Benton Ford from his bunk. 'My grandfather and uncle picked asparagus in New York twenty years ago. They're still there now.'

'My grandfather picked coffee in Cuba for three years,' said Ronald Chin. 'Married a Cuban woman and brought her home. My grandmother. She only speaks Spanish.'

'I thought you were part Chinese, like me?' the boy said.

'The other side is Chinese. My grandfather was Chin. And my other grandmother was half maroon. Blue black, you know? All that mix is why I come out so handsome.'

The boy laughed. 'When the lights are off, yes man.'

'No money on the island, no work,' Enoch said, ignoring them. 'What do we have? Our hands, our backs.'

'You're right,' said the boy. 'Maybe one day they'll want us for our brains.'

'At least they're paying us,' Benton said. 'Not like the poor Japanese over the way.'

'It's our labour,' Enoch said. 'That's all they want us for. That's all we have.'

'And thank God we do,' said Ronald. He yawned, stretching himself like a cat across his bed.

'Things are working out here. Things are working out just fine.'

'Things are fine, except for the food,' said George McLean. 'What is this scrambled eggs? It looks like ackee, but it's no friend of mine.'

♦

America was an adventure. There were dances in the town. The Jamaicans would dress in their best clothes and, under the bright lights of the community hall, swing the local girls back and forth, spin them and show a little fancy footwork. There was a day off in the week when they could sleep all day or walk into town to take a girl to the pictures. Or on nights at the barracks, the boy might run a game of poker or kalooki, skilfully shuffling the cards before cutting them in two and dealing each man's hand. They were light-hearted games played for pennies. The boy didn't try to cheat his friends, although he always had an advantage, knowing which cards were out of play.

Sometimes they would talk about Jamaica, how things were and what might change. Enoch's mother sent the *Gleaner* and they'd pass it from bunk to bunk, reading the news from home. Food prices had gone up because of the war, but still no exports. Crops were still rotting in the country with no one to sell them to. Strikes were happening all over and the leaders were being punished severely. Alexander Bustamante had split from the PNP to found a splinter group – the Jamaican Labour Party. Thomas Reid was in prison. He and many others had been locked up for weeks with no release in sight. The boy had kept quiet about his political activities in the year before, unsure how the other men felt, but soon it became clear that they all agreed big change had to happen. The colonial government was not interested in the plight of the poor man.

'I feel torn, you know, about leaving,' the boy said. 'Sometimes I think I should have stayed to help make things happen, to make a change. Anyone else feel it so?'

'Plenty of time for revolutions and uprisings,' Charles Dee said. He was a big man, too big for the small bunk he was lying on. 'We all need money first. May as well earn what you can here and now, then go back.'

'Jamaica is hell,' Ronald Chin said loudly from his bunk. He leant up on his elbow. 'I never want to go back. That country eat you up and spit you out.'

'What you say is right about Jamaica *now*,' the boy said. 'Jamaica as it is now. And the war making it worse, for sure. But the Jamaica of the future could be something different, you know. I believe in that.'

'I think it's better to stay here for now,' George McLean said. 'Just send money home, send help when you can. That's my plan. I'm having a good time here – I don't want to go home yet.'

There were murmurs of agreement around the room.

♠

But not everything was rosy. Charles Dee and Paris Brown went to the neighbouring town of Standon to see a movie, but were refused entry into the cinema. 'They didn't let us in because we are black, I know it,' Paris said. 'The manager just stood there smiling, saying, "I'm sorry, we are full. You boys will have to try elsewhere." Where is this elsewhere, man? It's the only picture house for twenty miles. No way were they full. It was because we were black men standing there.'

In the same town, Mervyn Simms was denied service in a restaurant. 'I sat there for half an hour,' he said. 'I thought the waitress couldn't see me, so I moved stools. Then I moved again. Then some other fellow came along, sat in my first stool, and he got served. Then another fellow sat in the stool I just left and he got served. I start thinking to myself, what's going on here? And I ask the waitress, but she look straight through, like she can't see me, can't hear me. I ask her is she feeling OK, but it's still the quiet treatment. She was the only one there. So I tell her thank you, and I left.'

The men related these tales as they sat at the table of their barracks, all gathered in the lamplight.

'We have to do something,' said Enoch. 'They can't be treating us like this.'

'No way,' said Charles Dee. 'We are here as part of the war effort. They should be grateful to us, and understand their nasty rules do not apply.'

The next weekend they put on their good clothes and boarded the Standon bus. Twenty of them walked up to the cinema, queuing orderly for their tickets at the box office while the manager in the foyer looked on, wringing his hands, his face turning red. They filed in silently to the screen and filled the two rows at the front. None of them turned to see the faces of the other cinema-goers in the flickering light of the trailers. On their best behaviour, the Jamaicans watched the film, crunching their way through boxes of popcorn. And afterwards, the same twenty crossed the road and walked fifty yards up the sidewalk, attracting the stares of people in the street, to the diner where Mervyn had been snubbed. It was the same waitress on shift, but who could ignore twenty hungry men walking in and taking whichever spare booths they could?

A ripple of surprise went through the white clientele, but the Jamaicans just smiled cordially at their neighbours and bid them good evening. With the black and white diners comfortably interspersed, the restaurant was full to capacity. The Jamaicans ordered beers and burgers and fried potatoes and plates of ribs and steaks, then more beers, ice-cream, pancakes, pie. The waitress ran back and forth all night, angry blisters forming on her heels, while the manager smiled on, thinking only of their bill.

♥

Everything changed in the autumn – the nights drew in and a chill wind blew across the fields. The harvesting work at Smithfield finished and the men were split up and sent to different farms. Then, later in that year, the Jamaican government revoked the Mason–Dixon Line rule – there was too much work in the South and not enough hands. Fruit was dying on the trees with no one to pick it. The boy and thirty other men went to another farm in Maine, a few went east to Pennsylvania, but over half went down to Florida. Bad stories came up from there. They sat on their beds as the boy read out Ronald Chin's letter:

'"These crackers think we are monkeys with tails. I didn't know people could be so backwards. The black people here are raging. We sit round at night and I listen to their talk. They want to burn the South down and I do not blame them. I would light the match myself tonight. I am scared of what will happen if I stay here."'

'Oh boy,' Roy Atley said. 'I don't want to go down there. I'm no monkey, and no one's calling me one.' They others agreed to stay north as long as they could, picking cranberries on the night shift in the white glare of floodlights. There were miles and miles of vines, the men walking through the deep red fields, picking until their arms ached and they couldn't bend down any more. Then they slept at dawn in the darkened barracks, dreaming of cranberries, buckets and buckets of them, the juice of cranberries running like blood onto their hands.

Then, suddenly, the work finished. The liaison officer came to tell them they would be moved on in a few days. But the days became a week, the week two weeks. There were problems all over, the liaison officer told them. There was enough work, but no one was sure where, or when. The men's contract guaranteed them work for two-thirds of their time, but because they moved around, no one was sure who paid for their downtime. The only thing they knew was that there was work in the South. They waited in their barracks, playing dominoes, writing letters home. It started to rain, and then it rained constantly, the world outside running in dirty grey streams.

'Let's go south, then,' said Charles Dee, stooping down to stare through the window. 'I'm bored here, man. We're not earning any money.'

Another week passed and the farmer came and told them he couldn't keep feeding them, not if they weren't working.

'I'm grateful for what you've done,' he said, 'but it's time to move on.'

Three more days passed. The men were hungry. All of them had credit they couldn't pay at the camp store. No one had ready money. The liaison officer had disappeared.

'We need to eat,' said the boy, and early the next morning they crept out in half-darkness, walking a mile through forest to the barbed-wire fence of the neighbouring orchard. It was a low fence, but with only one torch between them, they ripped their trousers and tore their hands on the steel barbs.

'Come on! Come on!' Roy Atley called, running forward to the trees. They ran and jumped into the air for the green apples above them, crunching into the fruit, chewing, biting, tossing the cores and picking more. Apple after apple until all of them were full. They leant at the bottom of the trees to rest, the sky getting light. A cold wind blew through the orchard.

'I've eaten eight apples,' Paris Brown groaned below a tree. 'I feel sick.'

'Eat another,' the boy said from under his tree. 'Who knows when we next going to eat?'

The next day they took the bus from Portland to New York, and caught the overnight train south. On the way they saw a chain gang of black men working the fields while white men with guns stood over them. 'Oh man,' said George McLean. 'This is a bad idea.'

In was mid-morning when the Jamaicans stepped onto the platform in Jacksonville, Florida, shading their eyes from the morning sun.

There was work here. There was money. They would do what needed to be done.

11

OI, NELSON!

Sticks and stones may break my bones ...

It was 1990 and there was a new scene happening – indie music coming out of Manchester and Liverpool and dance music everywhere. Kim and I were too young to go to the actual parties, but we knew all about them. People were taking Ecstasy at raves, dancing to sound systems in marquees and fields and warehouses, or in people's front rooms. Somehow the mores of that subculture diluted themselves into signs and symbols we could be part of. Boys grew their hair long. We wore T-shirts with yellow smiley faces on, hooded tops patterned with psychedelic suns and moons, strange new shoes called Wallerbees in lilac and pink.

Romford was our stomping ground, equidistant between Ilford, where I lived, and Upminster, where Pinners was, and not far from Kim's house. We were fourteen and looked it, but there was an off-licence there that would sell us bottles of dry Martini or Cinzano or Thunderbird. We'd walk the town centre, swigging straight from the bottle, my vision blurred and spinning from the booze – the shops and alleyways and bus shelters doused in refracted light. There were boys we saw around the town, beautiful boys whose names we didn't know. We didn't talk to them, but talked endlessly about them, watching from a distance as they knocked around a football, or stood smoking cigarettes, or sat perched on the back on a bench, high up, their feet on the seats where they deserved to be – kings of the shopping parade.

I'd tell my parents we'd gone to see a film, but really we were drinking and mooching until my father came to pick me up. I didn't swim at the Dolphin any more, but it was a landmark for him to fetch me from. The yellow Triumph had finally gone, replaced by the more economical Mini – electric green, a joke of a car, shameful when he came to meet me, shameful as he was, parked up under a street light outside the pool with a roll-up on the go.

Once, I was sick into my bag all the way home, sat beside him in the car. He pretended not to notice, didn't say a word as we swerved back to Ashgrove Road, and by the time we got there I was recovered, my head no longer swimming. I thought I'd gotten away with it but he walked through to the kitchen and told my mother. I was standing in the hall, holding a bag full of my own sick. In the living room, he flicked the television on and sat down in his armchair. Not a word from him the whole way home, but he told her, and as usual passed the problem – me – straight on.

◆

It was ironic that the most significant role my father had in my life was as a driver, since he was a notoriously bad one, the butt of a running joke between Uncle Terry and my mother. I don't know if he'd learned to drive in England or Jamaica, but his driving, according to her, was 'pure Jamaican'. I remembered driving in Jamaica the year before

– motorists overtaking at speed on the twisting roads, trucks zig-zagging up hills with hitchers clinging to their backs, cars aggressively nudging and beeping their way through the Kingston rush hour. In our hired Honda, my father joined in these practices with relish.

In England, his irreverence for road regulations endured. He seemed unable to keep the car between the white lines of a dual carriageway, veering dangerously into the path of other vehicles, oblivious to their drivers, who beeped and harangued him. Once a cab driver rolled down his window, shouting at my father as he passed, 'Oi, Nelson! Keep to your own lane, will ya!' My father's hair was mostly white by then and with his broad nose and face, he did resemble Nelson Mandela, whose release that year was constantly in the news.

My father's bad driving had a long history. My mother enjoyed relaying the anecdote about his run-in with police in the early seventies. At this time, he had been employed by a casino as a games inspector. Not realising my father was cheating constantly on their turf, the casino figured that his experience of cards and knowledge of card games made him perfect for the job. Every night they perched him up a stepladder above the card table to spot any irregularities in the punters' play, a poacher-turned-gamekeeper job he came to relish. On that particular night my mother had joined him for a drink after a night out with her friends. They had left together in the early hours, my father worried that he was over the limit to drive. 'But he'd only had two gin and tonics during the night,' she said, 'so I wasn't worried at all.' My father sat next to her as she told the story, talking about him as though he wasn't there.

'So we get in the car and he starts the engine. But he doesn't look in the mirror, not even a glance. Straight into reverse, foot down, then *clunk*. We've backed right into someone. We both sit there in silence for a few seconds and I'm thinking, Bloody Nora, maybe he is pissed. Then I turn round to look, and he's only gone and reversed into a police car! Can you believe it? I tell him what he's done and he just sits there, swearing under his breath. The air went blue, I can tell you.'

'I didn't see them,' my father said, holding his hands out innocently.

'But,' my mother carried on, 'that's not the half of it. Because there's only two policemen sat in the car. They must have had their eye on someone in the club. Then suddenly one is tapping on the window. "Excuse me, sir," he says. "You appear to have reversed into a police vehicle. Were you are aware we were parked behind you?" And your dad goes, "Good evening, Officer," in his best Queen's English. "If I had been aware you were parked there, I certainly wouldn't have done so, no." Of course they breathalyse him, and it turns out he was over the limit, so they nicked him for that *and* for reckless driving. How many points did you get?' She turned to my father.

'I think it was four,' he said solemnly, although I could tell he was pleased with his misdeed.

Another time, years later, the police pulled him over when I was in the car. He was giving me a lift to Kim's house, but somehow he'd turned the wrong way down a busy dual carriageway. It was dark and raining, the windscreen wipers going frantically, but through the blur of rain I could see other cars looming bigger as they drove straight at us, swerving dramatically out of our way. 'Dad?' I said. 'I think we're on the wrong side of the road.'

'Eh? What do you mean?' He leant forward, peering through the windscreen, then sideways at the other lane, where cars were travelling in the same direction as us. 'Oh dear,' he said with exaggerated formality, putting the brakes on and pulling up on to the inside kerb, just as a siren sounded in the other lane. A police car stopped alongside us on the other side of the railings. There were two policemen. One got out of the car, climbed awkwardly over the railings and indicated I should roll down my window. He leant his face in, two inches from mine. He was young. I could smell his breath as he spoke. 'Good evening, sir,' he said sarcastically. 'Mind if I ask what on Earth you're doing?' He produced a torch and bathed us in its yellow glare.

'Oh dear. I don't know what happened, Officer,' my father said, sounding shaky. 'I don't know what happened. Oh dear me. I'm on my way to drop my daughter at her friend's house, that's all.' The policeman looked between us, clearly confused that the old black man was father to a white teenage girl. I said nothing.

'Well,' he said, his tone easing a little. 'Didn't you see a sign, sir? This is a dual carriageway. It's very well signposted. You could have had a head-first crash there.' His 'sirs' sounded less sincere as the interrogation continued, my father repeating 'I don't know what happened, Officer' and 'Oh dear me' until the policeman gave up, sighing dramatically, bored with us.

'Well, well. Looks like we're going to have to get you out of this,' he said. He popped his head back out, and half a minute later he and his colleague were standing in the rain facing the traffic, hands raised to stop the oncoming cars so that my father could pull away from the side, turn round, and continue in the correct direction. All the other drivers were looking at us. I was mortified.

'Mind how you go, sir,' the policeman said. 'You're lucky I haven't arrested you.' He looked at us contemptuously. We pulled off into the rain.

'Oh well, Han,' my father said as we drove along, the rain bursting on the windscreen, the wipers going furiously again. 'Looks like we got away with it,' he laughed. 'Yes, my dear, we escaped the police!' But I didn't laugh. I was thinking how old and confused my father was. I saw it clearly, and the policeman had seen it too.

♠

There was an under-18s club night in two large carpeted rooms above the Dolphin. It was called the Academy. They turned the lights down and played the rapid, delirious music we wanted. No alcohol but you could drink your fill before or nip out to swig from a bottle tucked in the flower bed. I went with Kim and Pauline, our new friend from school. We pooled our money for two packs of Silk Cut from the machine. 'I don't even know how to do it,' I said, pulling on the cigarette, a foreign shape in my mouth, tasting its bitterness.

'Just breathe in, breathe out,' Kim said. 'Don't taste great, does it?'

It didn't, but we lit one cigarette from another, strolling around the Academy feeling pleased and proud of ourselves. *Oh they're smokers*, I imagined other people thinking with awe – *they must be part of an older, wiser, more complicated world.* I was sick for an hour in the downstairs toilet back at Kim's house, trying to make sure her mum didn't hear.

Aside from the Academy, there wasn't much for us to do. At fourteen we were too young for pubs, too old for the playground. Sometimes we went ice-skating at the new rink in Romford. It was a soulless place with rubber floors and plastic chairs, bright billboards and vending machines. Every time I skated, and no matter how many pairs of socks

I wore, the hired boots cut into my feet in minutes, leaving blisters like small gaping mouths on my heels. I couldn't go backwards like the others could. I could barely go forwards. The only way I could stop was to slam myself into the rim of the rink against the adverts for McDonald's and Tango. I preferred to sit out.

But the last time I went ice-skating, something horrible happened. I was perched in the spectator zone, watching the others spin and glide below the rink's stark lighting, when a boy clambered over the seats behind to reach me. I hadn't noticed the group sat back there – four girls in a row, drinking cans of Coke, their trainered feet propped up on the chairs. They were the same age as me, I think, but I didn't recognise them from school. In the boy's hand was a bright orange Post-it note he held out to me. I took it, turning it over to find a biro drawing of a stick man hanging from a noose and gallows. 'They want to fight you,' he said, gesturing to the girls. 'You're the hanged man.'

I turned to look at where the girls were huddled, staring back and laughing. I felt my stomach flip. Who was the boy? A younger brother? His nails were bitten to the quick. 'Why?' I asked him. 'I don't know them.'

'I dunno,' he replied. 'They don't like the look of you, I guess.' I noticed the splatter of freckles across his nose. 'They're gonna get you outside.'

I didn't know what to say. The butterflies in my stomach worsened. I'd never fought with anyone. Would it be four against one? I looked at my watch. It was half past one and my father was coming to pick me up at two.

'Tell her she's a slag!' one of the girls shouted. I glanced up. She was the smallest of them, her long brown hair scraped back with gel into a pony tail, a bright pink ski jacket.

'Did you hear that?' the boy said. He looked like he felt sorry for me. I wanted to cry. 'I think they've got a knife,' he added.

I sat for a nervous few minutes until Kim and Pauline came back and I whispered what had happened. 'Stupid cows,' said Kim loudly. 'They're not going to do anything. They haven't got a bloody knife.' She looked up at them and held a stare.

'It's *her* we want to give a kicking, not you!' shouted Pink Ski Jacket.

'I better go home,' Pauline said. She grabbed her bag from under the chair and changed into her shoes quickly. She had her own clean white ice skates. 'Bye, see you Monday!' she said, rushing off to the exit.

'So much for her loyalty,' said Kim as we watched her leave. She looked up again. 'I know those girls from the Academy. They go to Hall Mead.' Hall Mead was a rival school. Male pupils regularly challenged Pinners boys to after-school fights outside Lloyd's Newsagent – fights which galvanised the school's rumour mill all day, but rarely took place – but this wasn't the same.

Kim and I returned our boots to the hire booth, my hands shaking as I pulled my socks and trainers back on, sat on the rink's grimy white chairs, horribly conscious that the Hall Mead girls had followed, sitting opposite, still laughing and jeering. I was in a surreal panic, unable to look at them, desperately needing the toilet.

I prayed my father would be early as we walked out into the cold afternoon. The bright sun lit the empty car park. The Hall Mead girls came out behind us. 'What are we going to do?' I said.

'Keep walking,' Kim said, taking charge, and we did, crossing over the entrance lane of the car park.

'Where you going, slag?' shouted Pink Ski Jacket. There were footsteps behind me and, quicker than I expected, two hands shoving my back hard. I fell forward.

'Back off!' said Kim. She spun round to face the four of them, her small body puffed up, jaw clenched, fists gripped at her side. I pulled myself up from the ground, just as Kim said, 'There's your dad!'

Sure enough, the green Mini was weaving through the car park, my father at the wheel. He pulled up by us, leant over and pushed open the door, a lit John Player in his hand. My relief was palpable – those girls couldn't do a thing if an adult was there, even it was just my father – it changed the stakes.

'You're fucking lucky!' shouted Pink Ski Jacket, as we scrambled in.

'Is her dad a black bloke?' I heard another one of them say. 'Slag.' We pulled away.

'Who were they?' my father said, stubbing his dog end into the overflowing car ashtray.

'No one,' I replied, looking to the side to hide my tears.

'How are you, Mr Lowe?' said Kim brightly.

'Oh, you know, Kim,' my father said. 'Could be better, could be worse.'

I took a deep breath, watching the girls grow smaller in the wing mirror. I knew they didn't have a knife, and that I was a random target, but for years after I dreamt about that day – the hangman scrawled on an orange Post-it, the boy with the bitten nails, Pink Ski Jacket with her sharp, angry face, following me into that bright afternoon, the empty car park, my heart thundering in my chest, sure I would be badly hurt, or worse.

♥

I was jealous of my brother, whose social life seemed exotic and exciting compared to mine. He was eighteen and no longer interested in graffiti, much to my mother's relief. Instead he disappeared for whole weekends to raves in Essex. There were fliers on his walls for clubs called Rain Dance and World Party. He'd turn up on Sunday afternoons looking spaced out, wouldn't eat his Sunday lunch. There were new boys coming round for him, although they weren't boys really, though not men either. Tall, spotty boy-men in Duffer St George T-shirts and Adidas hoodies. They all had long hair. My brother grew his hair long too and I was jealous of it – dark, shiny hair that fell down his back, poker straight.

His friends sat on the floor of his room, listening to music, sometimes getting stoned. I knew the smell of hash from Charlie White, and then Craig Fox at school had brought some in and we'd smoked it on the shot-put circle at the back of the school field, four of us pretending we'd smoked dope before, hiding our coughs in our stripy Pinners scarves. I hadn't enjoyed it much.

On the landing outside my brother's door I would rack my brains for reasons to knock – I'd lost my book and wondered if he'd seen it, or did he know what time our mother would be home. I was Annoying Little Sister, Nosey Little Sister. I'd push open the door to find the room thick with smoke, and the faces of my brother's friends all turned at once – the twins, Colin, Mickey. I had a crush on them all, and I was suddenly shy, stammering over my words.

One time I came in and saw Solomon Kallakuri sitting cross-legged on the floor with a tin of Red Stripe at his feet, a cigarette in his hand. There were six or seven of them there, a record spinning on the turntable, the gentle thud of Soul II Soul. I was shocked to see Solomon. He was taller, bigger, filling out his green bomber jacket. His hair had grown long and was parted in the middle, like the others. He looked straight at me, but his look said *don't say a word, don't say a word*. Little Solomon playing at being grown. Something in his face had changed – he wasn't my friend any more.

I had become a thief again, but of a different kind. I can't recall the first thing I shoplifted. A lipstick from the chemist, was it; a pot of lip balm? It was something to do. Sally Ramwell first suggested it. She was an old hand and never got caught, she said. Every Saturday we went to the shops in Romford and spent an hour or two helping ourselves. Four girls conspicuously loitering in the aisles of Marks and Spencer, fingering the underwear we couldn't afford, or in the Body Shop, smelling lotions and bubble baths, waiting for the right moment, when the till girl was serving and the security guard had looked the other way, to shove a bottle in my bag. There was a thrill to stealing. My heart hammered hard in my chest when I walked back through the shop doors.

I was at it for months, coming home every weekend with new things I'd hide in my room, never enough of anything to raise suspicion. I didn't value the things I stole and none of them lasted – clothes fell apart or I lent them out and never cared to get them back. I'd lose the cheap necklaces from Chelsea Girl, the hairbands and hairclips. I remember feeling upset about stealing. I didn't want to do it, but I couldn't stop, even when the thrill had gone. What was wrong with me?

It occurred to me there was something wrong with both Sam and me, though it manifested itself differently. Where Sam was rebellious and angered by authority, I was sneaky and dishonest. Was it because I came from a home where dishonesty was an organising principle, where we all turned a blind eye to the shady goings-on of my father; was it my own boredom; or was it, as I suspected, just something I did because other kids did, just because I could?

Looking back, I can't believe we didn't get caught more quickly, and of course we were caught in the end – myself and Claire Fitzgerald. The others ran out the door when the security guard laid his hand on my shoulder. Upstairs, the manager had us tip out our bags in his small, hot office. They dimmed the lights and stood behind us as we watched the CCTV footage. The delinquent girl in the grainy picture was me, I realised, watching myself slip a box into my carrier bag from the shelf. On the table in front of me were tubes of anti-aging cream and eye cream, nothing I wanted or needed. The manager said the police were on their way and made us write down our phone numbers. Claire had the sense to give a false one, but it didn't cross my mind. Perhaps I wanted to be found out. When, after half an hour, it was clear the police hadn't really been called, the manager told us never to come in his shop again and sent us away. When I got home, my mother was ironing in the back room. She didn't look up. 'So you got caught,' she said, running the iron down a shift sleeve. 'Maybe it's time to stop, eh?'

My father said nothing about the shoplifting. It was not his place to tell me off. Nor did he say anything to Sam about the smell of dope outside his bedroom door, the late nights and early mornings, Sam's unruliness. But he'd been quieter anyway since our return from Jamaica. Nothing had come of the talk of going home. I doubted he'd even mentioned it to my mother.

When I see photographs from that time, I'm shocked by the image of a frail man standing in the kitchen, or sitting in an armchair, always smoking, never smiling. He was still taking medicine for high blood pressure; the stomach ulcer had gone, but he looked unwell. Often I'd come home from school to find him sitting in the thin light of the front room, staring at the net curtains, no book in his lap, no newspaper. He went out less often. There were no more trips to Newcastle, but he must have had one big win around then because one evening he announced he was opening a bank account for me. 'You need to save,' he said, trying to look wise. 'I'm going to give you fifty pounds a month.' He reached into his pocket and pulled out a wad of notes and peeled some off.

Fifty pounds. This was strangely generous, and I reciprocated with simulated seriousness regarding my financial education. Of course I would manage the money carefully, I promised solemnly, before going to Romford to spend it all on clothes I didn't even like and a mountain of sweets. I remember thinking I would be rich now, there'd be no temptation to steal with fifty pounds a month. But the following month there was no fifty pounds, or the month after, and my father was back in his armchair, the dog curled in his lap. One afternoon I found him rifling frantically through the living room bin. He pulled out a few dog ends, rolling the charred tobacco in a Rizla and lighting it. 'I can't afford tobacco,' he told me, exhaling a stale gust of smoke with relief. I didn't want to know. I wanted that fifty pounds – and not just for clothes and sweets. I wanted to live in a world where my father could make me a promise like that and be able to keep it.

♦

In line with my bad behaviour outside of school, my conduct in school worsened. Looking back, I'd like to say I was the architect of an insurgence against the school's authority, but this imbues my immature pranks with a grandeur they do not warrant. At best I was irreverent, at worst completely puerile. I was rarely acting alone – Emily Bonnyface was my main accomplice. As a twosome we were negative influences on each other, according to our teachers, and, looking back, they were right. When we were banned from sitting together in lessons, lunchtime became our witching hour – we sprinkled paprika and chilli onto the charity cakes we sold in the staff room, stole paintbrushes from the art room, bunked off cross-country running to hide out in the wood behind the school field.

A particular low point in our mischief-making was an incident involving an iced bun, for which we became notorious for a time – and which involved Kim. This was unusual since she was normally well behaved. But one lunchtime in the dining hall she dared me to throw a flat currant bun topped with glutinous pink icing at the school caretaker as he stood on a stepladder, fixing a window. My aim was always poor – hence my place on the second reserve teams for both rounders and hockey. But by some miracle, the pitch of the iced bun that day was perfect – it sailed gracefully through the air on a perfect arc, hitting the caretaker on his left cheek, sticking to the side of his face for a second, then slowly peeling off and dropping to the floor.

Kim, Emily and I were fixated by the spectacle, which seemed to play out in slow motion, the slap of the bun on the ground jolting us back to reality. Witnesses were all around, fellow students and dinner ladies, not to mention the red-faced caretaker, who stared across the room looking outraged. In these circumstances there was only one thing to do – scarper! We scraped back our chairs and hurried from the hall conspicuously, hiding out behind the bins for the rest of the lunch hour to formulate a 'story' we swore to stick by, despite its implausibility. We would swear on our lives that Emily had dared me to throw the bun at Kim's mouth; the throw had gone askance and the bun had hit the caretaker. We were desperately sorry. We ran away because we knew we wouldn't be believed.

It was Friday lunchtime. We anticipated being pulled out of lessons that afternoon. But by the end of the day nothing had happened. Perhaps the incident had not been reported after all. We went our separate ways for the weekend. But on Monday morning, in a manoeuvre reminiscent of a police raid, the three of us were removed from our different lessons at exactly the same time. I knew it was serious when Mr Harrington, our head of year, loomed up through the window of my French class. Little did I know the two deputy heads had gone for Emily and Kim. Like members of a resistance group, we stuck to our story religiously in the ensuing grillings. As I implored Mr Harrington to believe me, his moustache twitching irritably, the time I'd stolen my mum's meringues came to mind. What was it with sweet things that made me so fraudulent?

When the three of us were brought to the dining room an hour later, the game was over. We were ordered by our respective inquisitors to sit at separate tables in the hall. Mr Harrington handed us each a sheet of graph paper, a pen, a protractor and a compass, and asked us to draw an exact diagram of the events of last Friday lunchtime, mapping our places at the table, the position of the caretaker and the flight of the iced bun. We were not in a position to collaborate. When we had finished, Mr Harrington laid our drawings out and announced the disparity of our diagrams evidenced our duplicity and guilt. Admittedly we had drawn each other in different locations, with wild variations in the positioning of the caretaker. But what all of this demonstrated to me was the pedantic nature of the powers-that-be at Pinners, wasting a valuable morning of teaching on their petty investigation. Sadly, my mother didn't see it this way when Mr Harrington phoned to say I was suspended for a week and would be readmitted only after a parent–teacher meeting at which my 'immoral conduct' and 'burgeoning delinquency' would be discussed.

♠

My father was actually seven years younger than Nelson Mandela, who was born in 1918. In April that year, my mother bought us tickets for the Nelson Mandela Tribute Concert in London, to mark Mandela's release two months earlier. At one point, Mandela backed out of appearing at the concert because *bloody Margaret Thatcher*, as my mother put it, was still prime minister and supported the apartheid regime. But he changed his mind on the condition the speech he gave would be broadcast unedited on television.

Sam didn't want to go to the concert so I invited Kim, and we took the Tube to Wembley with my parents, joining the crowd of thousands in the stadium, my father receiving the odd glance by concert-goers who noted his resemblance to Mandela. I'd never been to a concert before, and the scale of this one was huge – hours of performances: Tracy Chapman strumming 'Freedom' on her guitar, Simple Minds singing 'Mandela Day', and as the sun went down, Anita Baker on stage belting out 'Bridge Over Troubled Water'.

What everyone was waiting for was the appearance of Mandela himself, his face broadcast in close-up on the big screens, very thin but standing proud, smiling and waving as the crowd erupted into cheers that lasted nearly ten minutes. Winnie Mandela and Adelaide Tambo stood behind him on stage, their fists raised in solidarity. We were high up in the stadium, standing in the night air, cheering with the crowd. There was a black South African family behind us, a man and woman, two children the same age as me, dressed in their traditional clothing – bright coloured robes and headdresses. It was clear they were deeply affected by the appearance of Mandela and his speech. He thanked the international community and paid long tribute to Oliver Tambo, the exiled ANC leader who was ill and unable to be there. I kept looking at that family so enraptured by Mandela – I wanted to know their story. When they played the South African national anthem, they sang along, their fists raised. I was stirred by Mandela's appearance too, the crowd's reception, the music, to be part of that momentous day. It made me want to live a different sort of life. I was a teenager with teenage concerns, I knew, but even so, my current existence was pretty contemptible. Life in and out of school was infantile and inconsequential, and just a bit grubby.

Suddenly I was tired of Romford, hanging around smoking, hoping boys would talk to us. I stayed home, read more, played the piano more. I was still having lessons with Maisie the punk, but by then I could sight-read well, and, with practice, play most of the music in the front-room cupboard. This housed piles of my mother's old manuscripts and my grandfather's piano scores, signed in his scratchy fountain pen.

It was there that I found an anthology of a black American composer, Scott Joplin – railroad labourer turned ragtime impresario at the turn of the century, a solemn portrait of him at his piano on the front cover. Joplin's music made me sad – his melodies both jaunty and melancholy in turn. They spoke to me of another time and place – the bars and saloons of Memphis and New Orleans at the turn of the century, America reconstructing itself post-slavery – my imaginings constructed from films and books.

I'd spend hours playing Joplin's pieces in the front room – straddling the left-hand chords of 'Bethena' and 'Maple Leaf Rag', the tricky runs of 'Elite Syncopations'. One version of Joplin's death says he went mad and died from syphilis contracted in a brothel where he was a pianist, but the biography of my anthology told a much greater tragedy: how Joplin's magnum opus – an opera named *Treemonisha* – was never published or performed because he was a black man. Faced by the will of a society whose racism was endemic and crushed his creativity, I read that Joplin died in the asylum of 'a broken heart'.

I was practising his 'Pineapple Rag' one day when the phone rang. My parents were in the garden making a bonfire. I answered to Emily Bonnyface's mother, a woman I'd never properly met, only seen at the school gates parked in her shiny black car, patting her blonde hair in the side mirror. She wore sunglasses no matter the weather.

'Is that Hannah?' she asked in a thick Essex accent. 'Is your mum there?'

'No,' I lied. The tone of her voice made my wary.

'Well,' she carried on, 'I want to talk to you. Emily's been in trouble. We think she's been stealing.'

I didn't know what to say. Why was she telling me? 'I've had a long talk with her dad and we've decided we don't want her to see you any more.' I hadn't shoplifted for months by then. 'We've *decided*,' her mother repeated, as though I had challenged her. She sounded flustered. 'Is that clear, Hannah? I'll tell your mum if I have to.'

'OK,' I said. She hung up.

After, I wished that she had told my parents because they would have stood up for me. I felt angry and misjudged. But something told me to keep it to myself. I phoned Kim and told her instead.

'Stupid woman,' she said. 'That's nothing to do with you. But Emily probably told her you came from Ilford and …' She paused. 'Well, she probably told her your dad was black. I heard her saying something nasty about it, and her dad would be pissed off if he knew. Sorry, Han.' Oh God, was that it? How stupid were these people? I felt enraged, but I also didn't want to talk about it. 'What's your art project?' I asked, changing subject.

Later I lay on my bed thinking. I had another year of Pinners. I was tired of the small-mindedness, the petty prejudices. One more year. I curled up with a book, impatient to leave school behind.

Alan Slade was a strange, gossipy boy, a loner in our class, but not shy, often in trouble with the teachers. He lived with his mother, a fierce presence in his life whom he talked about endlessly. Alan didn't register on the wavelength of the boys at Pinners, who were more concerned with rugby trials and football, but the girls ribbed Alan constantly – for his small stature, big ears and slight lisp, for his sometimes tatty clothes and unfashionable school bag. In the world of Pinners, taunting and derision were everyday occurrences, but the cruelties of one day were often forgotten the next. Alan had a survivor's instinct – no matter how harsh our heckling, he came back with quick and spiteful rejoinders.

It was Alan who labelled me 'white wog' at school – a name that gained widespread use for a time. He shouted it out as we jostled down the corridor after an hour in the French language lab, listening through huge headphones to François booking a hotel room *avec douche*, Michelle asking directions to *le banque*.

'All right, white wog!' Alan called out, coming up to me, laughing.

Peter Collins was standing next to us. 'Why's he calling you that?' he asked.

''Cos her dad's a wog, but she's white,' Alan said matter-of-factly, before I had the chance to speak.

'Oh yeah,' Peter said. 'That's funny. Funny-ha-ha and funny-peculiar.'

'No, it's not funny,' I said. 'It's racist and pathetic.' But I already knew I'd hear it again.

'Oh, come on,' Alan said, pushing his arm through mine. 'I'm only joking, aren't I? Can't you take a joke?'

'You shouldn't say things like that,' I said, but he wasn't listening. I let him drag me off to the dining hall.

◆

We bunked off school one Thursday afternoon, Alan and I. His mother was at home, so we caught the train to Goodmayes, walking cagily down Ashgrove Road to my house. It was a sunny day. I hoped my father would be out, or asleep, although I could usually rely on his obliviousness – he might not even notice I'd come home.

Alan had cigarettes and we shared one as we leant out of my bedroom window, letting the warm air in. It was a while before I heard Dad's footsteps on the stairs.

'Why aren't you at school, Han?' He came into the room just as Alan stubbed the cigarette out, flicking the butt from the window sill, standing in the corner looking conspicuous.

'Got the afternoon off,' I said, turning back to look out of the window, willing him to leave, but he didn't move. I turned again. 'What do you want, Dad?' I said.

'I don't want anything,' he said, 'I'm just wondering what you two are up to.' He'd adopted a sterner demeanour in front of Alan, who stayed silent, looking at the books on my shelf. My father was standing in the middle of the room, looking worn out, his old cardigan draped on his hunched shoulders.

'Nothing, Dad.' I said. 'Don't be stupid.'

The punch took me completely by surprise. I didn't know what had happened. Then I saw him standing before me, his first clenched at his side. I felt a sharp pain in my mouth and the taste of blood. 'Don't you ever call me stupid!' My father's face was up close to mine as he spat the words out. 'You hear me? Don't *ever* call me stupid.'

It took a while for the gravity of the situation to be clear to me. My father had just punched me in the face in front of a boy from school. Christ! I was mortified, and outraged.

'Just fuck off, Dad!' I pushed him, both hands on his chest. I was strong, and he was an old man. He fell backwards against the wall, looking winded and shocked. 'Just get out of my room! Fuck off!' I was shouting and crying and pushing him. How dare he, how dare he? He let me shove him out of the room, his body slackening under my palms, his face already softened. I slammed the door and looked down at the blood on my hands.

'Oh God, are you all right?' said Alan. He looked horrified.

'Yes,' I said, but I felt my split lip as I spoke.

'I'd better go,' he said, picking up his bag from the floor. 'Sorry, Hannah. Sorry. See you tomorrow, yeah?' He was halfway through the door.

'Don't tell anyone,' I said to his back. 'I'll kill you if you tell anyone.'

He turned, looking sympathetic. 'I won't. I promise.' I heard his feet knocking down the stairs and the slam of the front door.

♠

My father was gone for four days, banished from the house by my mother. The car was in the drive, so he must have gone somewhere on foot. My mouth was sore and swollen. I covered the redness with make-up for school the next day, where Alan Slade was as good as his word, acting as though nothing had happened.

But I had bigger things to worry over – Where was my father? When was he coming home? I knew I didn't deserve to be punched, I knew that, but I also knew I'd triggered that rage in him by what I'd said – that word, *stupid*, had struck a raw nerve. I was scared I could make him so angry. My mother was being very nice to me, but I didn't deserve that either. I felt I'd done something very wrong.

The bell rang at lunchtime on Sunday. I answered the door. My father was standing on the step, looking dishevelled and tired. In his hand, three Topic bars in their shiny red wrappers. He held them out to me, asking to be let back in. My mother came to the door, her mouth fixed in a thin, angry line. She pulled me back inside. I couldn't hear what they were saying, but that evening he was back in the house, sitting in the front room on his own watching television. The Topic bars were in the fridge. 'Don't you dare eat them,' my mother said, pointing her finger at me.

In the morning I bumped into him on the landing, coming out of the spare room in his pyjamas. 'Hello, Han,' he said solemnly.

'Hello, Dad,' I said.

Later in the day I heard him rustling on the other side of the front-room door as I was practising Scott Joplin. I didn't pull open the door to catch him as I used to, just played on as though I didn't know he was there.

The change in sleeping arrangements was not temporary. The spare room became his room after that, with a single bed, a bedside cabinet with his tablets and books, a narrow wardrobe for his clothes – just like a lodger's room. I was too young to understand my parents' relationship, its own stresses and strains – all I knew was that my father had been evicted from the marital bed, and the fault, I felt, was mine.

When Sam was a baby, my father used to look after him one night a week when my mother had a course. One night she came home to find my father sitting at the table crying. 'What's wrong?' she asked, sitting beside him, her hand on his arm.

'I don't think I should look after Sam any more,' he replied, looking down.

'Why not?' she asked. 'It's good to have time with him. What's wrong?'

'He's so small. I keep thinking I'll hit him, or shake him, or worse. What's wrong with me, what's wrong with me?' He held his head in his hands.

They went to the family doctor in Seven Kings, where my father confessed his dark thoughts to Dr Goldstein, who diagnosed depression, offering him pills or counselling. 'I'll have the pills,' my father said. He was always a great believer in medicine of any kind, and the thought of counselling, of exploring his past, probably terrified him. He took those pills for months and months – old-fashioned anti-depressants that made him too drowsy to drive, too tired to stay up all night. But the dark thoughts stopped.

They came back when I was born and he went back to the doctor for more.

There are photographs of me sitting on his knee, a fat smiling baby, his hands around my middle, or holding me high, delighted, in the air above his head. I look at them now and search his face for the fear he had of hurting me. *It was the way his dad had hurt him*, my mother said.

12
1946

*T*he boy walked back onto the island like he owned it. He had good clothes, a swagger in his step and $1,500 lodged with the Jamaican Post Office. He'd been gone for over three long years, working harder than he ever had before. He'd been up and down America and from coast to coast – never imagining landscape and weather so changeable, through the sweltering Florida summers cultivating corn and tomatoes, to the freezing winter he'd spent back in the north, hauling timber onto fuel trucks with raw and bleeding hands. The last four weeks had been spent behind the high fences of Count Murphy, Florida, with five hundred other Jamaicans, waiting for a ship to bring them home.

Sailing back, he remembered the people he'd met – men and women he'd worked alongside from Jamaica, America, Peru, the Bahamas; kind farm managers and ones that barked their orders; folk he'd shared a beer with, a game of cricket, a game of poker. Different people from place to place – good and bad – but none worse than in the South. In Florida, the Jamaicans quickly discovered the marching bands and apple pies were gone. No one gave a damn about their foreign charm or Britishness. A black man was a black

191

man, no matter where he came from. No more barracks, no more hot showers. They lived in tent cities – squalid canvas shelters with bare mattresses, no pillows, filthy shared latrines, supervised by gun-toting white men on horseback who summoned them with whistles to a daily roll call and picked and chose the day's workers.

The pay was worse than in the North, the hours longer. At first, they had resisted – refused the back seats of buses, the back doors of diners, stared down anyone who affronted them – but the punishments they faced were harsh. White southerners hated them for agitating, for rousing the black Americans to do the same. Troublemakers were sent to jail without trial, to languish until a ship could take them home. Seven hundred Jamaicans were caged in those Florida cells in no time at all. Roy Atley was gone within two weeks. Charles Dee a month later. For every man who left there was another waiting to take his place, a fact the farm leaders exploited. It still haunted the boy, the injustice of it.

Those who hadn't been repatriated early had to go home when their contracts ended. Demobilised American servicemen wanted their places back on the farms. The boy's feelings about return were conflicted – he had a daughter in Pensacola, Florida – a two-year-old girl he had seen three times, rarely near enough to visit her, not allowed to take leave. Her name was Gloria and her mother was Kathleen, a kind girl he'd married when she'd said there was a baby coming; he'd stayed with her two weeks before he had to leave again. She didn't love the boy, and if he told the truth, he didn't know what love meant, had only done what he thought was the right thing. He sent his daughter money from Atlanta, Wisconsin, Michigan – a card for each birthday, called her mother from downtown phone booths

– but neither of them said what needed saying: he wasn't coming back to the place she called home.

♣

Back in Kingston, the boy walked the streets, looking to see what was the same and what had changed. The city looked worn out. Rubbish rotted in the gutters, a cloud of pollution hung in the air. The island was scarred by the hurricanes that tore up the earth each year; the worst of them two years before had nearly wiped out the entire coconut crop. Houses and schools in Kingston were still waiting to be rebuilt.

'Things are bad here, man,' Felix told him. They were leaning on the wall outside a bar on Temple Street. 'Got worse when the war broke out. Now it's over, and things still as bad.'

The club on Barry Street had closed in the last year, putting Felix out of work. Mr Manny was running a smaller place in Chinatown – less rent and no money for servants. Now Felix collected empty bottles, selling them back to the factories for pennies. He looked older. Two of his teeth were missing, his skin dull and marked.

♦

The boy slept on the floor of Felix's room, waking the next morning alone, dressing without thinking. As though on autopilot, his feet carried him to Half Way Tree and onto the yellow bus to St Thomas. Only as they were waiting to depart did the boy question what he was doing, twice standing to get off, and twice sitting back down. And then they pulled away. Some part of him wanted to see his father, and the bus would take him there, out past Kingston Harbour, along the country roads, rattling over the familiar potholes, crossing the old bridge, the Yallahs River so high it lapped onto the road.

The shop looked as he remembered it – the flat tin roof, the small windows, crates of vegetables outside. He could smell the orange trees at the back. At least his father still had the place, the boy thought – it hadn't been razed or gambled away. He saw James Lowe through the door, his lean figure behind the counter in his white vest, his head bent over the ledger, a pencil in hand. It was as though time had frozen in the old shop, as if his father had stood there for three years. The boy held him surreptitiously in his gaze a little longer, holding that power for a moment, before walking in.

In the shop's dimly lit interior, nothing had changed – the high shelves were still muddled with goods, the same smell of salt-fish, the same battered mat lay on the floor. James Lowe looked up and saw the boy, his face moving through his emotions before settling on a frown. The boy looked back, holding his stare. His father looked exactly the same.

'So you back?' James Lowe said, as though the boy had been gone a week.

'Looks like,' the boy replied, a wind already rising in his body, churning his insides.

He had wanted to see his father, he told himself, he had to see him, and some part of the boy wanted his father to be proud of the money he had earned. He tried to hide the strain in his voice.

'How are things, Dad?' Silence. James Lowe just stood looking at the boy for what seemed like for ever. Then abruptly, he shook a cigarette from its packet on the counter, tapped it, lit it.

'How are things?' he said, mimicking the boy, exhaling. 'How are things?' A look of disgust passed over his face. 'Things are no good. You read the paper? Eh? No, you've been gone in America, making money, when your place is here.' He jabbed the cigarette in the boy's direction as he spoke.

The boy knew the ripple of his father's anger, how it could swell from nothing in seconds, but had told himself all the way here that he wouldn't take it any more, he couldn't take it any more.

'Yes, I read the paper,' he said. 'I know what's happening here. But I make my own choices now.' His father's face gave nothing away. 'I don't belong to you,' the boy spat out. But already he was backing towards the door, his body saying what his words did not – he was still terrified of his father.

James Lowe took long drags, blowing the smoke towards the boy, but looking off somewhere else in the room. 'I raised you,' he said quietly, the tempo of his speech slower. 'Put the clothes on your back, fed you, gave you a bed. You owe me,' he said. 'If you can't give the time, you must give the money.' He met the boy's eyes. His father was serious. He wanted the boy to pay for the years he'd been away, payment for the loss his absence had incurred. Like the injuries claimed by slave owners. Suddenly he didn't care for his father's pride at all.

Behind the counter, the dark curtain moved. There was a cry as a little boy came running through into the shop – two years old perhaps, wearing only a nappy. He had chubby legs, but moved fast. 'Vic!' a woman called, coming through the curtain after the baby. She was black and young, the same age as the boy perhaps. Pretty. His father's type. She grabbed the child and lifted him as he started crying, and her eyes locked with the boy's, her eyebrows raised in surprise. No one spoke for a second. The woman looked at his father, who tutted at her, flicking his hand in the direction of the curtain. Her face fell – she turned quickly and was gone.

Another woman, the boy thought. Another child, a half-brother. Nothing had changed.

His father said nothing, went back to his ledger. If the boy wanted more from him, he would have to do as he said – pay for it. James Lowe still hated him then, despite the years he'd been away. That's what he had needed to know. He looked once more at his father, fixed him in his memory. He wouldn't see him again, he told himself. He turned and walked back through the door.

The boy took a room down by the harbour. At night he lay on the bed reading the paper. The cane cutters were on a sit-in strike over wages. The wharf workers were refusing to unload trucks. The wages were low, lower than when he'd left. It was good the workers were still organising. He wondered about Thomas Reid. Much had changed in the island's politics in the years he'd been away. The boy wondered if he should get involved again, wondered who Reid supported now. The boy still believed Jamaica needed its independence, but in those years away he'd fallen out of touch, and worse, something inside him had changed – the idealism of three years earlier had gone.

He turned to the jobs section in the newspaper. What could he do? There were jobs for office clerks and accountants that required applicants to have finished school with qualifications. There were positions for curtain fitters and carpet layers, all of them insisting on skills and experience he did not have. He circled a couple of advertisements to look into – door-to-door salesman positions, one selling medicines, the other encyclopaedias. Both provided a bicycle. The boy imagined cycling with a suitcase of encyclopaedias balanced on his handlebars. He thought of his other options. Mr Manny's club was one. Another was his friend Rufus, who lived in Kingston now and wanted to open a grocery store, and had asked the boy to help him.

He dropped the paper to the floor, and lay on his bed thinking, listening to the dripping tap in the corner. It grew dark outside. The boy checked his watch, swung his feet down onto the floor, splashed his face with water at the sink and left the room.

Down in Chinatown, the noise was the same as ever – traffic and the clatter of hooves, the calls of the street merchants selling sugared ice and fried fish. This place at least hadn't changed. The laundry hung, ghostlike, on washing lines strung between buildings, fruit in bright piles outside the Chinese shops. The smell of ginseng rose from copper urns. He passed the same laundries, the same hairdressers, recognising faces as he moved between the night-stalls. Some of the Chinese recognised him, nodding quickly at him as he walked.

The door was down the narrow alley where Felix said it would be. The boy pushed it open, went in and stood in darkness. 'Hello?' he called out. 'Anyone here?' He saw a chink of light and could just catch the sound of low voices ahead. He went forward, reaching his hand out to push open another door. And there, behind it, was the low-hanging bulb above the big round table, a pile of money in the middle. Four men sat with fanned hands of cards. Three empty chairs. Felix was right – this was a dingier place. Mr Manny looked up.

'Chick?' he said, his eyebrows raised. He stood up, coming forward. 'Chick! Long time no see!'

'Yes sir, Mr Manny,' the boy took Mr Manny's outstretched hand. 'I'm just come home. Been gone three years.' They shook hands hard.

'Boy you grow up. Come in, come in. No way, three years,' said Mr Manny, chuckling. 'Well you see us fellows been sat here all that time!' He held his belly laughing. 'Good to have you back, boy,' he said, taking his seat again, picking up his cards. The boy took his place at the table.

Three months passed, and the boy had slipped back into the night-time routine of Mr Manny's and other clubs in Kingston, not dealing for money but playing cards five nights a week, the jobs in the paper forgotten, Rufus's grocery store forgotten. He played it straight and he played it crooked. In the small room on the harbour he practised and practised, laying down hands to check the probability of combinations. His memory was as sharp as ever. He was practising other skills too, things he'd picked up in America, bent to the room's lamplight with a razor blade between his thumb and forefinger. He carefully shaved the edge from a playing card, the thinnest sliver, invisible to the eye, but just detectable when he ran his thumb along the long side of the card. Or sometimes he gently punctured the card with a pin, the tiniest bump only he could find. Then he practised dealing the deck, his hands so quick and smooth, no one would ever see a thing amiss, but in truth, those skilful hands were looking for the marked cards, holding them back in his palm, dealing them to himself. His timing was perfect.

He only ever let himself win small, and certainly not every night. In the small room in Chinatown, the same men played again and again – the boy couldn't risk being caught, and he didn't want to cheat Mr Manny – he'd been good to him in the time before. But at the other club he took bigger risks.

Three months living nocturnally, sleeping the hot days away in the small room at the harbour. It couldn't go on. Despite his wins, his savings were half what they had been, the money gone on food, rent, clothes, a loan to Felix that he knew would not be returned. Something had to change.

'Oh, you're back,' was all Hermione had said when he'd called to her through the screen door of the little house. She'd put on weight since he'd last seen her, her clothes tight around her body. He followed her through the kitchen into the living room. She carried a jug of iced tea and poured it into two glasses. 'Well, well,' she said. 'I wondered when I'd see you again.'

They sat on the veranda, where she lit a white-tipped cigarette, the first time he'd seen her smoke. He told her about his time in America, making her laugh with his stories, her eyes widening when he told her about the South.

'You didn't get my letters?' he asked. Hermione looked straight at him, paused, shook her head.

'No,' she said, 'but the mail here is bad, you know. Always bad. Letters get lost, turn up a year later at the wrong address.' She blew a long tongue of cigarette smoke, and the boy knew she was lying. She'd received the letters but hadn't been bothered to reply.

'But I received the money,' she said, as though she just remembered. 'Thank you for that. You must have made a lot in America?'

'I did all right,' the boy said, thinking of his dwindling stash. 'Put a little away.'

'Things sure have been tough while you've been gone. Half of Kingston is out of work, you know.'

'It's worse for sure,' the boy said. 'We need to rule the island ourselves, you think?' Hermione said nothing, uncharacteristically quiet. 'It's about time,' the boy pushed it. Nothing again. 'Did you vote in the election?' He wanted to know.

'Oh, let's not talk about politics,' she said. 'Do you mind? It's so depressing.' He knew she hadn't voted.

'How about you?' he asked, changing subject. 'How you been keeping? How's Fay and Angela and Laura?'

'So-so, you know. I don't see them so often now. Not so much time to be visiting family. I've been working. Taking in clothes, sewing, repairs. Washing sometimes.' She held her hands out and turned the palms up then down. 'My poor hands are ruined from the soap!' The boy thought Hermione's hands looked as pretty as ever. Long graceful fingers, the nails neatly painted coral pink, but like Felix, she looked older, the skin on her face no longer as supple.

They chatted some more until Hermione looked at her watch. 'Oh dear,' she said. 'I didn't realise the time. I have a visitor coming in just a minute. Can you come back another day? I'm sorry to throw you out.' It was just like old times.

'No problem,' the boy said. 'I'll come next week.' He wanted to ask who her visitor was, wondered why she didn't tell him. At the door, she pecked him on the cheek, closing the screen quickly behind him, in a hurry for him to be gone.

The boy went down the steps and walked half the length of the road before stopping and turning back. The sun was hot in the sky and he cast a long shadow on the pavement. Who *was* the visitor? He really did want to know, walking slowly back towards her house, his eyes searching the street. He felt conspicuous, standing on the street corner. No one appeared, and after five minutes had passed the boy suddenly felt ridiculous. What was he doing, spying on her? He turned on his heel, ready to walk back towards the bus, and nearly crashed into a man coming in the other direction. 'Oh excuse me,' the boy said. He stepped back. The man was holding a brown paper bag under his arm and a thin bunch of flowers in his hand. He was Chinese. 'Hope I didn't crush them,' the boy said, looking at the flowers.

'Oh no, they look fine to me,' the man answered, turning the bunch round. 'Don't worry. But mind how you go now.' He continued up the street and the boy walked on, turning half a minute later to see the man climbing the steps to Hermione's porch. He knew his face. It was the Chinese shopkeeper from Barry Street. The boy had seen him last week in the shop. He and his wife serving behind the counter.

◆

'You see the notice in the paper?' Felix asked the next time they met at the bar near the harbour. 'Boy, I wish I had that sort of money. I'd take myself to England in a second.'

'What notice?' the boy asked. 'I didn't see anything.'

Felix pulled the crumpled page from his trouser pocket. 'I don't know why I'm carrying it around,' he said. 'I'm not going anywhere.' He smoothed the paper on the table and the boy bent over to read it. It was a notice advertising passage to England on the SS *Ormonde*, a returning troopship. It said the ticket would be in the region of £48, should it be possible for the vessel to call at Jamaica. There were two hundred berths.

'They don't even know if this ship is coming,' the boy said. 'Either it's coming or it's not.'

'I think it'll come,' Felix said. 'Because enough Jamaican boys would sell their mothers to be on that boat and be away. But forty-eight pounds is a lot of money, man. And forty-eight times two hundred is a whole lot more.'

They lifted their bottles and drank.

13
EVERY DOG HAS HIS DAY IN LUCK

If you can make one heap of all your winnings
And risk it on one turn of pitch-and-toss,
And lose, and start again at your beginnings
And never breathe a word about your loss

– Rudyard Kipling, *If*

My father had a heart attack at Coral's card club in Stoke Newington. Or thought he'd had one. It was early September and unusually warm – too hot and humid in the basement room where he'd been playing poker for close to five hours. When he keeled over clutching his chest, the other players gathered round him, laying him out on the carpet while someone phoned an ambulance. At 1 a.m. the phone rang at home, and a man my mother didn't know told her my father was on his way to the Homerton Hospital in Hackney. Without waking Sam or me, she phoned a cab, wrote us a note and left the house.

Before I saw the note in the morning, she called to say my father was fine. 'He's asleep, the lazy bugger!' she joked. In fact, he'd been asleep since she arrived, slept through the night, and was still asleep. He hadn't had a heart attack after all, but the doctors thought he might have angina and wanted to keep him in for tests. It seemed a regular occurrence – testing my father for one medical ailment or another, dispatching him with a new medication. The only difference was the more dramatic circumstances. I made myself toast and a cup of tea, packed my bag for college and left the house.

He was home that evening, laid up on the sofa looking serious. 'It was a terrible pain,' he told me. 'Up and down one arm. Across my chest. I thought I was dying.'

'It's the stress of gambling,' my mother said in the kitchen, out of his earshot.

'But he didn't have a heart attack,' I said. 'Did he?'

'Angina attack. Heart attack. It's the same thing. It's the stress of it all.' She lit her cigarette. 'He'll drop dead playing bloody poker. Mark my words. Or I'll drop dead of worry.'

The doctors told him to avoid stress, fatty food and cigarettes, and for two weeks my father stayed home, stopped smoking and ate more vegetables. His stash of pills increased, filling three of the bathroom cabinet's shelves. Pills for blood pressure and angina, statins to lower cholesterol, PPIs for his stomach ulcers, antacids, painkillers. He took them religiously, swigging them down before he put his front teeth in. But soon he was back on the cigarettes, cadging them from my mother because he couldn't afford his own.

'I'm getting old, Han,' he told me the next morning. 'My body's giving up.'

He'd been ill so often, and over so many years, that I didn't take it seriously. 'You're fine, Dad,' I said. 'Stop worrying.' I looked at the clock. I was late. 'Can I have a lift to college?'

♠

I didn't want to stay on at Pinners for A-levels, and I wasn't welcome to. The school had made quite clear that my bad behaviour had consequences. I wasn't allowed into the sixth form. Instead I went to the local college in Barking, where Sam had gone four years before. It was a relief to be away from that school. Maybe all secondary schools are harsh places where children vie for a position in the strict hierarchies of good looks, ability or popularity, but Pinners was harsher because of its own elitism. It instilled a sense of superiority that gave way to a firm pecking order and much bullying of those who didn't fit in. I'd spent five unhappy years enduring the long journey on the Tube and bus, stuffed into that regimental school uniform, hating it all. I quickly lost touch with the friends I'd had there. I was trying to forget.

Barking College was liberation – no uniform, no stuffy assembly or Lord's Prayer, no heavy-handed authority. It embodied the spirit of further education – community-based courses for adults and teenagers from all backgrounds, studying anything from further maths to drama to car mechanics. The academic curriculum was more radical than what I was used to. Two teachers, both named John, set books to study that my old school would never have taught – experimental novels, black women's poetry, the lesser-known Shakespeare plays. I found a new love of reading and a new engagement with politics through literature.

The Students' Union was run by Tim, a camp boy from Dagenham, who told scandalous tales of his encounters in the dark rooms of East End gay clubs while calling us to arms against the British National Party and the National

Front. I went on my first demonstration that year. Under the college banner, we marched in a sea of yellow placards with seventy thousand protestors to Welling, where the British National Party headquarters stood.

I had a sudden memory that day, of my father, years ago, his glasses perched on his nose, standing in the hall reading a red and white leaflet he'd lifted from the doormat. He'd crumpled it when he saw me, but I found another in the letter box a few days later. It was from the National Front. 'Enoch Powell Was Right' it said in bold letters across a Union Jack – 'Stop Immigration. Start Repatriation'. I'd asked my mother who Enoch Powell was, what repatriation meant, and as she explained I knew they wanted to send back people like my father, even after forty years in England. Who knows how many leaflets he had found before? I was glad to be marching against racism that hot May day.

We walked for an hour, chanting slogans, singing songs, until the procession came to a halt. It was fractious in the crowd as word came back of a police barricade at the crossroads. There was a strange, volatile energy, and things turned nasty quickly – police riding their horses into the crush, protestors in balaclavas throwing bricks and bottles, police on foot with riot shields and batons, dragging demonstrators across the ground to where their vans waited. The violence ebbed and surged. I was torn between wanting to witness what was happening and wanting to be away. When the crowd charged forward, we lost the Barking College banner. I was separated with my new friends, Holly and Ella, and we ran, scared and holding hands, over the rubble of a wall, through a graveyard, down an alley to the high road, where shoppers ambled, oblivious of the uprising streets away.

'Police protect the Nazis!' Holly shouted as we walked towards the bus stop, people giving her strange looks. On the top deck of the bus she yanked open the window, yelling, 'Down with the BNP! Down with Nazi scum!'

♥

I'd met Holly on the first day of college. She wore fashionable clothes and chain-smoked, flicking her long hair down her back. She lived in Forest Gate with her parents and sister, and another set of parents and their two daughters, Ella, who was a year younger than Holly, and Melissa, who was little. The two couples had pooled together to buy a big Victorian house overlooking a park. They were members of the Socialist Workers' Party, and Holly and Ella grew up in a house of political talk and protest. Unlike me, they were seasoned demonstrators. They could quote Marx and Chomsky, and every Saturday they sold the *Socialist Worker* newspaper at the railway station. I'd not met anyone like them before – my age and so politically engaged – but they were also products of their environment, had gone to the local secondary school, spoke with cockney accents and dated the local black boys – boys with thick gold chains around their necks, and expensive, spotless trainers.

I was flattered that they liked me, and secretly delighted to be invited to their house. I loved it there, and envied them the four narrow floors joined by creaky stairs, stained glass in the windows, the old-fashioned fireplaces. I loved their living room the best – the walls lined with books and records, and hung with film posters in bright wooden frames, a vintage jukebox in the corner – everything so stylish and chic, a far cry from the brash new wealth of pupils at Pinners, who lived in vast mock Tudor houses with stone lions at the gates and satellite dishes stuck to their roofs. I was confused about class. I wasn't sure whether class depended on your background – who your parents were and where you were born, the job you did, how much money you had in the bank – or something else.

Most of all, I envied them their familial camaraderie. There were long, sociable meals in the kitchen, fresh bread and bottles of red wine spread out, the din of conversation. Everyone got on, or so it seemed. Holly's dad was an ex-docker who had gone back to university and become a lecturer. Holly adored him and he adored her, would sling his arm around her shoulder, pulling her in for a kiss, and together they'd go to art exhibitions and gigs. My family life couldn't have been more different. Sam and I would sit at the dinner table long enough to eat our tea before returning to the enclaves of our rooms, where our parents were not welcome. I couldn't imagine sharing any actual activity with my father, and hadn't known his physical touch in years, except for that terrible afternoon two years before, which I was still trying to forget.

♣

It was at college that I met my first boyfriend, Jason, a druggy dreamer, five years older than me. He tied his long hair in a ponytail, wore baggy jeans that hung from his thin frame. We were in the same film studies class, but he only came to college one day a week and worked the rest at an industrial bakery, making apple turnovers. 'Bloody apple turnovers,' he said. 'Sometimes I dream I'm standing in a field of them, miles and miles of the sodding things.'

Jason lived with his parents on a dilapidated estate in Stratford. Until I met him, I'd never walked through an estate, only seen them from the road or on the television. From those viewpoints, council estates seemed like scary places – mazes of concrete alleys and minimal playgrounds, the high anonymous blocks. I could never imagine living sandwiched between people above and below, taking the wrecked elevator to my small box in the sky. But when I went to see Jason I saw that estates can be safe places for those who live there, havens from the world outside. There was a strong community where Jason lived – children who'd grown up together, adults who'd worked together for most of their lives. Most people knew each other, and soon I came to know them, through a wave and a smile on my way to Jason's place.

But too many people lived in his thin-walled maisonette with its cramped rooms – the three grown-up sons still lived at home with their parents. Jason's mum was a school cook. His dad and brothers all worked at the bakery. A lifetime of apple turnovers beckoned inevitably.

'What I'd like to do is direct films,' he said. 'Not big-budget action ones, but arty films about bands, you know. With mad dream sequences.' He was lying on his bed, rolling a spliff. 'Yeah, direct films, or maybe music videos.'

Jason had enrolled at three different colleges in the last three years, each time to study A-levels he didn't complete. He lasted six weeks studying at ours. 'I hate being told what to do,' he moaned, pulling on a cigarette as we stalked through the rain from the college to the bus stop. 'Why does that bloke think he knows more than me?' He meant our lecturer. 'And the films he shows are crap.'

'I don't think they're crap,' I said. That day we'd watched *The Life and Times of Rosie the Riveter*, an American documentary about women going out to work in the Second World War. I'd found it fascinating.

'They're crap!' he said, unwilling to enter a debate. 'Anyway, enough moaning.' He flung his arm around my neck. 'What shall we do tonight?'

We jumped on the bus to Mile End. I remember how new it all felt, catching the bus with a boyfriend who held my hand. He'd already had two girlfriends and was worldly-wise compared to me. I felt warm and snug, sitting beside him, wiping my initials on the steamed bus window as we rode through Ilford's drab town centre and down the Romford Road, walking through the alleys tagged in spray paint to his house, where he whisked me up to his bedroom.

The first time I visited, he'd lain on his bed and pulled a rectangle of paper from his pocket. It was wrapped in cling film. 'Look what I've got,' he said, unpeeling it. Inside there was a pile of white powder.

'What is it?' I said.

'Speed,' he said. He tipped it into a can of Tango, swilled it round and drank. 'Shall we?'

I thought about it for five seconds before taking the can and taking a swig. We passed it between us. 'Nice one,' he said, draining the dregs, wincing at the taste. 'Let the fun begin.'

High on amphetamines, we walked through Maryland and Leytonstone towards Wanstead Flats, car headlamps and street lamps magnified in our dilated eyes: a dazzling orange blur. We talked and talked, the drugs making every thought bubble excitedly to our mouths. Wanstead Flats at night was a haunting place, miles and miles of wild wasteland surrounded by distant tower blocks, the windows like dominoes of light. There was a lake in the middle, a wide stretch where the bold white shapes of swans glided on the black water. We kissed for the first time there, high as kites, laid out on Jason's coat, our bodies pressed hard together, kissing suddenly more exciting than talking.

I sneaked home early the next morning, hoping to avoid my mother. I hadn't slept. 'Where on earth have you been?' She was up already, standing in the kitchen as I came through the back door.

'Nowhere,' I said, then: 'But I'm here, look!' I prodded myself. 'Safe and sound, no damage.'

She wasn't having it. 'You're sixteen, Hannah. You're still a child.'

'I told you I was staying out.'

'Yes,' she said. 'But I'd like to know *where*.'

My father stood behind her, holding his tea. 'Your mother's right,' he said. 'You should tell her where you're going.'

'Oh, do me a favour,' I said, annoyed at his interference, stomping upstairs to lie wide awake on my bed.

◆

Since starting college, I had more free time in the day and was often home alone with my father. Since the incident at Coral's, he was home more too, and the phone rang for him less and less, as though his cronies had finally realised how old he was, how frail his health. He'd lost something that night.

At home, we were like tenants of the same building, occupying different rooms, rarely crossing paths. He still woke late, appearing in the kitchen at midday, barefoot in his dressing gown, making tea or rolling his first cigarette before his trip to Patel's, the newsagent, for the newspaper. He spent his days in the sofa with Chloe on his lap, reading or watching snooker. He'd nap away the late afternoons, waking just before my mother came home to make himself look busy in the kitchen. Some days Charlie White came round to drink tea and do the crossword. Unlike most of the men my father knew, Charlie was a proper friend.

On Tuesdays, my father could draw his meagre pension at the post office. He'd get up early on those days, returning via Patel's with the paper and a pouch of tobacco, and he always played cards on a Tuesday night. A club in Gants Hill ran a kalooki game that cost £10 to enter. It might be his only night out in the week – a tenner of the pension was always reserved for the game.

I had a job as a waitress at a pizza restaurant in Ilford, serving customers, refreshing the buffet's dehydrated pizzas with a water spray and, when it was quiet, going out into the street wearing a bright shell suit, leafleting shoppers with discount vouchers. Despite such humiliation, I liked my job – the feeling of independence, going off to work, collecting my pay packet at the end of the week. My father would often pick me up from a night shift and we'd drive through Ilford, the roads quiet of traffic, past pubs at kicking-out time, people crowding the fluorescent-lit kebab shop. 'Lend us a tenner, Han?' he would say on the way home, his face looking hopeful.

'I haven't got a tenner, Dad.'

'Oh come on, Han. I thought you were rich now you were working?'

I'd be annoyed. 'No, I'm not rich. Anyway, that's not the point – it's my money!'

But often I'd dig out a note from my purse. I hated him asking, and the fact that I pitied him enough to give it.

One day I came home early from college to a quiet house. I assumed he'd gone out. But from the hall, I heard him in the downstairs bathroom.

'What am I going to do? What am I going to do?' he was shouting. Then there was silence. Then he started again. 'What am going to do? Oh God, oh God.' Over and over again until his voice broke. I thought I could hear sobs.

Quietly as I could, I tiptoed up the stairs to my room and shut the door.

♠

Despite his weakened heart, my father continued to take Chloe for a daily walk up the road to the newsagent's, where he would tie her up outside the shop, make his purchases, pass the time of the day with Mr Patel, retrieve the dog and walk home. Five minutes left alone and Chloe would be whining with anxiety, convinced she'd been abandoned.

One day he forgot her. I was at home, engrossed in my essay on William Faulkner's *As I Lay Dying* while he watched Wimbledon downstairs. My father loved any sport he could bet on – horses, snooker, boxing – but he also loved Wimbledon for its Englishness. Before Nan died, Wimbledon fortnight brought a temporary truce to Ashgrove Road, Nan's prejudices put aside so she could watch the only television in the house, upstairs in our flat. She and my father forgot they hated each other, sat side by side, commenting on the players' form, the quality of rallies, drinking endless cups of tea. Maybe it was because he was so engrossed in the tennis that he didn't notice Chloe's absence.

'Where's the dog?' my mother asked, the moment she came in from work. 'Hannah!' she shouted upstairs. 'Have you got Chloe up there?'

'No!' I called down.

I watched my parents through my bedroom window, walking the length of the garden, calling for her, checking the hole in the fence which Chloe liked to wiggle her way through. My father stood on the lawn scratching his head. I couldn't hear what he was saying. Suddenly my mother turned and stalked into the house and he hurried in behind her. I came down the stairs as he was putting his shoes on.

'Your father's left the dog outside the paper shop,' my mother told me, incredulous, standing over him. 'He's only just remembered. He'd lose his bloody head if it wasn't screwed on. The same way he's lost the car, not once, but three times, in as many years.'

It was true: more than once in the last few years my father had forgotten where he'd parked the car, following nights of gambling. Once he'd even phoned the police to report it stolen before finding it parked on the street where he'd left it.

My mother was still ranting as he left the house, rushing down the path and up the road to see if, by some miracle, Chloe was still waiting patiently at Patel's, seven hours after being left there. Of course she wasn't, and that evening he walked the streets as the sun went down, calling and calling for the dog, bent to his knees looking under cars, searching front gardens. He scoured the local park and knocked on our neighbours' front doors to ask if anyone had seen her. It was past ten when he came in, sitting forlornly on the sofa, his head hung low. My mother had been phoning local animal rescue centres, but most were already closed.

'I'm so sorry, Bet,' he said. 'I don't know what's happened to her. Where can she be? Where's poor Chloe? Can you imagine how scared she'll be? Where can she be?'

My mother was kinder. 'Well, there's not much we can do now,' she said. 'It's late. We'll have to go to bed. Not that we'll sleep.' She dragged deeply on her cigarette. 'The dog will be having a nervous breakdown somewhere.'

'No, I can't go to bed,' he said. 'How could I go to bed? I'll go back out in a minute. I'll just have a sandwich, Bet, and go back out.'

Then the phone rang and she answered. It was our vet, telling us he had Chloe. He described the day's protracted chain of events: Chloe had been rescued from the newsagent by an old lady, who had given Chloe some food and rung the local vet. The vet had come by after work, collected Chloe and taken her to an animal rescue centre near his home. He hadn't recognised her, but by coincidence, a nurse at the centre who used to work for him remembered her. The vet took the now-identified Chloe back to Ilford to check the records for our number. They were just round the corner – we could go and pick her up. My mother was laughing as she relayed this to my father, but he went silently to stand at our back door, a cigarette in his mouth. I watched him from the kitchen. I couldn't see his face, but I could tell he was crying.

♥

'Couldn't you leave him?' I blurted out to my mother one night. She was in bed and I was sitting on the edge. My father was out somewhere. We were both rubbing Nivea cream into our hands.

'Leave your dad?' She stopped rubbing. I could see she was surprised. Then she laughed. 'Don't think the thought hasn't crossed my mind!' she said.

I knew this conversation was strange territory. I don't think I had any idea what I was asking. In the world of my friends, boyfriends were picked up and dropped with relative ease. I had no idea about the allegiances and obligations that might come with thirty years of marriage. I had no idea what it would be like to not have my father around. But my mum was still so young, and my father was such a burden on her. I wanted her to have a different sort of life. Another chance.

'I couldn't leave your dad, Hannah,' she said, turning serious. 'Where would he go? How would he get by?'

Who knows where he'd go, I thought. He probably wouldn't get by. Part of me didn't care. I was angry at him – for being old, for being ill and depressed, for losing the dog.

'Do you still love him, then?' I asked. The question was out before I could stop it.

She looked sorry for me, like she was letting me down, and I realised in that moment that she would never leave. She'd made her bed and she'd lie in it. She didn't want to be set free.

'I do love him,' she told me. 'He's a silly git, but I do.'

There was no doubting my father's health was getting worse, but he was also a dreadful hypochondriac, convinced that any physical discomfort was the onset of life-threatening disease. He worried constantly about his health and was a regular at the doctor's surgery, so much so that the receptionist knew his name and birthdate off by heart.

My mother thought his anxiety was linked to his lifestyle. *It was the instability of everything*, she said later. *Money, health. He never knew what was round the corner.* But even after the scare with his heart, she didn't take his ailments seriously and neither did I.

'Help!' he cried out from his bedroom one morning. It was late and I'd just woken up. My mother was at work. 'Hannah?' he said in a small voice, as though he could tell I was there on the landing.

'What is it, Dad?' I asked through the door.

'Phone your mother. I'm very sick.'

I opened the door of the dark room which smelt of sleep and sweat. He lay on the bed in his old dressing gown, sheets twisted around his bony legs, his head at an awkward angle on the pillow. His hands gripped his side of his mattress. 'Thank God you're here,' he gasped. 'Call me an ambulance.'

'What's wrong with you?'

'Terrible pain. Terrible. Get your mother.'

I phoned my mother at work. 'He's probably got indigestion,' she said. 'Make him a cup of tea and give him some Gaviscon. It's in the bathroom cabinet.'

I administered the Gaviscon to my father, two pink spoonfuls he sipped carefully, tears in his eyes. But an hour later he was still crying out, 'Help me! Help me!' writhing on the bed, kicking his feet. There was a slick of sweat across his brow.

I phoned my mother again. 'Oh bugger it!' she declared. 'Tell him I'll be home in an hour.'

I relayed this news to my father, who groaned. 'I can't bear the pain!' he panted. I wondered if I should call an ambulance. His face was pale, his eyes were bulging. It was hot and fetid in his small room. I opened the window to get some air. 'No light!' he cried.

Finally, my mother arrived home, took one look at him and dialled 999. The paramedics lifted him down the stairs on a stretcher, thrashing around and groaning. He was in hospital for a week, diagnosed with renal colic caused by kidney stones. The acute variety, which the doctor told us my father had, was considered to be more painful than a gunshot wound. Or surgery. Apparently it was more painful than childbirth.

♦

Jason and I lasted nine months together, until one weekend I made up an excuse not to go to his house. Something had changed. I didn't want to lie on his single bed drinking cider and stubbing my cigarettes out in empty pizza boxes. I wanted to get out into the world. Holly had tickets for *A Midsummer Night's Dream* at the Barbican and she and Ella wanted to go to a club after. I told Jason I had to study.

I surprised myself when I felt the same the next weekend, calling him from the payphone at college to say that I had to study again.

'I'm not stupid!' he told me.

'Speak up,' I said. I could hardly hear him in the busy hall.

'I know what this is,' he said loudly and slowly so I couldn't miss a word. 'Why can't you just say it straight? We're breaking up. Don't bother to answer. I know. I'm going to come round and get my stuff.' He hung up.

I was shocked, but I didn't phone back, suddenly realising he was right. I didn't want him any more. I wondered if his ex-girlfriends had grown bored of the weekend routine, watching Jason wasting his wages on a bag of weed, a wrap of speed, still talking about his dreams, knowing they would come to nothing.

When I came home that night, my mother was in the kitchen, drying her hands on a tea towel, looking concerned. After a shaky start, she had come to like Jason, preferring him to come to our house where she could keep an eye on us.

'Jason's been over, love,' she said. 'I think he's taken his things.'

My father hovered in the doorway, listening in. I had no idea what he thought of Jason – whenever he'd come over, my father would disappear into the back room. Upstairs, I looked around. Jason's things had gone – his old guitar, a battered copy of *Dark Side of the Moon*, a pile of sci-fi novels I hadn't read. There was a short note on my desk. I hadn't seen his handwriting before. It was a mess. He'd misspelt *beautiful*. At the bottom, a PS: *Are you sure you're sure?*

I sat in the chair and cried. I was completely sure.

♠

I spent that summer, my last before university, dancing in nightclubs all across London. Bagley's was my favourite, an enormous brick warehouse behind King's Cross – three dark, cavernous rooms that pumped melodic house music the clubbers gyrated to from midnight until dawn. A long concrete terrace overlooked the industrial estates of York Way, and as the sun came up, the drugged-up crowd paraded in their sparkly, theatrical clothes – girls in silver hot pants and headdresses, boys in denim shorts and braces, their tops off to show their slick torsos. I went with Maria and sometimes Holly or other friends from college. We didn't take drugs and hardly drank on those nights – there was a high enough in the experience of dancing to the uplifting music, meeting new people. At home, I raided the music from my brother's record collection – Frankie Knuckles, Inner City, Ce Ce Rogers. It wasn't just house music playing in the clubs back then, but old and new soul music and R&B from America and the UK.

After these nights out, feet sore, we hobbled to whichever side street Maria had parked on, driving home through the East End and towards Ilford. My father came to mind on those journeys – the same journey he'd made most nights of my childhood – the sky lightening as he came down from the adrenaline of the night, sleep heavy on his eyelids, the tiredness hanging on his breath. My mother would greet us at the door, just out of bed.

'Have a nice time then, girls?' she said.

'Yes, Auntie Bet,' Maria would say. 'But I'm starving now. Is there any toast?'

The sweat would still be drying on our clothes as we sat down to eat my mother's bacon and eggs, a round of toast, a mug of sweet tea. The sun always shone that summer. When Maria left, I'd pull the curtains tight, curl up in my bed and sleep the day away.

We were all on the move by 1994. Sam had already left for university in Nottingham. My cousins moved too. Susanna went to Liverpool to train as a teacher, Maria moved into halls in London to study science, and suddenly little Alf was grown, with a clan of misfit friends who dyed their hair in rainbow shades and pierced their lips and noses. Alf coloured his hair bright blue and shaved his eyebrows off. He looked like an alien. The spring he turned seventeen, he moved up North, ostensibly to study music but in truth to busk the streets of Barnsley.

That same autumn, I packed my bags and headed off to Sussex University. My parents didn't drive me, unlike the other first-year students. I was an adult now, I thought. I didn't want their chaperoning. Instead, Maria and her boyfriend Ben took me there – my clothes and tape cassettes and a duvet tucked tightly into the back of his car.

On the doorstep, my father pulled a ten-pound note from his pocket. 'There you go, Han,' he said, handing it to me. I looked at the money. He must have missed his kalooki game to give me it.

'Thanks, Dad,' I said, slipping it into my pocket. 'Bye, then.' I hoisted my last bag onto my shoulder. He stood behind my mother outside Ashgrove Road and as we pulled away, I waved, and they waved back. He was shielding his eyes from the sun with his other hand, his purple cardigan buttoned up all wrong.

Ben was a DJ and had friends in Brighton. There was a party the night we arrived. So rather than sharing a nervous drink with my fellow freshers at the halls of residence bar, I sat in a posh flat on the seafront, where people ten years older than me drank cocktails and a tall girl in a sparkly dress racked up wobbly lines of cocaine on a mirror.

'Who's got a note?' she said loudly over the music, looking around. 'Anyone?' Her eyes locked with mine.

I fumbled in my pocket, finding my father's tenner. 'Here you go,' I said, half standing from the sofa where I was crushed between two men who couldn't stop talking over me about graphic design.

'Ta!' she said, almost snatching it from me, rolling the note into a tube she then popped up her nose to snort with. 'Who's next?' she said, lifting the mirror with my tenner rested on it.

'Yes sirree!' shouted the man next to me, reaching for it.

Someone turned the music up and turned the main light off. Fairy lights sparkled around the high windows and people started dancing. And I lost track of that tenner as the mirror was passed from one pair of knees to another – all night long.

♣

If my father was addicted to gambling, his compulsion was masked because it was his work – his job, he might have said. We never used the word addiction. He said that gambling was 'in his blood', and blamed his father, whose penchant for *mahjong* was seemingly much more destructive than my father's compulsions. But my father – unlike his dad, unlike most gambling addicts who run up debts of huge amounts, who might purloin or commit fraud to fund their fix – rarely lost at cards or dice, because he cheated.

Aside from a few years driving a cab, it was the only work I'd ever known him do. If Sam needed new shoes for school, he'd play cards for it. If I needed money for a school trip, he'd play cards for it. My mother's income paid the mortgage and the bills, but for food shopping or clothes or treats, my father was dispatched to get the cash, and for many years, he did just that.

Aside from playing, he also dabbled in various other gambling-related ventures that might, if they had worked out, have earned him some serious money. The dice tables might have brought in an income if there'd been more demand, as might his foray into betting shops.

Sometime in the late 1960s, just as he met my mother, my father and a fellow called Leslie Jones rented some rooms above a row of shops in Ladbroke Grove. The government of the day made betting shops legal in 1961, but, still not wanting to encourage gambling, had decreed they had to be strictly functional places – no drinks or food, no television or advertising, no carpets, and windows blacked out. The buildings my father and Leslie secured were grand and Victorian. They set about painting and refurbishing the rooms, laying new carpet, buying comfortable chairs and sofas and installing a tannoy system with speakers in each room. There was an entry phone downstairs through which, after word got around, 'high class' punters could come to enjoy the ambience of the rooms, be served a drink and place a discreet bet. My father and Leslie laid off the bets to a bigger bookmaker who was willing to take them and who charged them a small fee for doing so. They, in turn, charged a large fee for entrance to the sitting rooms and people were willing to pay.

The place was entirely against the law, but was doing a roaring trade, no doubt because of the exclusivity of the sitting rooms, and because, between races, my father and Leslie would put the tannoy to another use. Leslie knew a prostitute called Gladys in Paddington, who, for a fee, would happily describe her services in great detail over the phone – which they would broadcast to the room. Men would stay for hours, buy more drinks and place more bets.

They should have been rich, but there were two problems. One was that Leslie was a crook with his hand in the till. He was pilfering the profits under my father's nose, knowing it would take my father a while to get his nerve up to say something. The other problem was my father's own gambling. He was like a child in a sweet shop, betting on every other race. When the landlord got wind of the illegal goings-on at the sitting rooms he put the rent up, but my father and Leslie were already out of capital. After six months, they had no choice but to close.

My father really was an addict. He lost a fortune on the horses, the biggest cause of gambling addiction. He spent countless afternoons at the local bookmakers, at home among the other punters whose camaraderie he must have enjoyed. All of them knew betting on horses was a losing game, but still they studied the form and hopefully filled in their betting slips. Unlike cards or dice, there was no way for my father to swing things in his favour. He lost like everyone else.

Sometimes he'd put on his best suit and drive to Kempton Park or Epsom. I have an early memory of Goodwood racecourse where my parents sometimes took us for a trip. I'm trackside in my pram, the thunder of the horses' hooves approaching, and I'm straining out my seat to see them – the sweat-dark animals, the jockeys in their rippling coloured silks. *You loved the sound of them,* my mother told me. *You used to shout out, 'C'mon horsey! C'mon horsey!'* And I remember how my father lifted me, high up above the crowd, so I could see them galloping past.

We should have been rich, but my father never saved a penny, never planned for a future when his luck had gone, or, more to the point, his health. But financial acumen and gambling don't go hand in hand – it wasn't as though casinos offered pensions to seasoned gamblers. Later, when he couldn't play because he couldn't take the stress, or his hands wouldn't work, or because he didn't have the cash to stake – his addiction showed itself the most. We needed money – to maintain the house or for car repairs – but my father couldn't make it. He'd take a handful of change to the bookmaker to try his luck, but rarely won.

Instead, he had to rely on my mother, a humiliation he found hard to bear, and she in turn amassed more debt. He couldn't have borrowed money if he'd tried – he'd never had a bank account and didn't understand the way they worked. He'd once made an appointment at the bank to enquire about a business loan to open a Jamaican café. He just walked into the local branch in Goodmayes, no business plan, no paperwork. *The manager took one look at him and laughed,* my mother said. It wasn't that my father had a bad financial history – he didn't have a history at all.

In the end he was depressed, frustrated and despairing – crying in the bathroom, his self-esteem crushed by his financial impotence. But more than that, I think he desperately missed his way of life – the thrill of playing through the night, all the shady characters he knew – fifty years of living off his nerve.

14
1947

*T*he boy sat on his blue leather trunk on the deck of the *Ormonde*. Waiting. They were two miles from England, the captain told them, but a thick mist obscured the sight of land. Before they could move on they needed clearance from the authorities, and so the ship was held offshore while it was decided if they would be permitted to dock. No one had expected this.

The boy walked along the deck, pulling his coat around him, so used to the rhythm of the ship on water. He wondered whether he'd be able to walk straight on land. It was March and the cold bit at his skin. All the fellows had their good suits on, polished shoes and smart coats, but the morning's excitement was waning. They milled around aimlessly, anchored for nearly four hours after three long weeks of sailing. Please God let them land today.

Three weeks. Three long weeks. What a journey. The boy had played cards the whole way, with chaps he'd met on the ship and some he knew from before. Rufus and he had planned to come together, had both bought their passage. But at the last minute – the day before the ship left – Rufus had knocked on the door of the boy's room to say he couldn't go. There was a girl he liked. He wanted to stay. So the boy had climbed aboard the *Ormonde* alone, only to find there were plenty of men he knew – some from Yallahs, some from Kingston and one he even knew from America: on the voyage's second day, he'd found Enoch Leaford sitting on deck with his nose in a book.

Some of the passengers were ex-servicemen who'd been in Britain before and told the others what they knew about their destination – fish and chips and rain, rain, rain, and documents. You needed paperwork and ration cards. You needed work permits. Others of the group had never left Jamaica, and said they were coming for a quick look-see. And no one planned to stay for more than five years. Make money, go home. Get rich quick, go back.

Among the passengers there was a sense of camaraderie – all of them doing this thing. When they found out there were stowaways on board, no one gave them up. Instead, clean shirts were found and the fellows let them share their sinks because nothing gives away a stowaway more than a dirty collar. When one was caught asleep in a lifeboat, they clubbed together to pay his fare.

Not all the men were Jamaican. En route, the boat had stopped at Trinidad and Havana. The boy had never met a Trinidadian before, but soon he was fast friends with Teddy Lyon from Port of Spain who joined him at the poker table most nights. And two boxers came aboard at Trinidad – Spike and Johnny King, brothers with a sponsor bringing them to England to fight. Most days of the voyage they would spar on the upper deck, marking a ring in chalk on the planking. Short and muscular, they skipped around each other in their long shorts, ducking punches, shooting quick jabs and uppercuts. Soon one of the fellows was running a book on them, and everyone was betting.

The boxers had an address to go to in Liverpool – a landlady their promoter had fixed them up with. They told the boy to come with them when they docked in case there was an extra room. The boy was grateful to them, but he knew why they'd asked him. Johnny King loved to play cards, had spent hours standing at the table, watching the boy shuffle and deal, and other times he'd ask the boy for card tricks – Follow the Lady and Slap the Deck, his eyes fixed to the boy's hands as though hypnotised.

The boy heard a muffled sound behind him and turned to see Haggai Tucker, a fellow he knew from Yallahs, all dressed up and sniffling into a hanky. 'Haggai, man. What you crying for?' he asked him. 'The English know we coming. They'll welcome us.' He put his hand on Haggai's shoulder. They had shared the walk to school as boys, chasing snakes and mongooses.

'I don't know why,' said Haggai. 'Just overwhelmed, is all. Happy too.'

And just then, a boom from the belly of the ship let them know the engine had started, and slowly the boat began moving forward, land appearing through the mist. Was it England? Yes! The sight had the same effect on all the fellows, all one hundred and fifty of them now stood along the rails of the deck in the dull light of March. The engines of the *Ormonde* were fully running and the ship sailed towards the dock, closer and closer. Were there hands raised in the distance? Yes! A crowd was gathered half a mile off, waving them in. One Jamaican fellow raised his hand, waving at England, then another, then the boy raised his hand, until all of them had raised their arms, and were waving.

And then all heads turned as they heard one splash, then another. 'Oh God,' said Haggai. 'What are they doing?' They watched as another man further along jumped from the ship into the water and began swimming – fast, frantic strokes towards the coast. 'There's got to be crocodiles in there!' Haggai said, staring into the murky brown water.

'It's the stowaways,' the boy said. 'I hope they make it.' There were eight men in the sea.

Haggai pulled himself up the rails. 'God be with you!' he shouted out to them. There were other calls along the deck.

'Good luck!' shouted the boy.

'Let them make it.' Haggai said. 'Please God, please God.'

◆

After the paperwork, the offloading and the long wait for stamps and documents, a nervous man from the Council stood on a crate at the side of the dock and spoke slowly to the Jamaicans, as though he were speaking to children. 'Some of you will go to London, under the care of the West Indian Servicemen's Association. Some of you will remain here in Liverpool to look for employment. Whichever the case, we wish you all good luck, and welcome you to England.'

The stowaways sat shivering in blankets on the dock, a policeman guarding them. They had been pulled from the water by the police and were to appear in court the next day, but all of them were fine. They raised their hands to wave as the other fellows began to disperse.

The boy went with the boxer brothers, each of them with a holdall, leaving trunks they'd come back for when they found the address of their digs. The sun was going down and it was freezing as they trudged uphill. Liverpool looked as uninviting as any place the boy had ever seen, with its ugly red-brick walls and ugly houses. The three of them walked in the direction they'd been pointed in, the address scrawled on a piece of paper, and the boy felt the eyes of everyone they passed on them. Suddenly he missed his old neighbourhood in Kingston, even the small room with its hard bed and leaking tap. He thought of the shop in Yallahs – the tumbledown shelves, the orange trees with their waxy leaves and heavy fruit. He thought of his father, the sun coming up there and James Lowe standing in the doorway of the shop with his cigarette, the first customers walking the road for cups of flour and jugs of milk. Something fell away inside of him. It was the talk of the boxers that kept him going, and the fact they were moving on either side of him that made him move too. All the excitement had transformed into a thick knot in his stomach, a sick feeling. He turned round and from the top of the hill could still see the funnels of the ship in the dock. The sea was a flat, grey sheet frozen on the grey sky. Where am I, he thought – Lord God, what am I doing?

15

CAN THE SUBALTERN SPEAK?

Turn your lights down low

– Bob Marley and the Wailers,
Exodus (1977)

It didn't take me long to fall in love with Brighton – the tall fairy-tale houses in pastel blues and pinks, the narrow lanes of ramshackle shops selling Chinese lanterns, incense, bohemian clothes. It was so pretty compared to Ilford. I went on long wintry walks along the seafront, the heavy grey waves crashing on the shale, and along the old wooden pier with its tea shops and seafood stalls and the ancient arcade. There were sweet little cafés and old, cramped pubs in which I drank with girls I'd met in my halls.

'Adam really likes you,' Jenny told me, over our pints of cider. 'You can tell by the way he looks at you.' Adam was a boy downstairs in my hall, whom I liked too. The day before, we'd been for a long walk over the South Downs, just the two of us. It was cold and misty as we stalked up the hill. I was perfectly capable of clambering over fences, but I'd let him help me, and I thought he might have kissed me when we stopped so he could tie his stripy scarf around my neck.

Instead, we both blushed and bumped into each other as we turned to walk back down.

I'd met him on the stairs of our halls on the second day. He was settling in, stepping around the stacks of records that took up half his floor space. He'd pinned an enormous poster of Bob Marley to his wall and one of Che Guevara. If these were student clichés, I didn't know it then. When we'd exchanged the niceties that characterised all my conversations that week – where we lived, what A-levels we'd taken, what we were here to study – and established that Adam was a devoted Tottenham Hotspur supporter, he invited me into his room.

'What sort of music are you into?' I asked, as he cleared a space on his single bed for me to sit.

'I like lots of stuff, but reggae the most.' I watched him moving things around. He had thick auburn hair, longish and a bit wild, and his features were strong – a long nose, thick eyebrows. He looked clever. 'I'll put some on,' he said, carefully slipping a record from its cover and resting it gently on the turntable. What he played wasn't like anything I'd heard before. A thick bass line resounded, pulsing slowly below electronic bleeps and reverb, and intermittently, the syncopated guitar of reggae and a man singing would filter in and out.

'It's dub reggae,' he said. 'Mixed up at Studio One in Kingston.' I hadn't a clue what he meant but I loved the sound. He reached into a drawer and pulled out a pack of Rizlas and a bag of bright green weed, rolling a long thin joint he tapped against his hand then lit. We smoked, listening to that feverish music, both lying back on his bed in a sweet cloud of smoke.

In the weeks to follow, Adam's room became a congregation space for dub reggae lovers – mostly white, middle-class boys – and the smell of cannabis wafted down his corridor to the hall's reception, the first thing you smelt when you came through the door. 'Blimey,' said the security guard to me one evening as I came down the stairs, flapping his hand in front of his nose, 'even I'm stoned! It's like this every year, I tell you, but this year is the worst!'

♠

'God, it's really white down here, ain't it?' said Holly, when she came to visit. We were in my room. 'And everyone's posh.' It was November, raining hard outside, the water streaming down the glass in grey streaks. I'd been so glad to see her when she arrived, dumping her bag and umbrella on the floor, flopping onto the bed and lighting a cigarette. Brighton was an hour from home by train, but I felt a million miles away, distanced more by the new people I'd met than by physical space. But I could tell Holly disapproved of my new life and friends when we went to the pub that night, and after, back in Adam's room, where a crowd of us got stoned, Holly sat back, quietly observing. 'Hannah's dad's from Jamaica,' Adam told the room. 'Mad, eh?' Holly pulled a face, and I cringed, seeing things through her eyes.

'No way, man,' said Piers, one of the dreadlocked regulars. His father was a millionaire who apparently owned a third of the world's rubber, but Piers always looked unwashed, wore ripped jeans and flip-flops even in winter. His only concession to the cold was his brightly coloured Ecuadorean cardigan. 'You don't look it, man,' he said to me, and I think I detected a trace of a put-on Jamaican accent. Holly tried not to laugh.

I had told Adam that my dad was Jamaican, but he hadn't met him, and I suspected he and the others might have thought my dad was an old Rastafarian sat at home in Ilford smoking from a chillum. But my father had liked jazz and blues and had left Jamaica way before reggae music had come around. At the time he'd lived there, Rastafarians were looked down upon, in fact. I wonder what he'd have made of those wealthy white kids with their dreadlocks and tie-dyed clothes. How different his Jamaica was from the one of their imagination.

'So, let me get this right,' Holly said the next morning. 'The boys smoke dope all day, and think they're black.' It wasn't a question. 'Rich idiots,' she declared. I was annoyed at her for judging so quickly, but there was truth in what she said. There was the wealth of the solid middle classes there. Most students I'd met had been to private school. Most were white. There were a few Asian students in the halls, but I'd not met anyone black.

'How the other half live, eh?' Holly said. 'Spending Daddy's money on a big bag of weed and their designer hippy clothes!'

♥

I spent most of my time that first term lying on Adam's bed, listening to reggae. We were a couple by then and I was a permanent fixture in his room, sleeping every night in a cannabis haze to the percussive hiss of a record still rotating on the turntable, the purple light of a lava lamp swirling low on the walls.

Late in autumn we caught the coach to London to the big student protests, marching with thousands of others through Piccadilly and Trafalgar Square. Afterwards, he took me to his parents' house, a big Victorian semi on a leafy street in north London. 'They're not back from France until Sunday night,' he said in his bedroom, 'but they can smell dope at a mile's distance.' I'd not met his parents, only knew his father was Hungarian and his mother was French. When he went home to watch the football, she sent him back with delicious tarte Tatin we'd devour at midnight, stoned and ravenously hungry. Now we leant out of his window, exhaling smoke into the cool evening air. Red leaves dropped from the trees onto the wide lawn. He pulled me closer. 'I love you,' he said and kissed me.

That night we went to the House of Roots, driving over the Thames to Vauxhall, parking up on a side street by the railway arches. 'Wait until you see this place,' Adam said. I could hear the bass line booming from outside, vibrating the red doors we went through. Inside, a single bulb lit a room with a low curved ceiling, beneath which half a dozen old Rastafarians were bent intently over games of chess and a woman in a bright headdress sold tea and ginger cake behind a counter. The bass thundered through the door to the main room, and as we went in, it hit me – a gust of noise that shook the walls and made the hairs on my arms stand up. Dim light inside, the speakers stacked in piles that reached the ceiling at the back, the strong sweet smell of cannabis, a white gauze in the air.

Men stood facing the front – Rastafarians whose dread-locks swung in thick ropes down their back, some in long robes that brushed the floor. They were entranced by the music and by the DJ, a little dreadlocked man who danced and swayed on the stage, placing records on his single turntable and twisting the knobs on his mixing station. This was the Aba-shanti Sound System, and Aba-shanti himself playing dub reggae, a phenomenon Adam had been talking about for months. Aba-shanti's shout of *Jah!* reverberated through the microphone as he bounced on the stage and the crowd called back, *Ras Tafari!*

'Amazing, isn't it?' Adam shouted over the noise, and it *was* amazing – the force of the music, the mood of the room, more like a religious service than a nightclub. I knew enough of Rastafarianism to know that, for some there, this was a genuinely religious ritual. If anyone objected to our being there, they didn't say. We were the only white faces. We danced for hours, passing joint after joint between us, and although I loved it, still I felt somehow intrusive, prying into a culture I didn't fully understand, acquiring only the elements I liked, namely the music and the dope. The walls around the room were draped in the Jamaican flag – black, yellow and green – and pictures of the Lion of Judah. The pale, thin face of Haile Selassie in fur cloak and crown looking disapprovingly down on us from his ornate golden frame.

The course on literary theory was bewildering. Each week, a small group of us sat on battered armchairs in the cramped office of Professor Jameson, pretending we understood the set reading. It was a whistle-stop tour through various complicated, philosophical approaches to literature – structuralism, post-structuralism, deconstruction, psychoanalysis and feminism. I don't think anyone in the seminar really understood the language or the basic concepts of the texts we read. At eighteen, we didn't understand enough about politics or history to situate the ideas. Each week left me more confused until I bought an idiot's guide to theory that explained the main points.

For the seminar on post-colonialism we'd been given a long essay, 'Can the Subaltern Speak?' by the Indian critic Gayatri Spivak. I'd spent two hours trying to make sense of it.

'So the question is, can the subaltern speak? Anyone?' Professor Jameson looked eagerly around the room, his eyebrows raised. They were an inch long and curled to the middle of his forehead. 'Hannah?' I jumped in my seat. 'What is your opinion? *Can* the subaltern speak?'

I'd discovered that week that the subaltern, in the context of the essay, were those who had been colonised – subaltern meaning 'lower in position', oppressed by those in power and stripped of power themselves. The question posed referred to whether they could ever speak for themselves, when they had continually been spoken for by those who had colonised them – or at least that's what I'd gathered from my reading. The example given was the ban of *sati* in India, the custom of self-immolation practised by women who throw themselves on their dead husbands' funeral pyres. Apparently there are endless accounts of this ritual written by the British colonisers, but rarely are the Hindu women invited to speak for themselves. Reading this, I could just imagine those women under the scrutinising lens of the British, making all kinds of conjectures about their lives and motivations.

'Umm,' I said, my mind racing. 'I'm not sure. Sort of yes and sort of no?' Professor Jameson's face told me he was waiting for me to elaborate, but I'd gone blank. I could feel my face turning red.

'Well,' he said, 'can anyone expand on Hannah's, um, point?' he asked the room, his disappointment evident. No one could.

But when I had to write a paper for the course, I came back to that essay. I thought about my father growing up under British rule in Jamaica. How his term for himself, 'West Indian', was actually a colonial term. I was learning academic terms for him – 'subaltern', 'other', 'colonial subject', and I understood a bit of what Spivak said – that Western academic writing about non-Western cultures tried to present itself as 'innocent' and without agenda, but in fact, always spoke from a place of power, always informed by the culture it spoke from, and by whom it was speaking to. In essence, it was white men in universities speaking to white men in universities about black men and women – describing and defining them. It struck me as ironic that my all-white seminar group were discussing these problems.

But it also struck a chord, one thought spiralling into another, moving back and forth from Spivak's essay. I thought of all the ways my father might be represented – all the stereotypes of him as a black man or a Chinese man; a Jamaican or an immigrant. What power did he have to define himself in any public way? He'd had no door to education, less chance of a decent job. In another world he might have been a mathematician or a politician or a teacher, a position to be proud of, one that used his mind – like the fathers of my new friends who worked as magistrates and diplomats and bank managers. Not a gambler or card sharp, scraping an immoral living in seedy clubs and dives. The gambling world, with its own hierarchies and allegiances, might have been the only place he had agency or authority, regardless of skin colour, but it never extended beyond the card club's walls.

It was a secret and silent life – a night-time existence in the underbelly of London, untraceable through official records or legitimate channels. My father had lived on the margins all his life, and not through choice. Born poor and black in Jamaica, the odds were always stacked against him. Most of all, I thought about how these academic thoughts and arguments weren't at all about abstractions – they were about real people's lives, my father's life.

◆

That Christmas I went back to the house in Ilford, where the Christmas tree stood in the front-room window, sagging under the weight of tinsel and too many baubles. My father had been in hospital for a stomach ulcer, but had come home that morning, looking thinner than ever. 'Hello, Han,' he said solemnly from the sofa, folding his paper.

'Happy Christmas, Dad!' I said brightly.

'Hmm. Happy Christmas, I suppose,' he said. 'But when you've seen as many Christmases as I have, they're no longer of interest.'

'That's the spirit – happy bloody Christmas!' my mother chipped in. She was arranging presents under the tree. 'Oh, I forgot to tell you,' she said, looking at me. 'Solomon Kallakuri died.'

'What?' I said. 'Solomon?' I hadn't thought of him in years. 'What did you say?'

'Yes, it's a bit bleak, I'm afraid, love,' she said, getting up. 'It was in the newspaper. And then a reporter phoned the house, asking did I know this, did I know that? Because I used to teach him, remember? When he was five. He was a little rascal then, but I didn't tell them that.' She left the room and came back with the paper, handing it to me, but I couldn't read it. I'd never known anyone my age who had died. I couldn't believe Solomon was dead.

I read the article in my room that night. It was worse than I could have imagined. Solomon Kallakuri had become a small-time drug dealer. He'd been sent to prison, not for dealing, but for GBH against a local man who apparently owed him money. Solomon had gone to his house, tied him up and, according to the paper, tortured him with a hot poker. Torture? I couldn't imagine Solomon doing anything like that. The paper used the words *mindless* and *frenzied*. Apparently he'd been sentenced to seven years in Belmarsh Prison, and was found dead in his cell two weeks ago. He'd hanged himself. God, I thought. What had happened to him? I remembered that day I'd seen him in Sam's bedroom, playing tough guy with the older boys; the day he'd come into school with his lip busted like a split plum. I lay on my bed and cried. Little Solomon, the first boy I ever kissed, the only boy in the gymnastics team. The first boy I had loved.

♠

Christmas Day followed the same routine as always. My parents and I sat in the living room, waiting for Sam to come downstairs in his boxer shorts and insist we open presents. He was back from Nottingham for Christmas. I hadn't seen him in months. 'Did you hear about Solomon Kallakuri?' I asked him when he appeared. I was older now and less in awe of him, and he less easily annoyed by me.

'Yeah, Mum said,' he replied. 'I hardly knew him, but he was a bit off his head. Sad, though.' It was sad, and I couldn't shake the sadness all day. My father was in a gloomy mood as well. I gave him his present – a biography of Nelson Mandela and a pair of socks. 'Happy Christmas, Dad!' I tried to be cheerful.

'Happy Christmas,' he said. 'If you insist.'

My father might have seen too many Christmases but he was still an aficionado of the traditional English Christmas rituals – pulling his cracker at lunchtime, wearing his paper hat, reading out his awful joke before carving up the turkey. But he hardly ate a thing, and by the afternoon he was asleep on the sofa in the back room, not waking until bedtime. 'Come on, you lazy lump!' my mother said, shaking him gently. I was standing in the door watching them. It took a long time for him to come round, and when he did he gripped his stomach in pain. 'What's wrong?' she said.

'Just very painful,' my father said. He was struggling to sit up, his arms wrapped around his middle. 'Must be the ulcer – back again already, do you think?'

'Maybe,' my mother said. She helped him to his feet. 'Or too much turkey,' she said jollily, pulling him to his feet, her face full of worry.

♥

After Christmas, I moved from halls into a dilapidated Victorian house in Brighton, sharing with three friends. It might have been nice once but now the walls were peeling, the window frames held cracked glass and bright green moss grew on the bathroom walls and ceiling. Still I loved the house – light poured in through the tall windows and you could climb onto the roof and sit beside the chimney, watching seagulls swooping between the rooftops. I was sitting there in the winter sun when the phone rang and I clambered back through the attic window, rushing down the battered stairs to pick it up. 'Listen, love.' It was my mother. 'I've got some news.'

It could have been anything, but I knew it was about my father. My stomach tightened.

'Your dad's just back from the hospital. And the doctor said he's got cancer. Of the stomach. They're going to operate next week.'

Cancer. Oh God. I thought of him at Christmas, looking so thin, his clothes hanging off him. 'Is it bad?' I didn't know anything about cancer, except it could kill you. But this cancer could be caught, my mother told me. They'd found it early. They would remove part of my father's stomach and kill the rest of the cells with chemotherapy.

'And he'll be right as rain,' she said. 'Will you come home next week and see him after the operation?'

'Yes, Mum,' I said. 'I'll come.' I paused. 'Is he there now?'

'Yes, he's sat here with his cup of tea. Do you want to talk to him?'

I thought about it for a second. I wouldn't know what to say. 'No,' I said. 'No, I won't. But tell him I'll come and see him next week.' I hung up.

I have a clear memory of going to see my father in hospital after his cancer operation. He is sitting up in the ward bed under the bright lights, a drip in one arm. On the bedside cabinet: a bottle of Lucozade, his glasses, a newspaper. The image reminds me of all the times I visited him in hospital as he recovered from one operation or another.

I remember him singing old Jamaican folk songs to the nurses. High on morphine, singing at the top of his voice, a nurse laughing but asking him to sing more quietly. 'Think of the other patients, Mr Lowe.' 'Call me Chick,' he tells her.

'I come from Jamaica. I used to sing these as a boy.' And something about the way he sings announces that he means to survive. Yes, the cancer has come for him, but no, it's not his time. Look what the marvellous NHS can do! They can dose you up and cut you, and pump you full of chemicals, stop the bad cells raging, stick a tube in here, a tube in there, hang a clipboard at the bed's end, covered in scrawl you can't understand a word of but the doctors can; the doctors understand, sweeping through the wards with pens in hand, a tick in this box, a cross in another, and hey ho you're fixed, and heading home.

In my memory, my father pulls his blanket up and raises his pyjama top, saying 'What d'you think of this, Han?' He is proud of the neat scar across his abdomen, a long thin smile, a little red at its puckered edges but already half healed.

But years later, my mother told me that I didn't go to the hospital.

'You came back from university the day after he had the operation. And I was driving to the hospital, but suddenly you had something more important to do. Shopping, you said. You had to get something from the shops in Ilford.' She was disgruntled, remembering.

'What?' I said. 'No, I definitely did go, Mum. I remember Dad singing to the nurses.'

'No, you didn't go at all. *I* told you about the singing. He was off his head on bloody morphine, singing to the nurses and to Mac and Sylvester. All the old boys went to see him, but you couldn't be bothered.'

I could tell from the way she said it that it was true. I didn't go. Why couldn't I remember what had happened? Why could I remember what *didn't* happen?

I could still hear him singing to those nurses, could still hear his good clear voice:

> *She had the man piaba, woman piaba,*
> *Tantan, Fallback and Lemon Grass,*
> *Minnie Root, Gully Root, Grannie*
> *Back Bone,*
> *Bitter Tally, Lime Leaf and Toro,*
> *Coolie Bitters, Caralia Bush,*
> *Flat o' the Earth and Iron Weed,*
> *Sweet Broom ...*

◆

I came home the following summer and worked back at the pizza restaurant. I was saving money for California, for the exchange year that was part of my course. It was a strange time, waiting to leave. Adam and I broke up in an amicable way. He was going to Italy for a year, and a year seemed like infinite time back then; more practical to call things off, but our pragmatism didn't stop me missing him.

My father's chemotherapy had finished and he'd been given the all-clear. He was cheerful, pottering around the house fixing door handles, putting up shelves. We fell back into our usual routine – him driving me here and there, and finally dropping me at the airport in September, insisting on wheeling my suitcases through to the departure gates, where we had an awkward goodbye as I joined the long queue. I turned back as I passed through the metal detector and he was still standing there, looking for me, as people passed to and fro around him.

♠

Santa Cruz in California was long beaches and small coves where the Pacific waves crashed on the sand. There was a giant rollercoaster on the boardwalk and a main street where old hippies lolled on the sidewalk with wrecked guitars, tattooed stars below their eyes. One side of town was wealthy – big timber houses painted in pastels set back from the wide, leafy streets. A river divided those avenues from a run-down neighbourhood of graffitied concrete duplexes – a scrappier, edgier place where Mexicans lived, and which we international students had been told to avoid after dark.

We mingled with the rich kids who went to the university, its campus on a rolling hill overlooking the ocean, a far cry from most British universities. There was an Olympic-sized swimming pool, a state-of-the-art gym, an amphitheatre where Shakespeare festivals took place. The faculty buildings had won prizes for architecture – the bold postmodern angles and colours contrasted with the redwood forest the buildings nestled in, giant trees shading the walkways and bridges, the tallest trees I'd ever seen. Students' families paid a hefty sum to send them there, and in return the university treated them like customers whose needs should be met. We were lucky. An exchange year meant an American student had paid their fees for each of us and taken up our place in England.

Browsing the brochure of campus accommodation before I left, I discovered there was the option to live in racially segregated halls. I couldn't believe it. You could choose the Pacific-Islander hall, the Afro-American hall, the Mexican-American hall. The logic, I think, was that some people preferred to live among their own kind, a position updated from its bleak origins in Jim Crow segregation to what was now a *positive* choice, to enhance the racial harmony on campus. I didn't understand it until I lived in America, and realised that the myth of the melting pot was just that – a myth of assimilation and equality. There was a non-white middle class, but generally to be black or Mexican in America meant to be poor, and this divide was reflected in the cities and towns I saw – San Francisco, San Jose, Los Angeles – where racial communities lived separately. This, to me, was much more evident than in Britain, and soon the segregated halls made sense – they reflected the real-world apartheid which, I assume, some students were comfortable with.

I was lonely in Santa Cruz at first – homesick for Brighton, for Ilford, for my family. The leaflet for foreign students told us to expect culture shock, but I wondered how different America could be from what I knew. I'd seen hundreds of American films, followed American bands, read American books. I knew the place I was coming to. But I don't think culture shock is about the superficial things like currency, or eating foreign food, or hearing different accents. It's the shock of realising that another world exists in parallel to yours. I lived in America now, but my old world carried on regardless with everyone I knew still in it – five thousand miles and half a day away. Even now I find it hard to accept that while people sleep away the night on one side of the world, the other side are busy and awake, let alone the belief of some scientists that there are infinite parallel worlds, all playing out simultaneously.

In my first days in America I thought of my father – the only person I knew who'd uprooted himself from one life to another – leaving Jamaica, his arrival in England. Had he felt what I felt now? I wondered. Disorientation, a sense of unreality, a longing for familiarity, any anchor of home.

A few weeks after I'd left, an airmail envelope arrived in the post. Inside was a long letter from my mother, telling me all the things she wished she'd said before I left, how she was suddenly lost for words as we drove away, how proud she was of me. It was uncharacteristically emotional.

And you know Dad's proud of you too, she wrote. *I know he can be a pain, but don't forget he's twenty years older than me and so pleased to see you both having chances and making the most of them. Things he never had a hope in hell of achieving. Think of where he came from – he regards your achievements as his, and in a way, they are.*

I folded the letter neatly and slipped it into my desk drawer.

♣

In the end, Santa Cruz itself was a rollercoaster of hedonism, facilitated by a crowd of gregarious new friends who, like me, were off the leash, unbound to partake in a range of iniquitous pleasures I don't think my parents would have been proud to see – whiskey and pear cider were my tipples at the local Irish bar, the only one in town that accepted my fake ID. My downtown room-mate funded his studies through drug-dealing, but was a pinnacle of abstinence himself. Such level-headed acumen was not my forte. I had a credit card that bore the brunt of my indulgences. I'd worry about the debt when I got home.

There were men I fell for. I always fell so hard. First Bill, ten years older, a college administrator. He was as lonely as I was, fresh from Boston with a broken heart. Then Peter, an art student who styled himself on Motown and made me mix tapes of Marvin Gaye and Al Green. He wanted to come to England the following year. It took me weeks to find the heart to tell him no. Then Richie, then Jake, then Saul from Costa Rica, a barman who played guitar and smoked cocaine. I wanted him the most.

My mother came to see me at Easter.

'You've put on weight,' she said, and she was right. I was drinking too much, not exercising, eating junk food. But she looked well, like a different woman. She'd given up smoking since I'd left, and lost two stone. We spent a weekend at Yosemite, a few days in San Francisco, a week in Santa Cruz. But away from home, my mother became shy – too reticent to ask directions or buy tickets or talk to strangers. I had to do it all. This wasn't her territory, and it was strange to see her lack of confidence. Two weeks was a long time to chaperone. I wanted to get back to my friends.

I was young and high-living, I told myself, pursuing no-strings decadence. It was a year removed from real life. But when I look back, the good memories aren't really good, not wholly good, more like a happy photograph where something bad lurks just outside the frame. I was learning that life was precarious, its foundations unstable. Somewhere in my consciousness, my father's cancer skulked. I hadn't forgotten the thin smile of his scar.

◆

Somehow I still managed to get top marks at Santa Cruz, proving that, for a time, the old ideal of *work hard, play hard* can be achieved, that a person can be two things at once. We had far more lectures than at Brighton, and a surprisingly radical course catalogue to choose from. I took yoga for a semester, the marks from which, albeit a tiny percentage, went towards my overall degree. Aside from this frivolity, I studied modules in Chicano writing, black American playwriting, ethnic memoir. Where the material conditions of black experience in America might still be unequal, the study of black culture and expression was sophisticated – way ahead of the UK. I was building a foundation in the study of black literature in its broadest sense, linked back to the interests I had developed in Brighton – how politics and literature aligned, how writing could resist oppression through testimony, dismantle stereotypes, challenge the status quo. It didn't occur to me then that these interests might be personal, linked to my family history, my father's life story. I couldn't see the picture that broadly then.

I made it back from America in the nick of time. When classes finished I wasted two months partying, not eating enough, not sleeping enough, somewhere between adventurer and girl on self-destruct.

♠

I saw my father before he saw me at the airport, taking in his wild hair, his shoulders slumped as he stood searching the crowd in an echo of the day he'd dropped me off.

'Hello, Han!' he called as I walked over.

'Hello, Dad,' I said. 'What are you doing here?'

'Thought you'd like a lift,' he said. 'Good flight?' We both knew a kiss or hug might fit this occasion better but awkward platitudes would suffice. I let him take my suitcase.

It had been my twenty-first birthday the day before, and to mark both that and my last day in America, a friend had driven me to a piercing parlour where a heavily tattooed man had driven a metal spike through the thick middle cartilage of my ear, fixing a stainless-steel ring in place. On the plane, I'd slept against it, but hadn't noticed it had bled until I looked in the car's wing mirror to see a thread of dried blood snaking down my neck and chest. It fitted the surreal drive home, the slate sky, the London streets looking particularly grey, my father full of gloomy prophesies.

'Tony Blair will send Britain to the dogs,' he declared on the motorway. 'Everyone thinks he's great, but mark my words, he's bad news.'

I'd stayed up watching the elections a few months before, all the British students glued to the television screen as 'Things Can Only Get Better' played, and after eighteen years of Tory government, the newly elected Prime Minister walked onto stage to tell the nation a new dawn had broken.

'But why do I care?' my father continued. 'I'm not long for the world. I doubt I'll see next year.' We crossed Tower Bridge, drove down the Romford Road, past the side streets where his old gambling haunts lay. He lit a cigarette, and I said nothing – no half-hearted reassurances, no expression of the irritation I felt. I was determined to be the cheerful returnee, pleased to see everyone – I forced myself to overlook the shadows on the picture.

By the time we reached Ilford, America already felt like a garish, edgy dream, and home a depressing reality. My father took up his place in his armchair, staring out of the window. I went up to my room. My mother had gifted my bed with sunny new sheets and pillow cases. I buried my face in them and cried.

♥

My last year of university was quieter. I rented a damp flat on the seafront, freezing cold through winter, but I loved the bracing sea wind, the trudge along the seafront where the burnt wreck of the West Pier stood in the water, starlings swooping around its charred frame.

I saw Adam now and again. He lived nearby, and I'd pop round for dinner, sitting with him in his room, listening to records like we used to. He was always so kind to me, not like the men I'd known abroad. His clear eyes looked at me and saw someone to be enthusiastic about. It always took me by surprise. 'Shall we get back together?' he asked one day. Even now I wonder how it would have been to say yes to someone so kind, how simple more time with him might have been.

But I said no. I wanted to be alone. America had left me with a hangover of sorts. I'd seen too much of the world, been too intrepid. I was more anxious, more prone to bouts of sadness that lasted for days. I wouldn't have called it depression back then, but there was a seeping melancholy I found hard to shake. I lost interest in clubs and parties, slept a lot in my small room, and, strangely, started to go back to Ashgrove Road, often for weeks at a time. I found my parents' presence comforting – even my father's dejection was something solid to rely on. I played Scott Joplin on the piano and wrote my dissertation at the computer in the front room, my mother bringing cups of tea, my father cooking dinner, the three of us passing the evening watching TV.

My graduation was a long, formal affair in a seafront hotel. Afterwards, we gathered in the bar to celebrate. In the photographs my mother looks well and my father looks happy. I remembered my mother's letter, her words about his pride in me. I was older now – why not let him feel my achievements as his own? It didn't seem to matter now. He pulled a packet from his jacket pocket, a small parcel in white tissue paper that he held out to me. I unwrapped it to find a thin gold bracelet set with diamonds, a thread-like clasp, much more delicate than anything I owned. 'George at the club had some rings and bracelets,' he said. 'I thought you'd like this one.' He looked hopeful.

It might have been off the back of a lorry but I was touched. My mother always bought our birthday gifts, our Christmas gifts. It was the first thing he'd ever given me himself. 'Thanks, Dad,' I said, allowing him to do it up for me. 'It's lovely.'

Across the road from the hotel my friends and I stood on the shingle beach and tossed our mortar boards into the air for the camera. When I look at the picture, I see the carefree, cocky young things we were – shouting at the sky, on the verge of our adult lives.

16

1949

*T*he boy was being shaken awake, a hand on his shoulder. 'Chick, wake up, man!'

'Eh?' The boy rolled onto his back, squinting at the light sloping in through the small window, half blocked by the silhouette of the man standing over him. It was Lionel, a Trinidadian he'd met in London, his friend and roommate. 'What time is it?'

'Time for me to be asleep, and you to be standing here,' Lionel said, jigging from foot to foot. 'Come on, man, it's freezing out here.'

The boy rolled up slowly from the warmth of the bed they shared in shifts, and Lionel jumped in, pulling the blankets up to his neck. He was taller than the boy and his big feet stuck out from the bed's end. He wrestled with the blankets until he was covered head to toe. 'Hmmm, good you keep it so warm for me.' He said the same thing each morning, his eyes already closed.

The boy dressed in the corner of the room. Vest, shirt, overalls, two pairs of socks, boots, coat, two pairs of gloves, a woollen hat. The black bricks of the room were wet with trickling water, a sound they were both used to now. This was the coal cellar of a crumbling old Victorian house on a run-down street in Paddington. The old lady who owned it lived on the two floors above in rooms the boy had never seen. They could hear her wireless and her slow footsteps through the ceiling, but the door to the cellar was a separate one which she had told them they must use. Stone steps led from their room to a trapdoor into the house, but she had had it bolted down, as though she were scared of the two black men.

Every time the boy knocked on the door to pay her rent, her face froze with fear before she recognised him, taking the envelope quickly from his hand. 'Everything all right down there?' she'd say coyly, as though she couldn't believe they'd pay the rent she'd asked and knew it was an outrage to let that dank cave to them, so cold their bare feet turned numb on the stone floor, no heating, no hot water, only a cold tap and plastic basin, a two-ring hotplate to cook on. She'd told them no women were allowed down there, no friends, no music, no late nights.

'Yes, Ma'am,' the boy would reply, silently cursing her. He had tried for two weeks to find a room – sleeping in a Lyon's Corner House until the manager had asked him to leave, walking the streets, sleeping in the dance hall – before this greedy old lady with her rheumy eyes had opened the door to him. He knew he was lucky to have somewhere. *No blacks, no dogs, no Irish.* He'd seen the sign in ten windows, and each time his stomach flipped – was it *him* those signs were meant for? Never in his wildest dreams had he imagined they would be so unwelcome. Sometimes he couldn't believe this was London, couldn't believe this was England. But this *was* London – a grey and broken place after the war – gaps like missing teeth in the streets where houses used to stand, barbed wire cordoning off the bombsites of rubble in the street, paving stones cracked and warped underfoot.

The boy had stayed only a week in Liverpool in a run-down guest house on the dock. There had been no room at the boxers' lodgings, their landlady had told them that the first day, eyeing the boy suspiciously. In the end, he'd taken the train to King's Cross, marvelling at London's vast brick buildings and the thousand chimneys spread on the horizon. He'd heard there was better pay here. All those chimneys must mean work, he thought, staring from the window and at the same time wondering where among those factories and houses a man might roll a dice or deal a hand of cards.

In the winter chill, he rode the bus across the Thames, back towards King's Cross to his shift at the Somers Town Goods Yard. He worked there for months as a shunter, assembling and breaking up the strings of freight wagons, the first job the Labour Exchange had pulled up for him. Each day he ran along the tracks beside the moving trains, already loaded with fruit or bicycles or sacks of flour, a bar in his hands to turn the brakes, lifting his feet from the ground to ride the air until the wagon came to a halt. Then he'd lock it to another one – click-clack, click-clack – just as the next came into view, running the tracks from the marshalling yard.

It was hard work and dangerous. He'd seen another Jamaican fellow knocked to the ground unconscious by a wagon he couldn't stop. They'd carried him off on a stretcher and the boy hadn't seen him since. He hadn't asked the other three men he worked with if they knew anything; knew they'd answer with only grunts or silence.

Harry was the worst. He said nothing to the boy's face, but he'd stand with the other men at break, jibing at the black fellows in the yard. Beside the milk and fish depots was an enormous shed where crate upon crate of bananas ripened, waiting to be sold at the market next door.

'Oi, Abdul!' Harry would call at a black chap walking past, pointing at the banana shed. 'Your lunch is in there!'

'With the rest of the monkeys!' another would call as they stood in their dirty clothes, laughing into their mugs of tea. They had nothing better to do.

Each month there were more Caribbean men at the yard, but still only a handful in the huge workforce. The boy knew them all. In this cold country, he was always grateful to see a black face. Sometimes he saw a black man on the other side of the street and called out to him, crossing over just to ask him where he came from and pass the time of day.

Of the white men, only Keith was different, and then only if the other two were gone. He was just nineteen and lived in Bow with his mother and grandparents. His father was missing in service. Some evenings it was just Keith and the boy on shift. They sat together at the side of the tracks with a flask of tea, the yard suddenly quiet for a moment between the clatter of trains. There was something beautiful about Somers Town, the boy thought – all that brick and metal, the hatching of tracks snaking off into the distance under a wide grey sky. They'd learned about the industries of Britain in his island classroom, but the boy had never understood what it might really mean – the smell of oil, the clunk of steel on steel, the vast size and scale of it all. Even a farm as big as Cranthorn's was nothing compared to this.

'So, d'you have trains in Jamaica?' Keith asked the boy. 'What about schools? What about the police? D'you have policemen in Jamaica?' Keith's curiosity about Jamaica was seemingly endless, and the boy would always fill him in.

'Of course we have schools,' he said, wondering how Keith, like the Americans he'd known, had never heard the word Jamaica until the boy's first day, as though it were planet Mars or the moon. 'And we have shops, and dance halls and cinemas, the same as you.'

Sometimes the boy would pull a pack of cards from his pocket, rubbing his hands for warmth before he held the deck out to Keith. 'Cut them anywhere,' he told him. Keith split the deck, revealing an ace of spades. 'That's your card,' the boy continued, lifting the deck to Keith's face. 'Now blow on it for good luck.' Keith took a deep breath, blew, keeping his eyes open as the ace disappeared, replaced by the four of hearts.

'Bloody 'ell, Chick. How d'you do it? What, you got it up yer sleeve or something?'

The boy laughed.

'You're like my uncle,' Keith said. 'He's always got a pack of cards in hand. Plays poker and all sorts in the back of the Nag's Head.'

'What's that?' the boy said.

'Pub round the back of ours,' Keith said. 'A right den of iniquity, my nan says.' He stood up. 'She won't set foot in there, and she'd kill me if she knew I did. The police are always raiding it.' He chuckled. 'Come on, we should get back on the job, I suppose.'

♣

After work, the boy's body hurt from head to toe. His hands ached from gripping the steel bars, his feet hurt from running. He caught the bus back over the river, glad for the smoky warmth of the top deck, the heat from other bodies, although sometimes the whole deck would fill, with only the seat next to him empty. The boy knew why.

How strange this country is, he thought. Some days he moved in a surreal daze through the city, made stranger because he knew the grand statues and landmarks, the red buses and phone boxes, so well – images from his school books and newspapers back home. But now they were disjointed from his imagination by the reality of England – the constant noise, the yellow lights, the dirt and the grime. And the people were nothing like the rich white men and women in Jamaica. Most of the English were poor. He had never expected that. And old. So many young men were lost or hurt in the war – grey old women cleaned the streets and old men took bus fares.

Often he thought of Mr Ho Choy, Felix and Mr Manny, and wondered what they were doing. He missed the warmth of his people, the easy talk, knowing where you stood with another fellow. He missed his mother. Even the memory of his father's face was a pang for home.

◆

That winter, it snowed. The boy had seen snow before in Maine and New Jersey, but it was Lionel's first time. Four inches settled overnight and in the early morning the street looked wonderfully clean and bright. 'The whole world's gone white!' said Lionel as he clambered up the basement steps and out into the road, marvelling at his sunken footprints. 'I never thought snow would feel like this,' he said, scooping a handful from the ground. 'Or be so cold.' He frowned.

'Like this damn country,' the boy said, bending to lift a handful. Two women were walking on the other side of the street. The shorter, squat one looked disapprovingly at them and tutted loudly.

The boy turned to her, suddenly angry. 'We're just two men stood in the snow!' he said, his hands spread. 'Is that a crime?'

The woman looked aghast. 'How dare you!' she said to the boy. 'You darkies come here and think you can behave any way you want. Well, we won't have it, we won't have it at all.'

'Come on, Maeve,' her friend said, pulling on her arm. She looked at the boy, her face friendlier. 'You can't go round frightening old women, you know,' she said to him.

'We don't want any trouble here,' said Lionel, coming up next to the boy, the snow still in his hand.

'We're not doing anything, Lionel,' the boy said. 'Just looking at the snow.'

'Well, that's no crime,' the kinder woman said. 'I don't s'pose you have it where you come from.' She turned, pulling her friend away, but the other woman hadn't finished.

'We won't *have* it, do you understand?' she said, red in the face. 'You darkies should go back to your own home.' She straightened her coat.

The kinder one yanked on her friend's arm. 'Good day to you,' she said over her shoulder.

'How can you be *nice* to them?' the boy heard the other one say. He shook his head as they stood watching the women walk away. 'You should watch yourself, man,' Lionel said, looking worried. 'I don't trust the English. Who knows who those old ladies gon' tell?'

♠

At Somers Town, they told the boy the marshalling yard was closed.

'Till when?' he asked, thinking of the rent due in a few days.

'Till there's no more snow, Chick,' the clerk in the entry booth told him. 'Go home and put your feet up.' The boy thought of sitting in the freezing cave watching Lionel snore. This can't go on, he thought.

It was lunchtime. He found a café on Euston Road for a cup of tea, then caught the bus to Bow, following the directions Keith had given him.

The Nag's Head was a run-down place on the corner, a hulk of peeling paint. There were the remnants of gold gilt on the horse's head on the sign over the door. Blacked-out windows at the back. Two men trudged quickly through the snow, their collars pulled up, glancing at the boy before entering the pub.

The boy blew on his hands, straightened his coat, and followed them in.

17

DOWN TO THE FELT

The art of losing isn't hard to master

— Elizabeth Bishop, *One Art*

It was bad luck to move from Ashgrove Road. My parents had lived there for thirty years, but the house was too expensive to keep. It was old and draughty with a leaking roof and the boiler on its last legs. My father's cancer was in remission but he was still unwell with high blood pressure and a poorly heart. He was barely earning any money. With Sam and me gone they didn't need the room, and so in my last year of university they sold the house. Only now does it seem to matter that I didn't have a chance to say goodbye to my old bedroom, the cherry tree, our mossy pond, even the dark, dusty loft that scared me as a child.

Our new house was my cousins' old house, a mile or so from Ashgrove Road. Perhaps it was my mother's urge for familiarity that made her buy it. Over the years we'd spent more time there than anywhere else. Now my cousins had left and Uncle Terry had moved away with his girlfriend. The new house was smaller with compact, boxy rooms, but it overlooked a big park with a lake, and there was a long garden and an attic room with a skylight that let light stream in.

Chloe kept running back to the old house. Each time, Irish Bridget would phone to say she'd found the dog on the path and my father would go and pick her up. Chloe was an old dog then, following a scent that led her over two main roads to Ashgrove Road. How strong her urge to return must have been.

The last time she did it, she was hit by a car. It was night-time, heavy rain, Chloe scuttling in car headlights, drivers skidding to avoid her. The first my mother knew was when a woman called to say Chloe had been hit but was still alive. At the vet's, my parents found her on the table, two broken legs, blood in her fur. Her tail slowly lifted and thumped when she saw them, but she was cold when my mother touched her, her breathing slow. The vet said she didn't have a chance. She died a few minutes later. They buried her in the back garden of the new house, but we all knew she should have been laid in the garden of Ashgrove Road, where her old rubber bones were buried and the familiar rattle of the trains might soothe her.

If my parents felt the loss of Chloe, or the old house, they didn't say so. Even as my mother told me Chloe had been killed, she was stoic, almost cheerful. I wished she would say how sad she was. She loved that dog. Chloe was part of our family. Sometimes, I wondered if my parents had their own emotional camaraderie, a private rapport behind bedroom doors, where they declared their love, or talked deeply and intimately, sharing their fears, their regrets and griefs, their hopes for us, their children. Perhaps to each other they confided the sorrow of leaving Ashgrove Road, where Nan had lived and died, where my brother and I had been raised, where they had socialised and loved and laughed, as well as fought and despaired. But I doubt it. I don't remember ever hearing them say they loved each other; can't recall a single kiss or hug.

The only open display of emotion I remember was when my father, not long before he died, lifted his head from his newspaper and said to me, 'Your mother is a good woman. One of the best.' And with that pronouncement, he went back to reading, and I pretended not to have heard.

♥

Soon after I graduated I moved into a house in Clapham with friends from university – a tall, decaying Victorian house on a street behind the railway. We were all trying to find meaningful work, wishing we'd taken more notice of the careers advice offered in the final year. What a fall from grace it was to discover that after four years of being encouraged to find my own voice, think independently and express my opinions, all prospective employers cared about was how fast I could type and whether I could use Microsoft Excel. I took the first job I was offered – in a university department, each morning catching the Tube to a dusty office on Baker Street where the head of department, a haughty professor of business studies, handed me a pile of scrawled notes to type and a stack of photocopying it took all morning to finish. No matter how I willed it on, the clock's hand ticked round more slowly as the day progressed.

I enrolled in a master's degree I saw advertised in the newspaper. Anything to stave off my rapidly-developing brain rot. The course was Refugee Studies, its focus on the 'lived experience of migration', studying the reasons people moved from one country to another, the psychosocial impact of migration, how diasporic communities formed themselves in exile. The other students were a mix – some were refugees themselves, from Sierra Leone, Rwanda, Bosnia, Palestine. Others were people who worked in the field as legal advisors or caseworkers. One of these was a human rights advocate, fifteen years older than me, with whom I embarked on a brief but passionate fling, attracted to him only because I admired his work.

I look back now and can see how my father's story, still half unknown to me, was the catalyst to my need to learn these other stories, not of economic migrants like he was, but of frightened, desperate people escaping war, persecution, horrors I couldn't imagine, and how they awoke in other lives – safer, yes, but uprooted, living the shock of displacement, subject to legal machinations and legislation, a popular media that sought to discredit them as strangers, scroungers, spongers. It was the same story over and over. They'd been coming for thousands of years, but this country didn't like foreigners.

'Your mum's ill, Han,' my father told me on the phone. It might have been the first time he'd ever phoned me. 'Can you come over?'

'What's wrong with her?' I asked.

'The doctor said it's Bell's palsy, but I don't think it is. Can you come?'

I admit, I was annoyed with him for phoning. Sam was home. Surely between the two of them they could work out what was wrong with my mother. It was because I was the girl. If anything ever needed organising or taking care of, it was always me my parents turned to, never my brother. 'Phone the doctor,' I said. 'See if he can come out and see her. I can't today but I'll come tomorrow.' I hung up.

I was just leaving the house the next day when the phone rang. It was my father again. 'Your mother's in hospital,' he said. 'We didn't realise. She's had a stroke.'

I remember the bus journey from the Tube to the hospital, the long walk through the corridors to the ward where my mother was propped up in bed wearing an old T-shirt. She looked the same, albeit dishevelled. She wasn't paralysed, she could still speak. I took those things as signs she was fine. The doctor said 'mild stroke'. She would be home in a few days.

It took weeks or months for the stroke's effects – not on her body, but on her mind – to show themselves fully, and they were severe enough that she had to give up work. There was nothing mild about the transformation she underwent. Where my old mother had been stoic and reserved, this new mother was confused, tearful and sentimental – she talked to her pets as though they were human, cried at the television, cried at the radio. My old mother had had endowment policies and insurance, had kept things just under control, but the new one was reckless, buying things she didn't need or want because the act of spending was a comfort. My old mother had kept an ordered house with everything in its place. The new one hoarded and amassed, decked the walls with wonky photographs in cracked frames, crammed every inch of shelf with vases and trinkets, until the whole house had the look of her mind – mawkish, over-brimming, disarrayed.

Each time I saw her, some new eccentricity would reveal itself, the effects of the stroke always in flux, more evident when she was tired, and sometimes I saw her old self in a fleeting glance. I found that the hardest. Other people thought the difference was subtle. They didn't know her well enough to see her mind was an unhappy muddle. She was depressed, wanting her old self back and things to be as they had been – a place she would eventually reach, but not before several years had passed.

I think of my parents in that house now – two sick people caring for each other, the blind leading the blind. I think they found a new peace after years of ups and downs, a different way of loving each other, knowing they might lose each other. They moved through the old routines in the way they always had – my father cooking, my mother tending to the garden in her new, haphazard way – crowding the patio with plants she didn't water, building a water feature in the middle of the lawn – too large and grand for its small patch of grass. They bought a new dog and called her Ellie, another mongrel, smaller than Chloe but just as neurotic. Some evenings that summer they took her out together, walking slowly around the park.

I found it hard to see them. I didn't visit enough. Instead I threw myself back into to a heady social life of parties and clubs, doing my day job sufficiently, my MA sufficiently, spending my wages on clothes and cigarettes and drink and taxis. I had a big group of friends in London – all of us single, our lives just beginning. If I felt different from them, I was desperate not to show it, desperate to fit in. Inside, I was a child, really – angry at my parents for their illnesses, for their lives veering from plan, for stopping me from being carefree.

One night I went to a party in Tooting – a gathering of friends who drank together in a bar up the road. It was a warm evening, a barbecue going in the back garden, and a gang of thirty were there, my age or older, sitting in deck chairs or sprawled on the grass, the sun going down, everyone waiting for dark to pop pills into their mouths and let the 'real' party start. I spent most of the night talking to a man I'd not seen before. His name was Sid – he was tall and very thin, blue eyes in a good-looking face splashed with freckles. Somehow in the light banter of our flirtation, he told me both his parents were dead – his mother when he was four, his father ten years later. He had a brother in Plymouth and one ancient Scottish grandmother, but he was alone in London, trying to get his own business together, but more often, he confessed, losing days to partying and its fallout. Even later, when I saw him pull a plastic bag from his pocket, dishing out pills to my friends who presented him with ten-pound notes, I remember wanting to know him, wanting to see him again, not just because I was attracted to him, but because I hoped he might help me through the dark days I was in, the loss I felt, the loss I knew and didn't know was coming, my sense of things falling apart.

When he phoned the next week, I was delighted.

◆

'Don't you like the bracelet?' my father asked, whenever I did see him. I suppose I was saving it for something special, but in the end, I wore it to meet Sid for a drink one night months later, just because. I remember admiring it on the Tube on the way and turning it on my wrist as I walked through the rain, excited to see him. But when we left the pub my wrist was bare.

'I have to go back,' I said, turning on my heel and running to the pub, crouching down to search the sticky floor. Sid helped me, but it wasn't there. I couldn't believe it. Outside, I walked off through Soho, retracing my route, scouring the wet pavement, Sid behind me trying to catch up. I must have looked mad, combing the streets with my eyes, thinking the wet stone glinting was the bracelet's diamonds, refusing to stop until finally he said, 'Hannah! It's gone, all right? It's gone.'

'It can't have!' We stood in the downpour, my hair stuck to my face.

'It's gone,' he said again, reaching his hand out to me, pulling me towards him.

'No,' I said again, sounding like a child.

'Look, don't worry about it. We can get another one, eh?'

'No. That's not the point. You don't understand. I can't have lost it.'

But I knew it was lost. Another bad omen. The rain fell more heavily as I stood sobbing into Sid's coat.

Despite my mother's confusion, she was still astute. She knew my father's cancer had come back. That Easter they booked a holiday to Crete but he was complaining of stomach pain, wondering aloud if it was his ulcer, as though naming the return of the ulcer negated the possibility of the return of cancer. Before they flew, he went to Dr Goldstein, who took him very seriously. *That's how I knew*, my mother said. *The doctor always laughed your father out the door before.* The doctor prescribed painkillers – the strongest type that needed diluting, and so everywhere they went in Crete they took a water bottle and my father's pills.

And he didn't eat, my mother said, although they sat for dinner every night on the veranda of the guest house. A local fisherman played guitar for the diners in the evening and my parents and he got to talking. His name was Stavros. His father had died of stomach cancer months before. He became my father's friend. Every evening after playing, Stavros slipped his elbow through my father's arm and walked him slowly from the hotel to the bay and back again, their heads together, talking.

'We've been to the hospital,' my mother told me on the phone, a week after they returned. 'It's a shock, love, but your dad's cancer's back. It's spread all over. There's nothing they can do.'

♥

Sunday lunch, a few days after the news. Maria and Alf were back in Ilford. A dismembered roast chicken rested on the table. We worked through the mound of food on our plates, making small talk, filling in the silences. My father was at the table, slumped so low his face almost touched the polished wood. His dinner was pushed aside. Suddenly he sat up straight and looked at me. 'You know I'm dying?' he said.

I was shocked to hear him be so blunt. 'Dad, don't,' I said. Ellie whined under the table.

'I'm going to die,' he said, looking around at everyone. We all looked away. He pressed the heels of his hands into his eyes to stop himself crying.

Nothing they can do. I hadn't believed it until then. My father had been ill so many times. There was *always* something they could do. They'd always fixed him – poked and prodded him, sent off samples for tests, delivered diagnoses, prescribed pills. It was a routine we all knew. But this wasn't the same. The shock of his prognosis had tipped him into a new place of despair – the loneliness of the banished man, told he will die, and nothing to be done, and no one to go with him there.

I remember the room that day – everything so familiar – the Welsh dresser my parents had had for years, the carved heads we had brought from Jamaica, the African prints on the wall – and my cousins, my mother, Sam, me, sitting at that table while my father looked around at the world he would leave very soon. He didn't want to die, his distress so acute it made the light of the room brighter, the air thinner, harder to breathe.

In the kitchen, I asked my mother what had happened at the hospital. 'Just what I told you,' she whispered. 'The doctor said it's terminal. He said your dad had weeks to live. Or days.'

'And what did Dad do?' I asked, and she gave me that do-you-have-to-know-everything look.

'He broke down in tears,' she said. 'He couldn't stop crying.'

I left straight after lunch. 'Can't you stay for a while?' he asked, looking up from the table as I shrugged my coat on.

I can't remember what excuse I gave.

I've had a hundred dreams that say the same thing since then.

I'm leaving a stranger's house at dawn after a party. No one knows me there, and the slam of the front door echoes my loneliness. I go down the steps, and there at the gate is the familiar car. It's winter, still dark, the engine running soft below a street lamp, and sitting at the wheel, waiting to bring me home is my father.

Or I'm on the phone to my mother and she says, *Oh no, love, no, your dad's not dead; whatever gave you that idea? No, he's not dead, but he doesn't live here now.* She gives me an address, and I go out into the thin blue light of morning, rushing up one street and down another, but every one is signless, and each one looks the same. And although I must see my father, I find myself in water, pounding up the fast lane of an outdoor swimming pool, the water freezing cold, but there's no way of getting out. I wake and nothing is resolved.

Or, in the worst of dreams, I'm leaving work on a hot day in summer, and there across the car park is my father's car. I walk across the asphalt, climb in and sit beside him, but he's crying, and when I look at him, I see he's dead already and decaying. 'It's too late,' he says. 'It's too late. I wanted to tell you, but you came too late.'

◆

I came back too late, with a rucksack of clothes, enough for the week the doctor said my father might have left, but the cancer was already at his brain. He sat in his old dressing gown on the single bed in the front room, his cup of tea rattling loudly on its saucer, a pile of unread newspapers on the floor. 'Hello, Dad,' I greeted him, but he didn't speak. He looked at me without recognition, his eyes glassy and distant. His language was gone.

♠

Two Macmillan nurses arrived at the door. 'Hello, Mr Lowe,' they both said, laying him out on the bed to undress him, clean him, wiping his arms and legs with wet-wipes, powdering his back and bottom, putting him into clean pyjamas. Naked, my father was just papery skin and bone, a concave stomach, thin chest, his stick legs marked by the scars my grandfather had made. His feet and hands looked too big for his body. Only his legs weren't covered in moles. They tucked him up in clean sheets, two pillows to prop him up, a morphine drip taped into his wrist.

'They're angels,' my mother said afterwards, and told me how, two days before, one had sat for hours with my father as he told her the story of his life, or as much of it as he could manage. Too late for me to hear, I thought.

♥

That night, we found him on the stairs on his hands and knees, the drip ripped out. He was nearly at the top.

'Oh no you don't, sunshine,' my mother said, blocking his path. 'He must want the toilet,' she said to me. 'We'll have to carry him back.' My father sat on the top stair, tears rolling silently down his face.

'I'll do it,' I said. 'Come on, Dad.' I scooped my father up into my arms and carried him down to the bathroom. His head lolled back. He was so light, the weight of a child.

'Look, he folds like a deck of playing cards,' my mother said, as I placed him on the toilet. Her stoicism amazed me. I left them alone for her to help him.

♣

The doorbell rang all the next day: Gloria, my half-sister, flown from America; Tom, my half-brother; Charlie White; Uncle Terry; Dionne from Peckham with a Tupperware box of rice and peas; Sid, who had only met my father once. The back room was full of laughter, chat and cigarette smoke; the front room lamp-lit and silent where my father slept.

The nurse told us he could still hear, so after dinner we went in one by one to fill the air with words.

And then who else was on the step but Auntie Lyn? It had been ten years. 'Hello, Han,' she said. 'I've come to see your dad.'

♦

'Mr Lowe, can you hear me? Can you hear me, Mr Lowe?' The doctor shouted, his face bent to close to my father's face. He was African, a bald shiny head.

'What will happen now?' we whispered in the hall door. He'd been asleep in bed for three days.

'Mr Lowe is very ill,' the doctor said. 'The brain cells are changing rapidly. Tonight, there'll be long gaps between his breathing, a rattle in his chest. Don't give him food or drink now. Just wet his lips.' He lifted his bag, turning away. 'It won't be long,' he said.

♠

I sat at the edge of my father's bed, remembering when I would creep into his room to watch him sleep – the curtains holding back the light, the rise and fall of his chest, the smell of sweat.

I leant forward and kissed him on the cheek.

The sun came up outside.

♥

In the morning, my mother shaved him. I passed the doorway as she held his face, a bowl of milky water on her knee, a razor at his chin. After she left the room, I went in.

'Morning, Dad,' I said.

♣

I went into the kitchen. 'Mum, I think he's dead.'

18

1952

*T*he boy, who was now a man, slipped through the red door on King Street, climbed the stairs to the hot room where already thirty or so others were sitting in rows of chairs. The stocky black man at the front stood up and turned to the group. 'Comrades,' he said, 'welcome to the fourth meeting of the West Indies Committee branch of the Communist Party. Happy to see new faces in the room, and hoping some of you will make it to the Allies for Freedom conference next month.'

The boy slipped into a chair, nodding to the folk he knew in the room. Plenty of Caribbeans experiencing the hardships in Britain but still caring about home politics had turned to the Communist Party. For a while, the boy had sold the *Daily Worker* outside the Tube station but had stopped when he realised the Party wasn't listening to his concerns. He, like many of them, had been quickly disillusioned with British communists, who, despite their shared politics, didn't seem to care about their plight with work and housing in Britain and the ongoing struggle for independence in the Caribbean. The boy and the others hoped for change through this new faction. He read *Caribbean News* and came to these meetings, staying in touch with the work of Thomas Reid back in Jamaica, still fighting the long fight for the island's independence.

The agenda for the meeting was the treatment of Caribbean workers, how to tackle the colour bar in employment. Since more of them had arrived, more were being channelled into the lowest menial work, way below their competence and terribly underpaid. The boy's experience at Somers Town was enough for him, but others didn't have the choices he had. The housing situation was worse too – women and children had come to join their husbands, living in cramped rooms in run-down quarters of the city: Brixton, Notting Hill, Finsbury Park. And there was more hostility too – the tuts and jibes of 'Watch it, darkie' or 'Why don't you go back to where you came from?', places they avoided for fear of trouble, and now, painted on street walls, *Keep Britain White* and *Blacks Go Home.*

But the boy didn't want to go home. He had friends here, a girl, a decent place to live. And he was making money, far more than he had as a shunter, playing most nights and half the day at underground dice games and card clubs, and sometimes at the chemmy parties up West. People knew him. He dealt and rolled the dice. He was using his skills.

◆

In a small, rented flat in Aldgate, the boy's friends sat around the table on comfy seats, the room thick with cigarette smoke. There was Lionel, Sue, John, Charles Dee and Enoch Leaford. It was March, bitterly cold outside, but inside the fire glowed in the chimney breast and the windows slowly steamed up. Calypso music played on the old gramophone

– Sam Manning, and Wilmoth Houdini, the boy's favourite singer. He sat at the table in the corner and sang along.

Elsie came through the living-room door with a birthday cake in her hands. It was iced bright pink and flocked with candles. 'Happy Birthday, Chick!' she said, setting it down front of him. 'Make a wish, then?' she said.

'Really?' the boy said, gently prodding the cake with his finger. 'You make a pink cake *pink*, Elsie.' He laughed.

'Make a wish, that's what you do.' She laughed, flicking her fair hair out of her eyes.

'You never had a birthday cake before, Chick?' Sue asked from the sofa. She was Lionel's girlfriend, a small freckly girl from Manchester. They were engaged to be married. Lionel's arm was hung around her neck, pulling her close to him.

'You know, I don't think I ever did,' the boy said. He closed his eyes and blew out all the candles.

'Hmm-mmm. Nice-looking cake, Elsie,' said Lionel, leaning forward to inspect it. 'I do love a nice bit of cake, don't I, Sue? And a cup of tea.' He raised an eyebrow at her.

'Make it yerself!' Sue laughed, pushing him.

'I'd love a cup of tea,' said Enoch Leaford from his spot in the corner, raising his head from the newspaper.

'Don't look at me,' Elsie said, slicing the cake, handing the paper plates round. 'But I'll have a cup if you're making.' Lionel huffed and sighed, finally getting up from the sofa.

'How old are you, Chick?' asked John from his armchair. 'No, let me guess, man. You twenty-five?'

'No,' said the boy. 'I'm twenty-nine. How old are you? I never think to ask before.'

'John look like him still in nappies,' called Lionel through the kitchen hatch.

'John can't be no more than twelve,' Charles Dee said, opening one eye. His big frame was squeezed into the other armchair, his head dropped back, listening to the music.

John gave him a bad look. 'I'm eighteen,' he said. 'And a half.'

'Oh boy,' Charles Dee said. 'No one counting halves any more, man.' He turned to the boy and raised his beer bottle. 'Many happy returns, sir.'

'Eat your cake then, old man,' said Elsie.

There was a knock at the door. The boy stood to answer it, coming back into the room with his arm around another fellow. 'Look who it is,' he said. The other man smiled, blinking in the lights of the room. One of his eyes was bad.

'Evening, Felix,' Charles Dee said. 'Look like the rain found you.' He laughed his big laugh.

'Evening, all,' said Felix, shrugging off his mac, laying his hat down on the arm of the chair. 'This damn weather. Now where you good folks going to squeeze me in? I need to get warm.'

'Squeeze in here,' Sue said, moving up on the sofa. 'I was just thinking of you the other day. What've you been up to?'

The music played and the room filled with talk and laughter. The boy sat listening and laughing, eating his cake.

♠

Later, when the party was over and everyone had gone home, the boy reclined on the sofa. They had moved three times before a Greek woman, a friend of Elsie's mother, had let them rent this place. It was a small flat, lacking light and a bit damp, but it was good enough – a world away from the wet, freezing basement he had shared with Lionel and the dank rooms he and Elsie had shared in other houses.

He sank back into the cushions, shutting his eyes. He was tired. It had been a good day, so good to see his friends. It was a month since he'd walked into the cellar club in Marylebone and seen Felix sitting at a table at the back, cards spread in his hand. He'd walked up behind him, placed his hand on his shoulder, making him jump. Felix had turned round and leapt up, grabbing the boy's hand and shaking it vigorously. 'Chick!' he exclaimed. 'I know I'm going to see you soon, just not sure when!' The boy hugged him. 'Long time no see, Felix,' he said into his shoulder. 'Long time no see.' He thought about the others, too – Charles Dee and Enoch, his old friends from America, Lionel, John from St Lucia. Before he left Jamaica, he'd never thought about those other islands, only knew that they were hundreds of miles away. But in London the islanders were friends – all in the same boat. Charles Dee said there was nowhere like England to make a man feel black.

Elsie came in, breaking his reverie. 'I forgot,' she said, holding out a thin blue envelope. 'A letter came for you. Looks like it's from abroad.' He opened it and sat reading in silence. Outside, the rain was still heavy, beating on the stone walkway that ran past their door.

'It's from my mother,' he said. 'Says she's getting married. To an American man. What a name this fellow has. Mr Walwyn Pennyfeather.'

'Pennyfeather?' Elsie said, and laughed. 'Does she say Happy Birthday? I thought it might have been a card. A thin one at that.'

'No,' the boy said, looking up. 'I don't think she knows when it is.'

'How can that be?' Elsie raised her eyebrows. 'Every mother knows the date their child was born.' She patted her stomach. 'I'll not be forgetting this one's birthday.'

The boy smiled. 'At least I know she's OK,' he said.

♥

The pavements flashed in the rain as the boy made his way down Oxford Street. He remembered what a fellow in Notting Hill had told him once. The London streets weren't lined with gold, but it rains so much, squint hard enough and you'll see the pavements shine with diamonds. He narrowed his eyes now and sure enough, from the right angle, there were diamonds stretched on the stone.

Five years he'd been in England, and he'd had good fortune, his share of diamonds. He had money – enough to send something to Kathleen in America, enough for rent, enough for smart clothes – the suit on his back was hand-tailored, his shoes good leather. But no, the boy thought, that wasn't right. It wasn't fortune, it wasn't luck. That morning he'd sat at the kitchen table for three hours, practising slipping a card from his sleeve into the deck in his hand. He could do it perfectly, in one swift move no one would ever see. Yes, gambling was luck and risk, but what the boy did was take the reins of chance and hold them tight. He wondered if Mr Ho Choy would be impressed with the move, forgetting for a moment the news that Felix had passed on from Mr Manny – Charlie Ho Choy was dead.

It was a Sunday night, quiet in the city, but as the boy neared the corner, he could see a queue moving outside the Feldman Club, 100 Oxford Street. He joined it, and bought himself a drink downstairs, standing at the bar, taking the place in. The lights were dimmed, the room packed with bodies. Smoke lifted in the coloured lights, making a strange haze in the room. When the band walked on stage and took their places, there was a murmur through the crowd. Four black men, one on drums, one at the piano, one with trumpet, and in the middle, the front man, his cousin Joe, tall and elegant-looking, his alto sax gleaming in his hands.

The air filled with their brash, jumpy sound. Bebop. The crowd took to their feet – black men swinging white women around, white men holding the hands of black girls – applause and whistling as the air grew hot with the energy of the dance. This was a different London, the boy thought – away from the unfriendly stares, the graffiti, the taunts in the street. Here, black people were respected and rightly so. The band looked so sharp in their suits, Joe howling through the sax he angled up into the air, his white shirt sweat-soaked, and on the stools around the room, women who weren't dancing lapped him up with their stares. The band played for an hour, and the boy stood at the bar the whole time, drinking his drink, nodding to the other punters, black and white.

After the show, Joe came through the crowd looking for him. 'Chick, you came.' He smiled his broad smile, reaching out his hand. The boy shook it.

'Long time no see, Joe,' said the boy. 'You looking good, man.'

'What you think of the music? We sound good?'

'Joe, you boys playing so well, looks like you on fire. Look like you get plenty admirers too.' He gestured to the girls, and Joe laughed. They chatted until the manager came to tap on Joe's shoulder.

'I have to go,' Joe said, 'but come for a drink in the back? Then we'll play some more.'

The boy looked at his watch. 'No can do this time,' he said, standing, his hand on Joe's arm. 'Sorry to miss it. I've got a game tonight, but next time, yes.'

'Fair enough, Chick. Take me next time, eh? Good to see you. You looking good, man, looking good.'

Out on the street, the boy hailed a cab, holding his mac over his head to keep the rain off. One pulled up and he jumped in. 'You can take me to the Edgware Road?' he asked.

'No problem, guv,' the bald driver said, pulling away along Oxford Street where the street lights were a white, starry blur in the rain. The boy watched from the window, remembering the rain at home, those quick, hot storms, and the light of the oil lamps flickering outside his father's shop.

'My other life,' he said to himself.

He'd swapped it for another.

The rain gleamed on the streets, and from the back seat of the cab, the boy saw diamonds again – there for a second, then gone.

This place was his home now – for better, for worse.

19

The Ace of Hearts

If wishes were horses, then beggars would ride

When my father went back to Jamaica in 1962, he placed an advertisement in the classified section of the *Gleaner* newspaper.

I am searching for my mother, it said. *Her name is Hermione Harriott. Also known as Ida. Last known abode on Altamont Crescent, Kingston.*

He'd listed his hotel details. He'd last heard from Hermione in a letter ten years before. He'd written back, but hadn't heard from her again. He didn't know if she was still alive.

He and Ray the Pilot were staying in Kingston for a few days before heading to Port Antonio for Ray to bake in the sun and my father to read books in the shade. The phone rang on the bedside table of his hotel room. My father answered, and on the phone was Dolores, a cousin he hadn't seen since he'd left Jamaica fifteen years before, when she was four or five. What a coincidence it was to learn she was now an intern at the *Gleaner*. She'd seen his ad and phoned his hotel immediately. 'And you'll never guess, Cousin Ralph,' she said, out of breath. 'I'm living with Auntie Ida!'

But you could call me Ida, Hermione had said. *That's what they call me around here.*

Dolores told him to wait there. She would pick him up and take him to see his mother in half an hour.

I've imagined this scenario many times – Dolores and my father pulling up outside the big white house on a corner in Liguanea, a wealthy neighbourhood far from the ghettoes and slums, an old man standing up on the veranda, a book and a pair of glasses in this hand. 'Uncle Walwyn,' Dolores ran up the steps of the house. 'You never guess who this is?' Pointing to where my father stood on the drive. 'It's Ralph! Auntie's son, all the way from England!'

'Ralph?' The old man seemed to search for the name in his memory. 'Ah, yes, Ralph. Of course.' He spoke with an American accent. He came down the steps, his hands held out to my father. He was well dressed in a shirt and blazer, shiny shoes. They shook hands. 'Good to meet you, Ralph. At last. I'm Walwyn Pennyfeather. I'm afraid Ida, um, your mother, is at the hairdresser's, but she'll be back soon enough. Come and have a drink. All the way from England, huh?'

They sat in the shade of the tall potted palms. Dolores brought lemonade. Mr Pennyfeather told my father about his businesses in New York and Jamaica. He had started out with one dry cleaners and now owned twenty. The two men liked each other, chatting away until a cab pulled up and Hermione climbed out. The boy caught her eye straight away, standing and coming down the steps to meet her at the end of the drive. She was in her sixties now, but still a good-looking woman. Well dressed as ever in a pink suit, her handbag clutched to her chest. Her mouth was fixed in a stern line.

'Ma,' he said, going towards her. 'I came to find you.' He didn't know what else to say.

'Shhhhh,' she said quietly, glancing up to the house. No greeting, no welcome hug. She looked shocked. 'You tell him you're my son?'

My father was confused, following the line of her eyes to where Mr Pennyfeather stood. 'Yes,' he said, feeling flustered. 'Dolores told him. We've just been –'

'Oh Lord,' she interrupted him, then whispered, 'I didn't tell him I had a son. I tell him I have a nephew in England. But not a son, not a son.'

My father hadn't known what to do or say, had remained rooted to the spot while Hermione went to greet her husband, to lie or say nothing or perhaps tell him the truth. My father stayed for an awkward half-hour – Hermione refusing to meet his eye, Mr Pennyfeather nervously joking – before taking a cab back to the hotel.

One night, years later, I heard my father on the phone to Dolores.

'I never understood it,' he said into the receiver. 'I still don't. Why didn't my mother tell him she had a son? Why did she lie about me?' Silence as he listened to Dolores's words. 'Maybe. Maybe. But so much time had passed,' he said. 'It still hurts me, you know. It still hurts.'

The day before they left Kingston, Ray the Pilot had driven them to Yallahs, and they'd found the shop where my father said it would be. It looked run down – the stained awning had sagged, the gratings at the windows had come loose. An old man shuffled out, squinting at the car. He was thin and stooped with white hair. It was my grandfather. James Lowe. Lowe Shu-On.

My father climbed out of the car and they stood talking, the old man pointing back to the shop, my father handing him something. A minute later he climbed back in, his father already back inside.

'We not staying?' Ray asked.

'No,' my father said.

'That was your dad?'

'For what it's worth,' my father said.

'What did you give him?'

'What I had in my pocket – a hundred dollars.' My father glanced back at the shop. 'Let's go,' he said. 'I shouldn't have come.'

Four years later, in 1969, the Salvation Army knocked on the front door of Ashgrove Road, asking for my father. They had come to tell him his father was dead. The same year, Dolores phoned. Hermione was dead too.

◆

My father had never forgotten his parents, then. I wonder if he thought of them in the last days of his life, as he called out for Jamaican food, his mind journeying back across time and space to his childhood in the shop. My mother had always assumed that the visit from the Salvation Army was part of a generic service – providing news from abroad, keeping families connected – but I always wondered how they would have known to come to our door. Later, I phoned the Salvation Army to check. A lady told me that my father must have used their family tracing service. 'He'd have had to have been looking for his father in 1968,' she said. 'He must have sent us a request.'

♠

He died peacefully at home, my mother told people on the phone in the days that followed, a platitude that was only half true. My father wasn't at peace. The winter sun streaming through the front-room windows hid nothing. His face in death was anguished and confused, his brow deeply furrowed, his white hair standing on end, framing his face on the pillow, exaggerating the look of shock. He'd had twelve days between prognosis and a death which caught him off guard and unprepared.

'At least he's shaved,' my mother said as we stood over him. 'Do you think I should put him in some decent clothes?' He was still in his old pyjamas.

'I don't suppose it matters,' I said. 'No one's going to see him. Are they?'

'Well, no,' she said. 'Oh, I don't know. He looks a bit dishevelled.' She leant down and brushed back his hair with her hand. In the end we left him as he was.

'I'd better phone Ken in Jamaica,' she said wearily.

At lunchtime the doctor came and signed his death certificate. Cause of death: *Carcinomatosis.* Cancer, disseminated. An hour later the undertakers arrived to take the body away. Afterwards I sat alone in the room where he had died – everything quiet, the single bed unmade, the pillow indented with the shape of his head. The air still held the power of his illness – the cancer that might have moved slowly three years before, but which in its finale was quick and ferocious. The light was still too bright, and there was a smell – faintly medical but also sweet, the ghost-scent of his sweat and talcum-powdered skin.

We had discussed already the business of the funeral. The crematorium and the Humanist funeral official had been contacted, and both could accommodate us the Friday of that week – only three days after my father's death, but it meant my half-sister would be able to attend the funeral. The official agreed to come to our house the next day to discuss the eulogy.

'He definitely wouldn't have wanted a church service?' Gloria asked, when my mother came off the phone.

'Oh no,' my mother said. 'He'd curse me if I did that. He'd turn in his grave.' She laughed half-heartedly. 'If he had one.'

I thought of that book, *The Case Against God*, my father's bible. I understood why people believed in heaven, the afterlife, reincarnation. The alternative was too sad. It was hard to believe in nothing. If only my father had believed in something, I could have believed in something too. I would have taken comfort there.

Upstairs, I lay on the bed of the attic room. On the floor, my rucksack, half full of clean clothes. He hadn't lived the week after all. I pulled the covers up to my chin. My regret was visceral, a surge and swell in my chest that pushed the tears out from my eyes. The moment I realised my father was going to die was the moment I wanted to ask him everything, to hear his story from his own mouth, to talk in a way we'd never talked. His death severed my connection to Jamaica, to China, to his secret life in London – all the history I'd never know, the chance to say *yes, Dad, your story is important; yes, your life has been meaningful*. Yet, wanting this, I was simultaneously repelled by it. Only time would have shifted the pattern of our relationship, the distance and silence so well entrenched. But time was what we didn't have.

I've never cried as I did that week, a ragged tissue clutched permanently in my hand, walking through the house sobbing, crying into the washing-up bowl, at the bathroom mirror, as

I sat on the side of my father's bed. Perhaps I'd wanted him to hear me. I wanted those tears to say 'I'm sorry. I should have stayed last week when you asked me.' 'I'm sorry. I should have talked to you.' 'I'm sorry, I'm sorry.' Over and over until that incantation spoke for twenty years of slips and blunders – for sitting, surly and grudging, on those endless drives, so curt in my responses he gave up trying; for lying about him to the other little ballerinas; for saying I wouldn't kiss him again – how could I have known my childish stubbornness would so solidly fix the distance between us?

A memory came back to me. Winter. Five years past. Before the cancer. My father in hospital for a prostate operation. I had gone to see him alone. It was night-time, black beyond the high windows of the ward, a dull lamp shining above the courtyard door. Sitting up between the sheets, he asked me for a cigarette.

'No way, Dad,' I said, annoyed already.

'Oh go on, Han,' he pleaded. 'I know you've got some.'

'No! I haven't.' I had. They were tucked in my bag. 'And even if I did, you can't smoke in here.'

He looked forlorn. 'Half the blokes in here keep sneaking off to smoke,' he said. 'You can hide in the courtyard. I've had one today already, but everyone's run out.' He sounded like a naughty schoolboy, confessing his crimes.

'Oh, Dad.' I was exasperated. 'I'm not giving you a cigarette and that's that.'

Walking away down the empty corridor, his voice called out behind me. 'Han!'

I turned to see him standing in his dressing gown, his hand around the drip he was still attached to. Bright lights on the green walls, the prints of silver birds. His face looked hopeful. He reached out the other hand.

'Please, Han, go on, please,' he pleaded.

'No, Dad! Go back to bed.' I walked on, but when I turned again, he was there ten feet behind me, shuffling in his slippers.

'Please,' he said.

'No!'

And I walked on, up the stairs, into the bright reception, through the swinging doors where the night air swept over my face. I rooted around in my bag for my cigarettes, lit up, exhaled deeply.

Lying there, I added that to my list of regrets. I should have given him that cigarette. What difference would it have made?

♥

In the evening, Sylvester knocked on the door, asking for my mother. I sent him through to the kitchen and went back upstairs. When I came down an hour later, she was at the table, looking upset.

'Has Sylvester gone?' I asked her. I thought he'd come to pay his respects.

'Yes, that bastard's gone,' she said, staring out into the garden.

'Why's he a bastard?'

'Because he just helped himself to dad's guillotine,' she said. 'While I was making tea he just went into the shed, came out with it, said he was taking it with him. He'd put it in a plastic bag.'

'How did he know Dad had it?' I said. 'I thought all that stuff was secret.'

'Not that secret,' she said.

'Why didn't you stop him, Mum?'

'Oh, I don't know,' she sighed. 'I don't even know where your dad got it from. It's no use to me or to you, is it? But it just seems so disrespectful to come and take it today. Most of those blokes were never your dad's friends. All they ever wanted was his money, or his way of making it.'

Gloria stayed for the week in our spare room. It was only the second time I'd met her. She was nearly forty years older than me. Small, with close-cropped hair. She wore stylish tailored clothes and lots of gold jewellery. My father had seen her only a handful of times since he left when she was a baby. But when I was eight or so, there were suddenly more phone calls, more letters. A package arrived with a US postmark, and two portraits of her daughters appeared on the wall on our hall. Dionne and Marlene, posed in soft focus – one in a pink jumper, one in blue – both grown-up by then, living and studying in New York. I used to stare at their photographs, marvelling that I was their eight-year-old auntie. A few years later, Dionne studied in London. My father was delighted to meet her, and so was I. She was pretty and glamorous. We used to drive across town to her flat in Baker Street to visit. She would throw her arms around my father at the door, saying, 'Hi, Grandpa!' in her thick Southern accent.

Her whole family came for her graduation – Gloria and her husband, Marlene, and, most surprisingly, Kathleen, my father's first wife, an old black lady I glimpsed for a second at the graduation ceremony.

'I never knew him as "Dad",' Gloria said, sitting in our living room that evening. It was just the two of us. 'I didn't really think of him as "Dad". I called my stepfather "Dad". But these last years, we spoke on the phone once a month at least. I guess I felt closer to him.'

'I didn't realise you talked so often,' I said.

'Oh yes,' she said. 'He used to phone in the middle of the night. You know, with time differences and all. He said he couldn't sleep. I think he was lonely. He used to say he was lonely. His health was bad. He sounded sad.'

'Oh,' I said again. 'I didn't know that. Poor Dad.' I wondered whether my mother knew about those phone calls.

'Well, I'm glad I can be here and see you all – my stepmother, who is younger than me. My white sister and brother.' She laughed.

'Yep, it's strange, isn't it?' I took a sip of my tea. I was thinking. I wanted to say something, but didn't know how to put it. 'I don't always feel white, exactly,' I blurted out.

She looked quizzically at me. 'Don't tell me you feel black?' she said, her eyebrows raised.

'No,' I said quickly. 'Not that, exactly.'

'Well, even if you do feel it,' she said, 'it's one thing to feel it, and another to be it, let me tell you.'

I felt embarrassed. She was right.

♦

The night before the funeral, my mother handed me a stack of photographs of my father.

'I thought it would be nice to pin them to a board in the hall for tomorrow,' she said. 'You know, to show his different sides.' She was cheerful. I don't think the fact of my father's death had hit her yet. She didn't know how much she'd come to miss him.

I sifted through the pile. There was a photograph of my father as a young man with baby Gloria between his hands; another with baby Tom; a black and white shot in a nightclub, my father in a black silk shirt, a coil of smoke rising from the cigarette perched in a cut-glass ashtray; photos where he swings my small body out over the lawn, or with Sam, a toddler, sat beside him in a dishevelled bed – my father in his vest, his glasses on, the newspaper open wide. It is early morning, likely he is just back from a game; or at the dinner table on Christmas Day, his arm dangling around my mother; or in his armchair smiling at Bobby, his grandson, playing his drum; or bent over a saucepan in the kitchen, or in the garden, loading up the bonfire in his anorak and wellingtons; and then the frail old man who loved his dog, holding Chloe on his lap, his nose pressed deep into her fur.

I made a collage using drawing pins. My father's many sides. I thought about it. Aren't all of us like this, versions of ourselves, each one different, performed for family, friends, neighbours, the people we work with – and variegated even more by their perceptions and prejudices? Perhaps what marked my father as different were the shifting and secret spheres he moved in, all the things we didn't know. But would we want to know them, if we could?

I remembered a version of my father, told to me by Tom, that I didn't like and didn't want to know. In the last weeks of his degree at Durham, my father phoned Tom to say he was in Newcastle with Ray the Pilot, and why didn't Tom catch the train over and come for a drink? My father took him to a seedy card-club-cum-brothel on a dingy side-street, where worn-looking prostitutes vied for the punters' winnings. Ray and my father kept cajoling Tom to go with one of these women, an offer my poor half-brother didn't take up, enduring their taunts and the half-hearted come-ons of a woman twice his age, who stroked his cheek and sat in his lap. Telling me this, Tom laughed at my father's crudeness, the smuttiness of it all. But I hated hearing that version of my father. He is a bully, a chauvinist, a man with too much cash. Once I'd seen that side of him, I couldn't help myself for asking more. Was my father a good father to Tom? Why had he and Elsie split up? 'There was lipstick on his collar, I suppose you'd say,' my half-brother said. 'He cheated. He was hardly there, and then he was gone.'

♠

The morning before the funeral we received a letter from my father's old Jamaican comrade, Thomas Reid, some of which would be read out at the funeral. He was in his eighties by then, living in England too, still writing books about the politics and history of Jamaica. Upstairs in my room, I read through what he'd written. It was his version of my father:

> Ralph cannot have been more than seventeen when I first met this idealistic and conscientious young man from St Thomas ... We were among pioneers in the great task of persuading our fellow Jamaicans that we were not preordained to perpetual inferiority but were a nation capable of administering to our own affairs. We have been friends and comrades for these many years. No doubt we have both been disappointed that our dreams for our homeland's future have not been more fully realised. I was delighted to renew his acquaintance in England and to learn he had found happiness here.

The versions of my father kept multiplying, even after his death. Many years later, I arranged to meet his old friend Mac, outside the Tube in Islington. He wore a suede jacket, a gold cross around his neck. *He's got a bob or two, that Mac,* my mother told me. *He's not stupid.* She was very fond of him. I knew he had a big house out in Essex somewhere, a house in Spain we had stayed in.

'I can't stay for long, luvvie,' he said as we hurried through the grey mush of snow to a pub on Upper Street, puffing on his cigarette. 'I've got places to be.'

We settled with pints of beer on stools in the pub's window. 'I wanted to ask about Dad, Mac,' I said.

'I did wonder, luvvie,' he said. 'Your dad was a good mate of mine. I miss him. What do you want to know?'

'Well, um ...' Suddenly I felt silly. Wasn't this a private world I shouldn't encroach on – an illegal world, a world of men? I wondered how much Mac would tell me. 'When did you meet?' I finally asked. 'How did you meet?'

'Well,' Mac scratched his head. 'It was 1965, I reckon. Probably. I can tell you where for sure. The Cubana in Ilford. I used to go in there to see a girl.' He laughed. 'One night she'd gone and I drank on my own until, just as I had my hat on, someone stepped through the wall – that's what it looked like. But it was a panelled door – the whole wall folded away and there it was – spotlights and baize tables, a little casino – I couldn't believe it.'

'Ha!' I said. 'That must have been a surprise.'

'Yes, luvvie, I'm telling you.' He rubbed the condensation on the window with his hand. 'There were thirty blokes in there, your dad in the middle, dealing. He had on a good suit, dressed for the occasion. And he shuffled the cards so fast and swish, like pulling ribbon through his hands. He was a real showman.' Once Mac had started talking, it seemed he didn't want to stop. 'That was the night we met. From then on we were pals. I respected him because he was older than me. He'd come all the way from Jamaica, he'd lived in America, he knew about politics, he knew about religion. He was clever.' He took a sip of his pint. 'He was always saying, "Mac, did you think about it this way?"'

'What about the cards, Mac?' I ventured. 'Did you play with him?'

'Course I did,' he said. 'We played as a pair. Your dad taught me everything I know. He's how I've got what I've got.' He shook his head, remembering. 'Some nights, we sat all night at the kitchen table, light coming up the walls. Your dad could make cards vanish up his tie or up his sleeve. I couldn't get it. He said, "Mac, just look," and he slowed it right down for me – that was how I learned.'

This was the first I'd ever known about my father playing – cheating – as one half of a pair. I had no idea. 'But if he made so much money, Mac, what happened to it all?'

'Ah, well, luvvie. That's a question.' He paused. 'I saved what I could. But your dad knew he could always get more. He didn't bother. Honestly. Money was never a problem.' He drained the rest of his pint. 'He was the man. Everyone knew who he was. One night we went to the Victoria to play, but the boss came down and asked your dad to stay away. They'd rigged the game and they didn't want him in 'cos he'd win it. Can you believe it?' His laughter turned into a cough. 'They didn't have a clue that he rigged half of his own games!' I laughed too, but what Mac said struck a chord. The gambling world was, as I supposed, the only place my father had any power.

Mac stood up. 'I'd best be off,' he said suddenly, as though he thought he'd said too much. 'But did you know I was with him the night you were born? We got back to your house at dawn and wet your head. Your dad never drank, so the only thing in the house was Cinzano. The two of us sat like a pair of girls.' He put on his hat. 'It was a heat wave that summer. All the ladybirds were dying. No rain in three months but that night it came down, when you were born.'

'One more question, Mac.' There was something I wanted to know. 'Wasn't there any racism back then?' I said. 'At those games? This was the sixties, right? The seventies?'

He sat down again. 'Let me tell you, luvvie,' he said. 'We used to play with Indian men, chaps from Africa, Polish blokes, Italian blokes, you name it. You know who loves gambling the most?' I shook my head. 'Jewish women!' he said. 'Blimey, they used to give your dad a run for his money. It was a community of gamblers. No racism – everyone got on. But you know why?'

I shook my head again.

'Because all of us were hopeless addicts,' he said. 'That was the only thing that mattered. I didn't give a hoot what colour a fellow was. We just wanted each other's money.' He stood again. 'Good to see you, luvvie. I miss your dad so much. He was my good mate. Give my love to your mum.'

The morning of the funeral I went to my father's room to look through his things. His was the box room, overlooking the park. It was a dull day, perfect for a funeral – a slate sky full of clouds, a few grazes of rain on the window's glass.

I flicked the lights on and looked around. There wasn't much – the bedside table loaded with painkillers, a bottle of dark red medicine, an old glass of water. His slippers were still tucked under the bed. Hanging in the wardrobe were his clothes, his shoes neatly lined up at the bottom, the old patterned jumpers in a pile on the shelf. I held one to my nose. Tobacco and wool. My father's smell. Then I pulled his old suits out, one by one. I hadn't seen him wear a suit in years. There were five in all, old-fashioned styles, old fabrics, beiges and browns. I looked at the labels. *Pierre Cardin, Hermès, Gieves & Hawkes*. Expensive, once.

In the top drawer of his chest, among the socks, I found a pair of red dice and a scuffed cufflink box. I remembered the cufflinks he used to wear – thick gold with onyx stones. I lifted the lid, unsurprised to find it empty. The cufflinks would have gone to the pawn shop, months or years ago, the box kept in case he'd ever had enough cash to get them back. I dug around. An old pack of Rizlas, a small red notebook. He'd had those notebooks all my life – they went hand in hand with the half-length betting-shop biros, always chewed. He made notes in those books on racehorses' form. I flicked through. Pages of numbers I could make no sense of, columns of horses' names – *Pay Check, Salem, Daddy's Overdraft* – I nearly laughed. *All that Jazz. The Ace of Hearts.*

In the corner of the drawer was my father's Post Office account book. The nearest thing he'd had to a bank account. I opened it. His balance was £4.25, the last withdrawal over a year ago. And there was something hard inside a pair of his socks. I turned them out and found a pack of cards with swirling red-patterned backs, the kind he always used. They must be marked, I thought, for him to keep them there. I shuffled through them. They looked perfectly ordinary. Of course. I slipped them in my jacket pocket.

I heard my mother calling my name. It was time to go. Outside, the hearse had pulled up, the coffin visible through the glass. Along the street, neighbours had come to stand at their gates. I looked to the park, where the treetops swayed back and forth in the wind. The rain was falling more heavily. I closed my father's drawer, shut the wardrobe door. Turned out the light. Went down.

EPILOGUE: IMAGINARY HOMELANDS

The corridor ran the length of the world
and you weren't there

– Ron Butlin, *Ryecroft*

Kingston, Jamaica, 2013. Devon Chang and I stand on a balcony looking over the dirt and dust of Barry Street. There are few Chinese here now. Black women kneel on the pavement selling their hotchpotch of goods, ragga music blasts from speakers above the cacophony of car horns. It is an edgy place. The public car lot where we have left Devon's car is run by street gangs who charge to wave vehicles into parking spots. They are skinny boys passing a vodka bottle between them who, Devon tells me, will quickly turn nasty if anyone refuses their service.

'All of this used to be Chinese,' he says sadly as we walk towards the temple, looking for signs of the old Chinatown. It is a scorching day and I am without a hat, the sun already burning my neck and shoulders. I feel a little dizzy. I am four weeks pregnant, still stunned by the knowledge there is a tiny thing inside me, already growing, leading my body in its strange woozy, fluttery dance. He carries on. 'The bakeries, the laundries. Washing lines hung across the street. People lived above, hopping from roof to roof to each other's houses. You see the signs?' He points to the white Chinese characters painted on the blue wall of a store. They are faded and chipped.

I don't tell him that what I really want to know about are the gambling dens tucked away behind these shops and down alleyways, where my father played sixty years ago. I'm not sure if this is a secret history, one Devon might not know or not want to share. He points along the road. 'These buildings were cafés and groceries. All Chinese. Can you imagine?'

Yes, I think, I can try.

♣

The Chinese in Jamaica are a close community who pride themselves on their success in business. Most made their money as shopkeepers. Now Devon runs a bakery that makes a third of the island's bread. They are also highly conscious of their ancestry and culture. 'We're more Chinese than the Chinese in China!' he says as we enter the tall temple, disused for years now, guarded by two peeling stone lions at the front, and round the back, the live-in caretaker, who only wakes when his black Dobermann barks and snarls at us.

We climb the dusty stairs. 'Years ago newcomers in need stayed here,' he tells me, waving his arms around the temple's spacious first floor. I picture the rows of single beds where men just off the boats would sleep. No women at first – wives sometimes came later. All of them were ethnically Hakka – 'guest people' – migrating thousands of years ago from northern China to the south, many later migrating again overseas. There are eighty million Hakka worldwide, living in every continent. I find out all the Lowes in Jamaica come from two Hakka villages in Guangdong, travelling to Jamaica first as indentured labourers after slavery, and then in the early twentieth century, many, like my grandfather, joining relatives, escaping poverty.

'Migrating is in our Hakka blood,' Devon says, and I think of my grandfather and father's migrations, two gambling men swapping hands they knew for ones unknown, and how migration is so much more than a physical relocation, but a transference from one realm of being to another – a translation of oneself.

Despite the community intimacies of the Chinese, the proximity of Yallahs to Kingston, where most of them live, the close generational ties of families, only one person can be found who remembers my grandfather – a woman called Marjorie Chong, who now lives in Canada. The network of the Chinese Benevolent Association helped me trace her. She remembered the old shop in Yallahs and the man she knew as Lowe Shu-Bak, meaning 'uncle' a common term of respect. She also remembered Lowe Shu's son, Ralph, who went to England.

I am strangely dazed to hear this – a stranger's memory suddenly solidifies the lives of my father and grandfather, the details of which have slipped and slid around my head for years. It makes them more than just a story. But the absence of more memories of my grandfather also confirms what I have always supposed – he was an outsider, moving from one isolated rural village to another, separated from the wider Chinese community, and, I suspect, largely unbound by its manners and mores.

Devon is part Chinese and part black, like my father. He tells me that this mix is accepted now but as a child some elders looked down on him for not being pure Chinese. They called him *ship yit diam*, meaning 'eleven o'clock child' – the clock's hand stuck, not reaching twelve, not quite good enough. *Half-Chiney* and *half-brain* were other terms. I wonder if this is the answer, or part of an answer, to why my grandfather treated my father so badly – because he wasn't pure Chinese, because he was half black?

♦

Today I am visiting the Chinese cemetery, where, to my great surprise, my grandfather is buried. Apparently all Chinese on the island are buried there and the work of the CBA make them easy to trace if you know a name and a year of death. It's less easy to trace Hermione. The records of her birth and marriage have been destroyed in a fire. Not this time, but another time, I'll have the heart to look up the records where I know her ancestors will exist – the island's slave registers.

The cemetery is a sprawling field of knotted pink bindweed and white graves, their marble headstones long ago stolen by the gangs whose territory is just the other side of the cemetery's walls. There are above-ground tombs strung with makeshift curtains, claimed by vagrants who sleep their days away on the cool stone shaded from the sun. I'm with a group of CBA volunteers involved in long-term restoration work – rebuilding the crumbling walls, cleaning graves, setting new headstones. We are accompanied by Mitchell and Delroy, burly men with gold-tooth smiles. They are security guards to protect us from thieves and shoot-outs.

Only up close do I see that some graves are almost completely concealed by the tangles of vine and pink buds.

'You know what we call this weed?' Patty Hogarth asks me. She's the secretary of the CBA and has been helping me negotiate Kingston. 'Rice and peas!' She laughs. 'But it's our number one enemy! Swallowing our ancestors' graves.' As we walk, she hands me a map of the whole cemetery, divided into sections – BABIES, CHILDREN, OLD SECTION A AND B, NEW SUPERIOR, WEALTHY, HONORARY, FREE. 'Your grandfather is in New Superior,' she says. I wonder what this means. Then she hands me an aerial photograph of five graves, one circled in red pen. 'This one is his,' she says. Below the image are his English and Chinese names. 'For your records,' she adds seriously.

There are loud bangs – the sound of a car backfiring, I think, but Mitchell and Delroy are suddenly on guard, tense, glaring around. 'It's gunshots,' Patty says, pointing to the wall. 'Over there. But it doesn't sound too close.' The gang violence that has sullied Kingston for decades is linked to old political rivalries between the PNP and JLP, rival gangs allegedly funding political campaigns. The gangs have deep roots in Jamaican society, making money through protection and selling drugs, but some of the proceeds are invested in creating a parallel state – building schools and clinics and handing out food and money to the poor. Not everyone thinks the gangs are bad.

We keep walking, nervously, finally stopping at a row of indistinguishable graves. Daniel Jin, another volunteer, walks the line, counting and referring back to his map. 'It's this one,' he says, standing at the foot of a dilapidated grave, bent over, pulling the tough handfuls of pink flowers from it. I stand beside him above the tomb that holds my grandfather's bones. 'He died 25 January 1969,' he says. 'Do you want to write his name on?' These are temporary markers until the headstones are replaced. He hands me a pen.

Hannah Lowe

'This is an amazing day for you, huh?' says Patty. 'What an honour, to pay your filial duty to your grandfather.' She lifts the camera hanging around her neck. 'Let's take some photos.' I smile as the camera snaps. And here we are – three generations out of four: my grandfather, me, the speck of an unborn child.

♠

'What was your dad's Chinese name?' Devon Chang asks me, when I show him a photo of my father – a young man, sharply dressed, standing on the front step of a house somewhere in London. From nowhere I remember that my father did have a Chinese name but it's lost from my memory. But surely he had enough names. Ralph, his real name. Chick, Chin, Chan, his nicknames. It was years before I asked how he came by them. *I don't know why they called him Chick*, my mother said, but she remembered Chin was for the old song 'Chin Chin Chinaman'. There are in fact at least two old songs with that name, both by white composers, both reworking stereotypes of the Chinese. In the 1917 version 'Old John Chinaman' is a subservient launderer with an appetite for gambling. It might be related to the 1898 version, about a down-on-his-luck launderer who gets caught cheating:

> *Chinaman no money makee*
> *Allo lifee long!*
> *Washee washee once me takee,*
> *Washee washee wrong!*
> *When me gette catchee cheatee*
> *Playing piecee card,*
> *Chinaman they allo beatee*
> *Kickee welly hard!*

Chan was better, my mother said. *Chan for Chan Canasta,
off the telly. He was a card magician. Amazing hands.* Chan
Canasta was actually Chananel Mifelew, a Polish immigrant,
made famous in the 1960s by his appearances on the BBC.
Always dressed in a dinner jacket and bow tie, Canasta
was gracious, humble and well spoken – he believed that
making an occasional mistake gave his act more credibility.
He was a 'mentalist', skilled in feats of mental magic, able to
predict which cards his celebrity audience had picked from
a deck, or recall the precise number of vowels on any given
page of Shakespeare. He spent hours refining his memory.
My father must have been given his moniker because he too
had an eidetic memory and in the old days, like Canasta, was
well dressed, refined, eloquent. Strange now to think that
the old man who shuffled through our house in crumpled
clothes, his hair uncombed, who searched the kitchen bin for
dog-ends, might have once, like Canasta, been the epitome
of charm.

♥

On my last day in Jamaica I take the bus to Golden River in
Above Rocks, the place we found Auntie Fay all those years
ago, but also, Dolores tells me, the place where Hermione
gave birth to my father. The bus swerves dramatically up
the hill, higher and higher, the road turning rugged, tall trees
bending precariously on the banks, the views on either side
of the thick forest, shadowy, deep-green, the air suddenly
cooler, thick with the scent of the vegetation. We are closer
to the sky swirling purple overhead, half set on a storm.

Years after my father died, Sam described a dream he was
having nightly – a kind, consoling dream I envied. In it, our

father, a young man back in Jamaica, was climbing the lush mountain footpaths. 'He can't turn round,' my brother said, 'but I know he's home again and I know he is happy.' Only now does it occur to me that Golden River looks like the place of my brother's dream. Far away from James Lowe, perhaps these mountains were my father's sanctuary. A sudden movement in the trees catches my eye, but there's nothing there except the wind driving through the leaves.

I came to Jamaica to find my young father, as though the young man might help me make sense of the man I knew. I came to find something of my grandmother and grandfather too. But high up in these mountains, it dawns on me – they are no more here than where they have always been: in my mind, residents of my imagination, imbued with idiosyncrasies of manner and expression, voices I can hear, almost as real to me as my own face in the mirror. They live their lives in the landscape I've created, the one I recognise, fashioned in that house in Ilford thirty years ago where johnny cakes fried on the stove and my father sang calypso. It was there that Caribbean men came to the door in Ashgrove Road asking for Chick or Chin, exchanging their greetings – *Long time no see.* Knowing this, what am I left with? A father who was both familiar and a stranger, constructing his life from my memory and the memory of others, through guesswork, inference, conjecture. Not because he is dead, but because he was always only half real, half imaginary, known to me for a long time but never wholly seen – bound to the silence of his own secrecies.

Postscript

On my trip to Jamaica in 2013, I was briefly reunited with my father's brother Ken (the young boy who visits the shop in the 1930s and tells Chick he's his half-brother), later my uncle 'Honey' with whom we stay in Discovery Bay. Shortly after I returned home, I was very saddened to hear that Ken had been murdered in his house on the hill.

In memoriam, Kenneth 'Honey' Lowe
1931(?)– 2013

Acknowledgements

I would like to thank the following people, texts and
organisations for their help, which has been invaluable:

Michael Bucknor, Armando Celeyo, David Chang, Vincent
Chang, Marcia Harford, Robert Hew, Jeanette Kong,
Patrick Lee, Rupert Lewis, Daniel Lowe, Keith Lowe, Ken
Lowe, Mickey Lowe, Parris Lyew-Ayee, Jock McGregor,
Josephine Metcalf, Herbie Miller, Richard Price, Alan
Robertson, John Siblon, Lorna Simms.

Mike Atherton, *Gambling*, London, Hodder and Stoughton,
2006.

Stewart Brown (ed), *Caribbean Poetry Now*, 2nd edn, London,
Edward Arnold, 1992.

John Burnside, *A Lie About My Father*, London, Vintage,
2007.

Ray Chen, *The Shopkeepers: Commemorating 150 years of the
Chinese in Jamaica 1854–2004*, Kingston, Periwinkle, 2005.

Cindy Hahamovitch, *No Man's Land: Jamaican Guestworkers
in America and the Global History of Deportable Labor*,
Princeton, Princeton University Press, 2011.

Richard Hart, *Towards Decolonisation: Political, Labour and Economic Developments in Jamaica, 1938–1945*, Kingston, Canoe Press, 1997.

Andrea Levy, *Small Island*, London, Headline Review, 2004.

Mike Phillips and Trevor Phillips, *Windrush: The Irresistible Rise of Multi-racial Britain*, London, HarperCollins, 1998.

Alan Robertson, *Joe Harriot: Fire in His Soul*, London, Northway Publications, 2011.

Phillip Sherlock and Hazel Bennett (eds), *The Story of the Jamaican People*, Kingston, Ian Randle Publishers, 1998.

Marika Sherwood, *Claudia Jones: A Life in Exile*, London, Lawrence and Wishart, 2000.

Gayatri Spivak, 'Can the Subaltern Speak?', in Cary Nelson and Lawrence Grossberg (eds), *Marxism and the Interpretation of Culture*, Chicago, University of Illinois Press, 1988.

Chee-Beng Tan (ed), *Routledge Handbook of the Chinese Diaspora*, London, Routledge, 2012.

Douglas Thompson, *The Hustlers: Gambling, Greed and the Perfect Con*, London, Pan Macmillan, 2008.

Ian Thompson, *The Dead Yard: A Story of Modern Jamaica*, London, Faber and Faber, 2009.

Robert Winder, *Bloody Foreigners: The Story of Immigration to Britain*, London, Abacus, 2005.

Kerry Young, *Pao*, London, Bloomsbury, 2012.

The Alpha Boys' School, Jamaica
The Arts Council of England
The Chinese Benevolent Association of Jamaica
The Institute of Jamaica
London Transport Museum
The Salvation Army
Scuola Holden, Turin

NEW FROM PERISCOPE IN 2015

PRINCESS BARI
Hwang Sok-yong; translated from the Korean by Sora Kim-Russell
'The most powerful voice of the novel in Asia today.' (Kenzaburō Ōe)
A young North Korean woman survives unspeakable dangers in
search of a better life in London.
PB • 204MM X 138MM • 9781859641743 • 248PP • £9.99

THE BLACK COAT
Neamat Imam
Months after Bangladesh's 1971 war, a simple migrant impersonates
the country's authoritarian ruler – with shocking results.
PB • 204MM X 138MM • 9781859640067 • 240PP • £9.99

THE MOOR'S ACCOUNT
Laila Lalami
'Brilliantly imagined ... feels very like the truth.' (Salman Rushdie)
The fictional memoirs of a Moorish slave offer a new perspective
on a notoriously ill-fated, real-life Spanish expedition in 1528.
PB • 204MM X 138MM • 9781859644270 • 336PP • £9.99

DRINKING AND DRIVING IN CHECHNYA
Peter Gonda
A disaffected Russian truck driver winds up at the centre of the brutal
bombing of the Chechen capital, forced to engage with reality as never before.
PB • 204MM X 138MM • 9781859641057 • 240PP • £9.99

THE GARDENS OF THE IMAGINATION
Bakhtiyar Ali; translated from the Kurdish by Kareem Abdulrahman
A group of friends search for the bodies of two murdered lovers in this
haunting allegory of modern Iraqi Kurdistan.
PB • 202MM X 138MM • 9781859641255 • 448PP • £9.99

A MAN WITH A KILLER'S FACE
Matti Rönkä; translated from the Finnish by David Hackston
A detective's orderly life is upended when a missing-persons case draws
him into the Russian–Finnish criminal underworld.
PB • 204MM X 138MM • 9781859641781 • 288PP • £9.99

THE EYE OF THE DAY
Dennison Smith
'Remarkable ... beguiles and enchants on every page.' (Ruth Ozeki)
A privileged boy and a hardened fugitive cross paths mysteriously beginning in
the 1930s, across North America and on the battlefields of wartime Europe.
PB • 204MM X 138MM • 9781859640616 • 328PP • £9.99